Coaching and Mentoring in the Asia Pacific

T0382793

Anyone involved in coaching and mentoring in the Asia Pacific region will welcome this book. It includes chapters from experts in the field and provides a fine overview of the challenges faced and how to tackle them. The book is a very useful contribution to our understanding of coaching and mentoring in this developing context.

Dr Elaine Cox, *Principal Lecturer and Programme Lead for Coaching &*
Mentoring, Business School, Oxford Brookes University, UK

Coaching and mentoring as management approaches have spread rapidly across the Asia Pacific region. Basic concepts of supporting people in their learning, in their career journeys and in the acquisition of wisdom are deeply rooted in all cultures, yet today there is little agreement about what constitutes good practice.

Coaching and Mentoring in the Asia Pacific is the first book to put coaching and mentoring into an Asia Pacific context – exploring the challenges, benefits and differences in application, both in concept and practice. Opening with a foreword from Anthony Grant, this book provides commentaries and practical case studies from a wide variety of countries, sectors and perspectives. The authors show how organisations in the Asia Pacific region can make effective use of this powerful developmental tool, in cost-effective, culturally relevant ways.

This book will be invaluable reading for students and practitioners based in, planning to work in or curious about coaching and mentoring in the Asia Pacific.

Anna Blackman is an Associate Professor at James Cook University in Queensland, Australia. She is also a Fellow of the Australian Human Resources Institute.

Derrick Kon works on CEO challenges, strategy, global leadership development and innovation. He is a Professional Certified Coach (PCC) with ICF and a Certified Solution Focused Coach (CSFC) with multinationals, consulting and academic experience.

David Clutterbuck is Special Ambassador for the European Mentoring & Coaching Council and Visiting Professor at three UK universities – Oxford Brookes, Sheffield Hallam and York St John.

Routledge-EMCC Masters in Coaching and Mentoring
Edited by
David Clutterbuck
and
Irena Sobolewska

This series is published in collaboration with the European Mentoring and Coaching Council (EMCC).

Routledge-EMCC Masters in Coaching and Mentoring provides critical perspectives in coaching and mentoring. It aims to avoid the overcrowded basic coaching/mentoring textbook market and focus instead on providing a toolkit for topics outside of core theory but are necessary to become a mature practitioner.

The series will appeal to those studying to obtain certificates, diplomas and masters in coaching and mentoring, alongside experienced practitioners who wish to round out their practice using selected essential reading as part of their continuous professional development.

Coaching and Mentoring in the Asia Pacific
Edited by Anna Blackman, Derrick Kon and David Clutterbuck

Coaching and Mentoring in the Asia Pacific

Edited by
Anna Blackman,
Derrick Kon and
David Clutterbuck

Routledge
Taylor & Francis Group

LONDON AND NEW YORK

First published 2018
by Routledge
2 Park Square, Milton Park, Abingdon, Oxon OX14 4RN

and by Routledge
711 Third Avenue, New York, NY 10017

Routledge is an imprint of the Taylor & Francis Group, an informa business

British Library Cataloguing in Publication Data
A catalogue record for this book is available from the British Library

Library of Congress Cataloging in Publication Data
Names: Blackman, Anna, editor. | Clutterbuck, David, editor. | Kon,
Derrick, editor.
Title: Coaching and mentoring in the Asia Pacific / edited by Anna
Blackman, David Clutterbuck and Derrick Kon.
Description: New York : Routledge, 2018. | Includes bibliographical
references and index.
Identifiers: LCCN 2017031445| ISBN 9781138642409 (hbk) |
ISBN 9781138642423 (pbk) | ISBN 9781315630014 (ebk)
Subjects: LCSH: Executive coaching–Asia. | Executive coaching–
Pacific Area. | Mentoring in business–Asia. | Mentoring in business–
Pacific Area.
Classification: LCC HD30.42.A78 C63 2018 |
DDC 658.4/07124095–dc23
LC record available at https://lccn.loc.gov/2017031445

ISBN: 978-1-138-64240-9 (hbk)
ISBN: 978-1-138-64242-3 (pbk)
ISBN: 978-1-315-63001-4 (ebk)

Typeset in Bembo
by Wearset Ltd, Boldon, Tyne and Wear
Printed and bound by CPI Group (UK) Ltd, Croydon, CR0 4YY

Contents

Figures

Tables

Contributors

Mike Armour heads up the leadership and talent function for a mid-sized insurance organisation where coaching and mentoring have been key elements of the leadership framework and have been an essential part of developing skills and capabilities for the future. He completed a Master's degree in Business Coaching in 2012 and is currently undertaking a PhD through the Sydney Business School, University of Wollongong focusing on coaching supervision. He can be contacted on mike.armour@bigpond.com.

Vasudha Bhide is an Assistant Lecturer and doctoral student in the School of Management, Massey University, Palmerston North, New Zealand. Her research interest is in the area of women and leadership and her doctoral research focuses on the diverse experiences of workplace sponsoring among women in New Zealand. She is also interested in and actively involved with leadership development programmes for young women and students. She can be contacted on justvasudha@gmail.com.

Anna Blackman is an Associate Professor at James Cook University, Australia, in the College of Business, Law and Governance. She is the Course Coordinator for the Graduate Certificate in Australian Rural Leadership for the Australian Rural Leadership Foundation and is a Queensland Councillor for the Australian Human Resources Institute. Her areas of expertise and research interest include coaching effectiveness, human resource management, business management and leadership. She can be contacted on anna.blackman@jcu.edu.au.

Alison Carter is a Principal Research Fellow at the Institute for Employment Studies (IES) in the UK. Her current research includes mindfulness applications in the workplace. She also writes, speaks and consults on a range of human resources, organisational development and coaching issues. Alison was a founding Director of the European Mentoring and Coaching Council (EMCC), Co-Chair of the 2nd Harvard International Coaching Research Forum, Chartered Fellow of CIPD and member of the US Academy of Management. She can be contacted on alisoncarterdba@aol.com.

Chérie Carter-Scott is a #1 *New York Times* best-selling author with books in 40 languages. She has been the MMS Coach Trainer since 1974 with over 10,000 coaching hours and an Executive Producer of the LEAP coaching documentary and writer of *The Workshop* musical production. She is the only MCC in Asia who is also a certified Mentor Coach and a certified ICF Assessor. To contact her: www.drcherie.com, drcheriecs@gmail.com.

David Clutterbuck is Visiting Professor in the coaching and mentoring faculties of three UK universities: Sheffield Hallam, Oxford Brookes and York St John. One of the two original founders of the European Mentoring and Coaching Council, he is now its Special Ambassador, tasked with spreading good practice internationally. He is a pioneer of the evidence-based approach to coaching. His book, *Everyone Needs a Mentor*, first published in 1985, remains the core text for mainstream developmental mentoring. He carries out continuous research, with current focus on effective supervision of coaches and team coaches and on how coaches and mentors assist clients in managing ethical dilemmas. He has been named as one of 'HR's most influential'. He is author, co-author or editor of more than 65 books, about half of them in the field of coaching and mentoring. He can be contacted on david@davidclutterbuckpartnership.com.

Vanessa Fudge is the founder of the consulting and coaching firm Leading-Well Group. Currently she is authoring a programme called 'Leading Well' with FeelGood Leadership UK. She is a registered psychologist specialising in organisational system dynamics, a coach supervisor and a member of the European Mentoring and Coaching Council (EMCC). She can be contacted on vanessa@leadingwellgroup.com.au.

Anthony M. Grant is globally recognised as a key pioneer of Coaching Psychology and evidence-based approaches to coaching. He holds a BA (Hons), an MA in Behavioural Science and a PhD in Coaching Psychology. In January 2000 he established the world's first Coaching Psychology Unit at Sydney University where he is the Director of the Coaching Psychology Unit. He has over 100 coaching-related publications. He is a Visiting Professor at Oxford Brookes University; a Senior Fellow at the Melbourne School of Business; and an Associate Fellow at the Säid School of Business, Oxford University. In 2007 he was awarded the British Psychological Society Award for outstanding professional and scientific contribution to Coaching Psychology. In 2009 he was awarded the 'Vision of Excellence Award' from Harvard University for his pioneering work in helping to develop a scientific foundation to coaching. He was a 2014 Scientist in Residence for the ABC – the Australian Broadcasting Corporation – and in 2016 was awarded the Australian Psychological Society 'Workplace Excellence Award for Coaching and Leadership'. He enjoys playing loud (but unfortunately not particularly Claptonesque) blues guitar.

Kasia Gurgul is a modern leadership and management coach, mentor and trainer, working internationally with leaders to develop high-level communication and coaching skills to empower their team, boost engagement and tap into diversity. Her background is in science and technology. Having lived and worked in Australasia, the Americas and Europe, she brings a global mindset and perspective to her work. She can be contacted on kasiagurgul01@gmail.com.

Sue Hubbard is an executive coach and the director/owner of Learning Partnerships Australia. She coaches people through a process to vary their mindset and learn to deal with the blocks they face in their professional lives with a view to building people to be their best. She can be contacted on suehubbard@learningpartnerships.com.au.

Peter Hudson's teaching career of 38 years includes 10 years as a school principal and lecturing in universities. He held four substantial Australian Commonwealth grants to advance educational practices. His model of Mentoring for Effective Teaching (MET) is at the forefront of his work in schools. He can be contacted on peter.hudson@scu.edu.au.

Suzanne Hudson is the Director of Professional Experiences at Southern Cross University and was the Project Leader of the 'Teacher Education Done Differently' (TEDD) program at Queensland University of Technology. She can be contacted on sue.hudson@scu.edu.au.

Derrick Kon is with The Conference Board which is a global think tank headquartered in New York with knowledge areas that include, among others: Strategic Human Resources, Global Economy and Corporate Governance. He has worked in management positions with multinationals and in global Human Capital consulting organisations such as Mercer and Mercuri Urval. He has served as the President of the Strategic Management Interest Group, with the Singapore Institute of Management. He is passionate about top management challenges in the areas of strategy, leadership and executive coaching. He is a Professional Certified Coach (PCC) with the International Coach Federation (ICF). He has published work in academic journals and global reports. He holds a Doctor of Business Administration from Victoria University, Australia and an MBA from RMIT University, Australia. He has taught at National University of Singapore Business School and Nanyang Technological University. He can be contacted on derrickkon@yahoo.com.

Ya-Hui Kuo earned her PhD degree in Educational Psychology from Auburn University in the USA. She was the Program Director for the C2 Educational Centers, Inc in Bethesda, Maryland, USA and now is an Assistant Professor in the Department of English at Wenzao Ursuline University of Languages in Kaohsiung, Taiwan. Her research interests focus on mentoring in higher education, international education and issues related to teaching and learning. She has a keen interest in qualitative research studies. She can be contacted on 94101@mail.wzu.edu.tw.

Charlie Lang is the founder and managing partner of Progress-U Asia. He is known for his innovative approaches towards leadership and coaching. He combines the latest findings in research with his own international coaching and leadership experience. He has 15 years of corporate experience, holding top positions such as Managing Director and VP Sales and Marketing for APAC. As an expert in corporate culture development and executive coaching, he accumulated over 4,000 hours of executive coaching experience and completed numerous coaching assignments with executives in senior management positions such as CEOs, managing directors, board members, etc. He is an avid writer, having published over 200 articles and two books, *The Groupness Factor* in 2005 and *The Coach Factor* in 2012. He can be contacted on charlie.lang@progressu.com.

Siqiwen Li's research interests include financial risk management, banking, financial crises, risk-based prudential regulation in the banking sector, financial risk modelling, behavioural finance, catastrophe risk management & insurance and environmental finance. She collaborates with researchers from finance, science, economics, management and other backgrounds in multi-disciplinary teams. She can be contacted on Siqiwen.Li@canberra.edu.au.

Doug MacKie is a business psychologist, executive coach and director of CSA Consulting. He has over 25 years' experience in the assessment and development of executive, leadership and team capability within top companies in Australia, Asia and the UK. He has a particular expertise in positive leadership development and has pioneered the development of strength-based approaches to developing transformational leaders with organisations. He has presented at international conferences and published in leading journals on positive leadership development, the importance of effective evaluation and assessing ROI in coaching engagements. He is the author of the definitive text *Strength-based Leadership Coaching in Organizations* based on his research in this area. He can be contacted at doug@csaconsulting.biz.

Morné Maritz is Principal at Morné Maritz and COO for Fiscus Capital and Fiscus Strategy. He holds a Master's degree in Organisational Psychology from the University of Johannesburg, and an MBA from Melbourne Business School (Melbourne University). He helps organisations to understand, apply and profit from innovation and change, leadership enablement and high-performance coaching. In that respect he is a disrupter of the status quo and helps his clients to answer two important questions – "Should I/we do this?" and then "Why?" Once they have a clear common understanding of those, he helps to bring an understanding of "How" to accelerate and realise the full potential of ideas, strategies and strengths. Prior to founding his current practice, he worked and lived in the UK, South

Africa and the US in various roles. He has developed a unique high performance framework while researching the national rugby team of South Africa. He is currently an associate with Melbourne Business School where he is responsible for the design and implementation of the overall governance and engagement framework for Executive Coaching. He can be contacted on morne@mornemaritz.com.

Tony Mathers is Chief Executive at the Institute of Executive Coaching and Leadership (IECL). He combines leading the company from Sydney with coaching a number of senior executives in the corporate, government and academic environments, both in Australia and Asia. He is an executive coach with many thousands of hours of one-to-one coaching experience and a business career spanning the UK, Asia and Australia, including a global leadership position in financial markets and later regional responsibility for Asia for a leading Australian bank. He was early into the executive coaching space back in 1999 and approximately 100 of the people he has coached have been based in Asia. He can be contacted at tonym@iecl.com.

Julia Milner is a Professor in Leadership at EDHEC Business School, France and a management consultant working internationally with leading organisations, focusing on leadership development and business coaching. As the Director of the International Centre for Leadership Coaching she has extensive work experience in Australia, Asia and Europe. She can be contacted on julia@coaching-int.com.

Marion Neubronner graduated from Harvard with a Masters in Human Development and Psychology and is faculty with the Behavioral Coaching Institute. With over 20 years' experience in coaching, mentoring, training and development, she has transformed clients (like Oracle, Google, Singtel, Schneider-Electric) with her expertise in leadership, multi-generational workforce, business growth, positive psychology and resilience. She can be contacted on marionneubronner@gmail.com.

Donnel Nunes is a family learning consultant with expertise in behaviour, education and mentoring relationships between family members. He is the founder of PVA Knowledge Group (pvaknowledge.com), a boutique firm that offers advising for individuals and organisations with a focus on family owned businesses. He is an associate of the Aspen Family Business Group and the Hawaii regional representative for Coaching and Mentoring International. He can be contacted on donnel@pvaknowledge.com.

Christopher Nunn is internationally recognised for his leadership qualities and strategic thinking. He has a passion for assisting people reach their potential. As a motivated individual himself he has the ability to assess the current situation, find the opportunities for growth and develop goals aimed at providing a successful outcome. He can be contacted on chris@chrisnunn.com.au.

Padraig O'Sullivan is the President Asia Pacific of The Leadership Circle and The Full Circle Group. He is also an Honorary Fellow at Sydney Business School, University of Wollongong where he lectures on the Masters of Business Coaching Degree. He works across Australia, South East Asia and the Middle East. He is the author of the *Foreigner in Charge* series of books and has contributed to three other books. He has written extensively on 'C' level transitions into the most senior leadership roles based up his 15 years' experience working in a coaching capacity. He can be contacted on padraig.osullivan@fcg-global.com.

David Pierce is an executive coach and a Professional Certified Coach with the International Coach Federation. He works with leaders at all levels to identify what matters to them and helps them to discover their purpose. The definition of purpose leads to setting goals and implementing the actions to get there. He can be contacted on enzocons@bigpond.net.au.

Jenny Plaister-Ten is the Director of 10 Consulting Ltd and a Global Executive Coach with a background in international marketing. She spent more than a decade living and working in the Asia Pacific region. She is the author of *The Cross-Cultural Coaching Kaleidoscope* (2016). She worked in a regional role for ICL Asia Pacific setting up a new PC division, before founding her own regional consulting practice based in Singapore. She has a Master's degree in Coaching and Mentoring Practice and now specialises in coaching global leaders and multicultural teams. She can be contacted on jenny.plaister@10consulting.co.uk.

George Quek is a leadership coach and consultant who has helped numerous organisations set up their Structured Mentoring initiatives as well as equipped their mentors and mentees. In 2004, he launched the first programme in Asia Pacific on 'How to Set Up a Structured Mentoring Programme' for HR/LD professionals. Besides mentoring, he focuses on talent assessment and development. He can be reached at george@distinctions-asia.com.

Ram Ramanathan (http://coacharya.com) is a leadership coach and trainer and spiritual wanderer, blending eastern spiritual wisdom with modern psychological and neurobiological knowledge to create mindless awareness. He can be contacted on ram@coacharya.com.

Akram Sabbagh has extensive experience as a board member, business founder, board advisor, business and executive coach. He plays a pivotal role in enabling numerous executives and businesses across a diverse range of sectors realise their growth objectives, transition to the next phase of their development and achieve challenging commercial and cultural objectives. He can be contacted on akram.sabbagh@altusq.com.au.

Vimala Suppiah is the Principal of GameChange Coaching Consultancy. She holds the ICF Professional Certified Coach Credential and is the co-founder and current President of the Association of Coaching Supervisors and Mentors (ACSM). She coaches leaders and executives to gain new perspectives, insights and tools to lead people and organisations. She can be contacted on suppiahvimala@yahoo.com.

Ross Swan is a behavioural leadership coach who is committed to reducing the stress for executives in managing their people. He is also focused on improving employee engagement in the workplace in order to give people a greater sense of purpose in their working day. He can be contacted on ross@soul-inspired-leadership.com.

Beth Tootell is a Lecturer and the Director of Teaching and Learning in the School of Management, Massey University, Palmerston North, New Zealand. Her research interest is in Human Resource Management and the broader area of people's experiences at work. She has a passion for teaching and learning and is most interested in the diverse experiences of different groups at work. She can be contacted on B.L.Tootell@massey.ac.nz.

Tammy Turner is based in Sydney, Australia and is originally from the USA. She is Managing Director of TPC Leadership Australasia and Founder of The Centre for Coaching Development and Supervision. As a Master Certified Coach, she has worked with key industry and government decision makers and trained, mentored and supervised many hundreds of coaches. She has been Director, ICF Australasian Professional Standards' team and led the ICF's global task force on coaching supervision. As a visionary in the international coaching field, she has been a contributing author to articles and books on coaching, mentoring and the power of leadership at every level. She can be contacted on tammy@developingcoaching.com.au.

Foreword

An overview of coaching and mentoring in the Asia Pacific region

Anthony M. Grant

Coaching is now pretty much a globally used methodology for enhancing performance, well-being, productivity and for facilitating positive change in corporations, government institutions, businesses and education settings. Indeed, it is hard to think of a sector of society that does not use some type of coaching methodology. For those of us who have been involved with the development and practice of coaching for some years, we have seen coaching throw aside notions of faddishness and hyperbole, and over the past 25 years we have witnessed the emergence of an evidence-based approach to coaching. We have seen the development of a solid empirical evidence base, as well as the development of conceptually coherent theories that can ethically inform our coaching practice. From both the empirical evidence and our own practical experience as coaches, we know that coaching and mentoring can be a powerful methodology for creating positive change. We have seen and experienced the positive impact of working with others in a supportive goal-orientated coaching or mentoring relationship. Although it may sound trite, we know that good coaching or mentoring can be a life-changing experience – and the empirical evidence is resoundingly supportive in this respect. This is wonderful. We have come a long way. But there is more to be achieved.

The fact is that most approaches to coaching have been developed from a Western perspective. For example, the origins of life coaching sit firmly within the American self-help genre. Similarly, the notions of executive and business coaching have mainly arisen in American and European business contexts, and the cultural and theoretical influences on contemporary organisational mentoring follow similar lines, as David Clutterbuck and Tammy Turner's chapter so concisely outlines.

Although many contemporary approaches to coaching and mentoring incorporate aspects of Eastern philosophy, for example, acceptance and mindfulness practice, my impression is that the coaching and mentoring industry per se has tended to merely appropriate and adapt such notions to make them fit within a Western paradigm. I should emphasise at this point that I do not want to position cultural perspectives in a dichotomous fashion; 'us' compared to 'them'; 'East' compared to 'West'; or 'individualist' versus 'collective'. Such crude dichotomies can polarise, subjugate and dehumanise, producing the very antithesis of the coaching and mentoring mission.

However, different countries and different cultures do have different values, expectations and working practices. The kind of coaching or mentoring that might work well in a New York stockbroker's office may be of little value in coaching or mentoring under-resourced, bureaucracy-burdened social workers working with acute at-risk cases in impoverished areas of Europe. The same caveats about generalisations hold true for using Westernised corporate coaching and mentoring methodologies in the Asia Pacific region. It is both foolish and patronising for coaches schooled in Westernised approaches to coaching to assume that they can go in and 'fix' organisations globally. Of course, few coaches really hold such fixed or authoritarian mindsets, but to date there have been few attempts to document the key issues to pay attention to when coaching in the Asia Pacific region, and there are few books that present a comprehensively curated anthology that can act as a practical guide for the ethically grounded and evidence-based coach or mentor. In a sense, such an endeavour has little chance of completely succeeding – not least – as Derrick Kon and Anna Blackman discuss – because of the vast differences in this massive region. Nevertheless, this book provides some important pointers towards enhancing the effectiveness of coaching and mentoring in the Asia Pacific region.

Padraig O'Sullivan's chapter provides an illuminative example of how to best coach expatriate executives who are seeking to work in new cultural environments in the Asia Pacific region. His work reminds of us the value of bringing mindful reflective practice to such challenges. The skill set required to help expatriate executives acclimatise and adapt their existing leadership styles to unfamiliar cultural context is perhaps one of the more common applications of coaching and mentoring as Ram Ramanathan and others discuss.

A significant challenge for those of us who work in this region occurs when trying to develop the coaching and mentoring skills of the indigenous workforce. A key point that resonates for me throughout much of the book relates to fully utilising and, where necessary, working with aspects of the client's indigenous culture, rather than simply imposing pre-existing (typically 'Western') coaching values and mores onto the client's culture. Christopher Nunn adroitly discusses his experiences with working in the Pacific region and highlights how much importance is placed there on a nurturing, personalised leadership approach, compared to the transactional style we so frequently see in the Westernised commercial world.

Along similar lines, Akram Sabbagh and Vanessa Fudge provide us with a useful example from New Zealand, and focusing on how aspects of Maori culture which already echo coaching and mentoring methodologies can provide an effective foundation and framework for contemporary New Zealand coaching and mentoring practice. Similarly, Chérie Carter-Scott's chapter provides intriguing insights into the experience of coaching in Thailand, and Chérie's example of using the Thai concept 'sanuk' (meaning that everyday life should be fun) is a beautiful example of using specific cultural constructs to help the coachee reframe and rearticulate their goals. It seems to me that we all can benefit and learn from each other's cultures in many respects!

Charlie Lang's chapter neatly outlines the very real challenges of cross-cultural coaching, and highlights a number of issues that many professional coaches will have faced. First, and this is an issue that has not as yet been discussed much in the coaching literature, are the opportunity costs that often flow from a poorly implemented coaching programme. Poorly implemented coaching and mentoring programmes can have the unintended consequence of increasing cynicism and resistance to subsequent change programmes. As far as I know there has not been any research into financial costs of poorly implemented coaching and mentoring programmes, but one can safely assume that they could be substantial on both financial and human capital levels. In Charlie Lang's chapter this issue was addressed by presenting the new programme as a 'Mentoring for Sales Leaders programme'. Second, as Charlie Lang concisely and forthrightly articulates, there are significant language barriers to be overcome. Indeed, it strikes me that it is not enough to merely translate the words of a leadership development programme or coaching technique from (say) English to (say) Korean or Japanese, we need to be able to capture the subtleties of the meanings embed in the language and convey those meanings. In a sense such cross-cultural programmes go well beyond the transmission of technical methodologies. Rather, they involve a genuine recreating of coaching principles and the ability to rearticulate those from within a different cultural reality. This is not an easy task and this book will provide useful insights for those of us engaged in such endeavours.

As Doug MacKie neatly reminds us, we seek to help our clients identify and utilise their personal, cultural and collective strengths. Regardless of geographic location, good coaching and mentoring helps individuals, groups and organisations construct and move towards better futures and positive outcomes. In this way good coaching and mentoring truly can be a universal methodology for creating purposeful positive change; let's use it well.

Part I
Setting the scene

1 A brief history of coaching and mentoring

David Clutterbuck and Tammy Turner

Overview

In this chapter, we provide a brief history of how coaching and mentoring have developed internationally and how this has influenced the Asia Pacific. We highlight the foundations of the models and schools of coaching and mentoring, along with well-established and emerging applications. We also review some current themes and trends relating to the continued evolution of coaching and mentoring.

Where do coaching and mentoring come from?

The 'untrained' person uses the terms coaching and mentoring interchangeably, although both scholars and practitioners tend to insist that there are fundamental differences. Our investigation shows that there is little agreement on what the differences are, though amongst the 'trained professional' the nuances of both creates passionate debate!

There is agreement, however, that the terms coaching and mentoring are of European origin, that the word mentor originated almost 3,000 years ago in Ancient Greece, and the word coach in England in the 19th century (a relative neologism!) adapted in both form and meaning from the Eastern Europe word *koc*, meaning a high-class horse-drawn carriage (Garvey, 2011) – yes, it was a joke that stuck! Many of the core concepts, which underlie coaching and mentoring, also emerged independently in many cultures of the Ancient World, most notably in China and India. The earliest account with echoes of coaching and mentoring is the Mesopotamian Epic of Gilgamesh dating from about 2100 BC, in which Gilgamesh, King of Uruk embarks on a learning journey, accompanied by Enkidu, sent by the gods to help him become wiser.

A short history of mentoring

In Homer's *The Odyssey*, the goddess Athena guides King Odysseus on his 20-year journey of self-discovery. His son, Telemachus, who sets out to find his father, takes with him an old courtier, Mentor, who is actually an incompetent old fool. Fortunately, Athena impersonates Mentor and also appears as a traveller Mentes. She engages both father and son in dialogues that make them reflect on their actions and choices, learning from experience. She also, on occasion, intervenes on their behalf – for example by hiding Odysseus under her *aegis* or cloak of invisibility. Some 2,500 years later, the French cleric Fenelon (1699) carried on the story with a book of further dialogues between Athena and Telemachus.

The Odyssey was a product of its time – violent, superstitious and in a world where slavery and cruelty were the norm. It's therefore not appropriate to adopt all of the precepts presented in the dialogues and actions. And, indeed, different Western cultures have taken different aspects of the story, on which to base their understanding of what mentoring is. In the US, the emphasis has been on Athena's role as the goddess of martial arts, as the sponsor of Odysseus and Telemachus and as their protector – hence the term protégé (literally, one who is protected) for the learner. A pedagogic model of mentoring emerged, which emphasises doing things for a younger person, one-way learning and the power of the mentor to exert influence on the part of the protégé. This appears to be compatible with what might be expected from a highly individualistic culture (Hofstede, 2001). For example, the teacher who has knowledge to impart to the student has followed suit and is the model that has traditionally been used in primary education.

In Europe, with its stronger roots in philosophy, psychology and with cultures that place more emphasis on collectivism (though not necessarily to the extent that many Asia Pacific cultures do) it was Athena's role as the goddess of wisdom that influenced the concept of mentoring. The idea of the mentor intervening directly on the mentee's behalf is seen as inappropriate within an egalitarian society as, generally, mentoring is between boss and direct report where the power dynamics can distort the learning process. Mentoring relationships in Europe tend to be based on two-way learning.

Of course, when we talk of 'European' and 'US' mentoring models, the terms encompass a wide variety of localised perceptions and expectations – just as in the Asia Pacific region. However, it can be a helpful short-hand to think of the US model as *sponsorship* focused and the European model as *developmentally* focused, accepting that examples of both can be observed on each side of the Atlantic and indeed within the Asia Pacific region. Examples of both models can be seen across Asia Pacific and, particularly, in Australia.

Kochan and Pascarelli (2003), in a review of mentoring programmes funded by state or national governments and aimed mainly at disadvantaged or excluded groups, found that culture appeared to have an impact on "how the projects were funded, their purposes, and the level of control exerted over them by the funding source" (p. 418). This issue of control seemed directly related to the societal ideas about the role of the government in people's lives. Governmental programmes were most often initiated in countries that tended to have formalised social services for their citizens – meaning they had a notion of the collective – thus viewing mentoring as a way to provide support within the social structure of the 20th century, where the target audience was disadvantaged youth in inner cities. Towards the end of the 1970s, Ted Levinson (1978) described mentoring as a significant phase in the developmental life of adults. He describes the generative effect, in which men in their later middle age feel the need to pass on their experience to younger people and gain self-fulfilment through the achievements of these younger persons, as much as or more than through their own accomplishments. Kathy Kram, a researcher in Boston, built on these insights at the beginning of the 1980s to capture the essence of a sample of informal mentoring relationships. She identified a number of psychosocial and career functions that these mentors played for their mentees and a series of phases that these relationships typically went through. At roughly the same time, some US corporations began to experiment with formal mentoring as a means of supporting young professionals entering the workplace.

David Clutterbuck began to research and write about mentoring as a result of reporting on Kram's initial findings. Focusing on formal mentoring within European and wider international programmes, he quickly found that both the functions of a mentor and the phases of the relationships were different in a number of respects that replicate the sponsorship-developmental model split. Clutterbuck and Kram published their seminal books almost simultaneously in 1985. Other academics in North America (notably Belle Rose Ragins, Lillian Eby and others) and in Europe (notably David Megginson and Bob Garvey) contributed to the development of theory, concept and practice, increasingly underlining the cultural difference between the sponsorship and developmental models.

A key factor in the rapid explosion of interest and practice in mentoring was the development from informal ad hoc *relationships* to formal or supported *programmes*. This appears to have happened in three simultaneous and largely unconnected spheres (business, education and community) at the beginning of the 1980s, first in the US and Europe, then across the rest of the world. In business, the primary motivator was attraction, development and retention of talent. In education, programmes addressed issues such as supporting new faculty (and particularly female faculty) and doctoral students, or the needs of disadvantaged schoolchildren. Community programmes addressed issues of deprivation or the rehabilitation of ex-offenders.

Early initiatives in Asia Pacific included Tata Consultancy Services' introduction of career mentoring in 1990, as an element of employee engagement and strengthening communications between leaders and talent at other levels. Mentoring has been relatively commonplace in the Indian IT sector since the turn of the century, although it appears that the term is applied to a wide range of developmental and supervisory activities, which are more about instruction and tutoring than mentoring. Manju George, reporting a case study of IBS Software Services, describes a shift from a heavily bureaucratic approach to much more informal learning partnerships.

International organisations have contributed a great deal to introducing supported mentoring to the countries in which they operate. For example, in the 1990s, Shell demonstrated the effectiveness of mentoring as a means of supporting indigenisation (replacing expatriate with local talent) in Brunei and Malaysian oil company Petronas, which created an extensive in-house mentoring capability to support the development of high potential staff. The Petronas programme was highly innovative in that it offered mentees two mentors – one in their own company or function (but not in the reporting line) and one in another company within the group. More recently, Youth Business International's mentoring programmes have reached tens of thousands of young entrepreneurs, from China to Sri Lanka.

Unlike coaching, which we shall explore next, mentoring did not develop a truly global and influential body to promote good practice. Even today, the International Mentoring Association remains a largely US-based organisation, with very little presence overseas at all; and the European Mentoring and Coaching Council has only recently started to have an influence in the region.

A short history of coaching

The modern origins of coaching lie in philosophy, psychology, sports, self-improvement and academia. In the 19th-century novel *Pendennis* (by William Makepeace Thackeray), a comparison is made between the horse-drawn coach, in which the characters are travelling, and the role of a tutor at Oxford University. Other references to coaching in England during the 19th century (Garvey, 2011) describe:

*   tutoring for academic attainment;
*   improvement in performance in boating and rowing;
*   teaching the defence of the wicket in cricket;
*   developing subject matter expertise, particularly in science;
*   teaching parenting skills.

Some academics have linked coaching to the stone age under the premise that early humans must have helped each other to thrive by sharing knowledge of fire and/or making axes (McDermott & Jago, 2005; Zeus & Skiffington, 2000) and the skill of coaching to classical times and, especially, Socratic dialogue (de Haan, 2008; Hughes, 2003; Neenan, 2009). As previously mentioned, the link to the performance nature of coaching has historical references from cricket and rowing in the 19th century (Starr, 2002; Wilson, 2007) though more contemporary coaching concepts did not arise until the mid-1970s, when Timothy Gallwey's (1974) *Inner Game of Tennis* incorporated elements of psychology and self-insight into the development of tennis skills.

These modern coaching concepts were quickly adapted to a wider audience, lending themselves to more universal appeal. In business, as a tool for managers, Megginson and Boydell (1979) describe coaching as "a process in which a manager, through direct discussion and guided activity, helps a colleague to solve a problem, or to do a task better than would otherwise have been the case" (p. 5). In 1988, Sir John Whitmore published the seminal book *Coaching for Performance* (Whitmore, 2002) with its omnipresent GROW model (Goal, Reality, Options, Will), although at least two other people claim that they were its original source. In recent years, Whitmore has openly recognised the limitations of the GROW model, which has utility primarily in the context of short-term performance, relatively simple, explicit and non-transformational objectives. These concepts spawned trainee and apprentice programmes, still in practice today.

There are also many, many definitions of modern coaching, which we won't go into here. As a result, the coaching industry has yet to agree on a single universal definition and many coach training institutions and associations maintain that their definition is the most comprehensive. Regardless of the definitions, the authors of this book agree that adult learning principles are at the heart of coaching and underpin what makes coaching work:

- andragogy, the theory of adult learning introduced by Malcolm Knowles in the 1970s;
- experiential learning as propounded by David Kolb (1984);
- the transformative learning theory of Jack Mezirow (1990).

As it has matured, coaching has borrowed concepts from psychology, adult learning, philosophy and mentoring, which have evolved into a range of coaching approaches … just to name a few! Each of these presents a different methodology and approach. The ones we have listed here can be considered 'mainstream' in the sense that they are established and tend to have both a body of literature and an evidence base. In addition, coaches may draw upon a wide range of other philosophies or disciplines to inform their practice, from counselling and psychotherapy (which, in turn, have their own multitude of schools and schisms).

Despite all of these specialities, most coaches (and mentors!) use an eclectic approach in their work. The result often presents the buyer of coaching and mentoring services with bewildering and often contradictory choices about what kind of service will best suit their needs; this continues to challenge the industry.

Table 1.1 Key influences on the evolution of modern coaching

Cognitive development	Organisation and relationship systems	Psychodynamic
Evidence-based	Performance	Solution-focused
Narrative	Person-centred	Team
Ontological	Positive psychology	Transpersonal

Global professionalisation of coaching and mentoring

How does this impact on consistency across the global? For the foreseeable future, there will probably be debate amongst the associations and their members as well as clients to better define what 'good' looks like. We hope there will be further research and continued professional development as the industry grapples to define itself and the service.

Defining an andragogic learning environment. Regardless of the label of coaching or mentoring we believe the outcome is growth created through an adult learning process. Although there may not be agreement on the approach that facilitates growth, we believe the basic core concepts must include:

- opportunities for the learner to make profound change as an active participant in their journey of self-discovery and, then, apply their current knowledge to new understanding;
- involvement of a wise person to enhance the learner's wisdom and understanding;
- the learner partaking in self-assessment, defining their change and taking accountability for progressing their learning;
- emphasis on a *learning dialogue* to access different perspectives and ways of thinking, which include:

  - conversations that stimulate reflection;
  - powerful, challenging questions;
  - underscoring important concepts or, perhaps, introducing new ones;
  - using story, including the learner's language palette and metaphor.

- the nature of the relationship between the learner and the coach or mentor is characterised by:

  - high levels of trust;
  - established boundaries agreed by both parties;
  - belief by the coach or mentor in the other person's ability;
  - mutual honesty.

In our experience, these elements help to ensure an andragogic learning environment which exemplifies best practices, promotes equality between the learner and coach or mentor and creates the conditions necessary for growth.

Global industry standards. In moving toward greater industry consistency and standards, the industry is attempting to better clarify and understand the nuances between coaching and mentoring as well as provide quality assurance. This is a bit more complex than it sounds. Currently, each association has its own definition of coaching, mentoring and measuring 'what good looks like'. However, a challenge these professional bodies face is that, to increase their membership numbers and/or to expand into emerging markets, creates pressure to minimise standards to accommodate coaches and mentors who are at various levels of development. There may be a potential conflict of interest as associations are also guardians of identifying and measuring minimum standards, which their members must be able to meet to have an industry-recognised qualification. To add to the complexity, each association has their own continuous professional development standards. Additionally as the industry is self-regulating, there are individual coaches and mentors who do not participate in supervision, are not members of a professional body and/or do not want to be upheld against professional standards. It is definitely a buyer-beware market!

Asia Pacific. Many Asia Pacific coaches have been trained using United States and European coaching and mentoring standards and continue to belong to GCMA member associations (see below), with ICF currently being the dominant player. Of those who have been educated at a postgraduate level, most of the training began in the early 2000s using methodologies borrowed from the helping professions or from programmes designed in collaboration with their USA and European academic counterparts. Since then, many coach training providers, who also have developed their materials from the USA and European counterparts, have evolved.

Asia is a large region and depending on the country, the culture and the desire on the part of the client to work in an adult learning (andragogic) fashion, there is wide variation. In countries such as Australia, New Zealand and Singapore, for example, coaching is considered mainstream and there would be many of the 'core concepts', discussed previously, evidenced in mainstream learning environments. Countries such as China, Malaysia and Papua New Guinea would be considered as emerging markets and more of a pedagogic approach to learning is expected by the client, which has hampered the flourishing of some of the 'core concepts'. We anticipate as training and/or more exposure to an andragogic way of learning is experienced, this will create more consistency in the region.

Industry consistency. To create more industry certainty, there is a desire amongst the associations and their members to better define and ensure a consistent practice so clients have more assurance in their decision-making and overall results. To this end, an alliance of global, professional coaching and mentoring bodies, currently made up of the Association for Coaching (AC), the European Mentoring and Coaching Council (EMCC) and the International Coach Federation (ICF), created the Global Coaching Mentoring Alliance (GCMA) in 2012. Their stated purpose is to "professionalise the industry in the field of coaching and mentoring and express a shared view of the practice of professional coaching". After a few years of member surveys and conversations, the GCMA released a press announcement on 16 December 2015, stating "the GCMA found there was considerable alignment in the commonalities across each body's coaching and mentoring competencies". The GCMA hopes this provides "confidence to coaches and the wider coaching market that there is cohesion in what constitutes effective coaching and mentoring practice" (GCMA, 2015). As a result, the EMCC and AC have released a join Global Code of Ethics for Coaches and Mentors and the

ICF has released a new Code of Ethics and Standards for its members. Consequently, the GCMA will no longer work on this. Despite all of the differences between coaching and mentoring histories, there may be more similarities than what many are prepared to admit.

This spirit of co-operation and collaboration is a welcome sign and all of the bodies involved can be congratulated for their persistence (especially in the face of their own internal politics and external pressures!). In the pipeline also, is greater collaboration on recognition of each other's credentials and accreditations. Worldwide consistencies in professional qualifications, methodologies and standards gradually move the industry toward a more uniform global standard, equal measurement and a more consistent client experience. However, given the complexity of the range of coaches and mentors, as well as markets at various levels of maturity, this may take a number of years to achieve.

Maturity factors to support consistency

Critical trends and themes in modern coaching and mentoring

Establishing strong regional identities for coaching and mentoring within Asia Pacific will be an essential element in this process. In order for this global transfer to fully emerge, these critical maturity factors must be considered:

- quality measurement of both internal and external coaching and mentoring, based on an international standard;
- established coaching cultures;
- coach/mentor tenure or maturity – defined by a large percentage of coaches working full time for a minimum of 5–10 years;
- existence of local supervision, peer review and learning from reflective practice;
- expectation that coaches and mentors are credentialed/accredited;
- locally generated research based on current coaching/mentoring deployment;
- the shift of focus from one-to-one to group and team coaching;
- university/postgraduate levels of education and continuous professional development.

As coaching and mentoring continue to mature, we hope that an even more constant transfer of innovations dynamic will emerge as a result.

As we've mentioned, coach/mentor as well as market maturity plays a considerable role in the moment and overall consistency of delivery. Various studies and ways to more accurately measure what 'good looks like' have been undertaken. Factors such as Continual Professional Development (CPD) including coaching supervision and reflective practice seem to be a thread that maintains increasing quality. In this section we explore some of the detail behind this and the work that needs to be further undertaken.

Coach/mentor tenure and maturity. Experience might make people wiser, but it does not necessarily make them wise. Wisdom comes from reflecting on experience in ways that stimulate new and deeper understanding of oneself and the world around us. Some of this comes from experience; some comes from reflective practice. Observation from coach assessment centres has provided insights into the mind-frames of coaches at different levels of maturity (Clutterbuck & Megginson, 2011) and these insights are captured in the Coaching Maturity Model (see Table 1.2).

At the earliest stages of learning to be a coach, people typically can cope with one, simple, conversational model or approach. The models-based phase of coach maturity can be described as *doing coaching to* a client – making the client and their issue conform to the model. It is characterised by high focus on the initial, presented goal, rather than allowing the goal to emerge and evolve; by overuse of stock questions and a very limited toolkit, such as scaling; and driven too much by the coach's need to feel useful and achieve some result.

In the next phase another significant mindshift occurs; this time from doing coaching to *being* a coach. The philosophy-based coach has a great deal of experience, has acquired a diverse range of tools and techniques, has explored multiple schools and perspectives of coaching and has integrated this with their wider experience of life and their professional and personal identities.

For a smaller percentage of coaches still, there is a further, substantial mindshift. Systemic eclectic coaches have continued this integration of self and role to the point where they are able simply to "hold the client, while the client has the conversation that they need to have with themselves"

Table 1.2 Four levels of coach maturity

Coaching approach	Style	Critical questions
Models-based	Control	How do I take the client where I think s/he needs to go? How do I adapt my technique or model to this circumstance?
Process-based	Contain	How do I give enough control to the client and still retain a purposeful conversation? What's the best way to apply my process in this instance?
Philosophy-based	Facilitate	What can I do to help the client do this for her/himself? How do I contextualise the client's issue within the perspective of my philosophy or discipline?
Systemic eclectic	Enable	Are we both relaxed enough to allow the issue and the solution to emerge in whatever way they will? Do I need to apply any techniques or processes at all? If I do, what does the client context tell me about how to select from the wide choice available to me?

(Clutterbuck, Whitaker & Lucas, 2016, p. 172). They are able to see the client and their issues from multiple, interconnected perspectives. They simultaneously exude both calm and creative energy. They speak less than a fifth of the time that models-based coaches do, but the impact of what they say is many times greater. (Almost all of the original, powerful questions asked by coaches in coach assessment centres come from philosophy-based or systemic eclectic coaches.)

With practice and experience comes confidence to be more flexible and to view coaching as something *to do with* the client. It becomes a shared endeavour, in which the coach brings a wider toolkit and offers the client choices of whether and how to use them. The coach is relaxed enough to let go of the need to control the conversation and its outcome. For the vast majority of coaches, this is the final stage on their journey of maturation.

Some of the implications of different maturity levels have been explored by Otto Laske (2008), who observes coaches from a perspective of general socio-emotional maturity (Kegan, 1982) and cognitive maturity. Among critical questions raised from his analyses are:

- To what extent can a coach be effective coaching someone, who is at a substantially higher level of maturity than themselves?
- What are the implications for team coaching, when members of the team are at different levels of maturity (especially if the team leader is at a lower level than some team members)?

Internal versus external coaching. Until recent years, the general consensus in the coaching literature was that executive coaching was an externally resourced activity delivered by paid and accredited professionals, while coaching by managers within an organisation was delivered by relative amateurs. Indeed, some commentators still maintain that line managers cannot really coach, as they lack the required training and there is an inherent conflict of role that makes truly open developmental conversations difficult to achieve. This neat distinction, if it was ever true, has largely unravelled.

First, many organisations have invested in developing their own internal pools of accredited executive coaches who bring to their coaching the additional resource of deep knowledge of the business and its culture. We have not been able to find any credible evidence that external coaches are generally or automatically more capable or competent than their internal counterparts, who have undergone similar training.

Second, experiments in a number of UK organisations in retail, utilities and education suggest that line managers can be effective coaches if they create a coaching culture within their teams, i.e. one where everyone, including the manager, takes responsibility for their own learning and that of their colleagues. What is gradually emerging is a more complex picture, in which the most senior leaders are typically coached (or mentored) from outside the organisation, while a more flexible range of different options is on offer for the rest of the organisation. An additional complicating factor is the rapid growth of reverse mentoring, in which senior leaders are mentored by people significantly more junior than themselves, to help become more technically aware or to give them insights into the world through the eyes of people from a different gender or background.

As internal coach pools become established, an unexpected problem has arisen – coach *ennui*. It seems that some of these coaches become bored with their role after a couple of years or so. One of the solutions being tested is creating opportunities for them to continue to develop professionally as a coach, by taking higher levels of qualification or by training them as ethical coaches or team coaches (see below).

Some recent research done by Anthony Grant at the Coaching Psychology Unit at the University of Sydney identifies three 'generations' of workplace coaching. In the first generation, in the 1990s, the focus was on performance management – helping line managers have performance-oriented conversations after or as part of periodic appraisals. The emphasis in this context was remedial, addressing poor performance rather than building on strengths. The second generation, in the late 1990s and early 2000s, was driven by the need to retain and develop talent. Grant describes this as "a more humanistic, goal-focused version of performance conversations", but points out that it was limited in effectiveness by jargon and excessively bureaucratic structures. The third generation takes a more systemic perspective of development and change – "a more flexible, more frequent performance conversation cycle" (Grant, 2017, p. 11). It also incorporates wider perspectives, such as well-being, taking a longer-term, more holistic view of development. All three of these generations can be seen in organisations around the world, including in the Asia Pacific.

Coaching culture. Since the book *Making Coaching Work* (Clutterbuck & Megginson, 2005) crystallised experience in creating coaching cultures, there has been considerable research and development of good practice and increasing evidence of the value of making coaching approaches integral to the way people in the organisation think and behave. There are now effective tools for measuring progress in achieving a coaching culture and for establishing a pragmatic and effective strategy to achieve the cultural shift.

Existence of professional supervision, peer review and/or reflective practice. Supervision has an ongoing developmental component and is valued by coaches to better understand both their coaching and the wider system in which they're working. The EMCC, the AC and some other professional bodies require all professional coaches and mentors to demonstrate that they receive regular supervision as part of their continuing professional development.

The ICF differentiates supervision from coach mentoring for credentialing, which is included as part of supervision in the other professional bodies, which muddies the waters. This differentiation has created extensive resistance to supervision in the USA, as there seems to be an expectation that once the coach has become a credentialed coach, their developmental work is completed. In a step toward a more universal professional standard, in 2015 the ICF recognised coaching supervision hours for credential renewal purposes.

We believe that supervision is an important part of maintaining the quality of the coaching profession, of safeguarding clients and coaches themselves and of sustaining continuous professional development (Bachkirova, Jackson & Clutterbuck, 2011; Clutterbuck et al., 2016; Hawkins & Shohet, 2012). A starting place for this, which is not often taught though we'd like to see that, is through learning circles, peer review and/or reflective practice which could be in-built into coach training curriculum. There seems to be a wide variation of what is required to encourage peer review and/or dialogue about delivery and/or ethics, topics covered in supervision in all regions, including the Asia Pacific. Being able to openly receive and provide useful feedback as well as better understand yourself as a practitioner is a sacrosanct core element for continued industry growth. As emerging markets mature, so too will the value of professional supervision as an indicator of longevity.

Expectation that coaches and mentors are credentialed/accredited. Although we've talked about the role associations play in credentialing/accrediting members, it is important to highlight further the role the associations also play in educating coaches and mentors as well. As was previously mentioned, there are many coach training schools around the world ranging from postgraduate to one-day foundational coach training programs. For each of the main philosophies of coaching there are many training providers to choose from.

To some extent, the quality of training is overseen by the ICF, ICA and EMCC as the accrediting bodies who give a 'stamp of approval' to the content being taught and link it to their codes of ethics and/or competencies. These bodies also offer individual coach credentialing/accreditation after the training has been completed, to measure the coach's competency. However, as there are no agreed standards and metrics, international bodies vary considerably in their approaches to the credentialing/accreditation process. Each association places a slight difference on the emphasis of input measures (courses attended and number of hours of coaching done) and output measures (evidence-based, demonstrated competence of live coaching, essays and/or research). Additionally, the various bodies do not recognise each other's credentialing/accreditation process and, sometimes, training hours from another professional accrediting body. This is further complicated by university training that has different requirements to demonstrate competence, inconsistent with that of the professional bodies. This is often due to the fact that university courses may be more skewed toward knowledge of approaches and research, with less emphasis on the practical application of coaching skills, which are emphasised in coach-specific training programmes.

Despite programmes being accredited and/or evidence-based, coach assessment centres in Europe regularly find that 60–70 per cent of coaches observed fail to achieve even a basic level of observed competence. Comparative data from North America and Asia Pacific are not available, as the coach assessment centre approach has not yet become established in these regions. Perhaps, where there is an opportunity in introducing supervision and/or reflective practice methods earlier, maturity will advance in line with skills development. Until some further research into this topic and/or agreement on the overarching consistency about 'what good looks like', the complexities of education and measurement of competency will continue to challenge the marketplace.

Locally generated research based on current coaching/mentoring deployment. The vast majority of research into coaching and mentoring is Anglo-centric, but the balance has been adjusting steadily since the turn of the century. Ontological coaching owes much of its evolution to South American and Australian theorists and researchers. Much research has come out of the universities, coach training providers and more recently coaching consultancy and/or service providers to bring awareness to the buyer and to provide market differentiation.

The research that led to coaching standards originated in Europe. However, as one of the first areas to offer coach training at both a university and at a training provider level, much of the research is coming out of Australia. As a leader in the region and in an industry attempt to define and measure quality, a workgroup comprising 35 universities, coaching consultancies and buyers of coaching services in Australia produced the world's first comprehensive handbook on coaching in organisations (Standards Australia, 2011). In neighbouring New Zealand, Jennifer Garvey-Berger and Keith Johnston have published their view on coaching in systems and continue to research the systemic effect of coaching in organisations. More recently, studies have started to emerge to look at the impact of cross-cultural interventions such as a study led by Fiji National University in 2013 in collaboration with Victoria University in Wellington NZ and the University of Saskatchewan, Canada (Ruru et al., 2013). ICF Singapore's Vision and Mission is to "Engage members and community for coaching awareness, excellence and advancement". In 2014 they established a research committee whose Vision and Mission is "to bring trending academic research to the forefront, create a professional dialogue to enhance the effectiveness of coaching, and conduct projects that advance the development of coaching in industry".

We see a steady flow of papers from all regions, including the Asia Pacific, from Hong Kong, India, Australia and New Zealand, which indicate an increased focus. Research in languages other than English is slow to arrive in Asia. As Spanish and French are becoming more common around the world, we are hopeful that, with China and Malaysia entering a more mature phase of development, more will be published both on cross-cultural research and in national languages.

University/postgraduate levels of education and ongoing learning. Throughout the Asia Pacific, university and coach-specific training is readily available. The presence of dedicated faculty in coaching and mentoring represents a significant step forward in the capacity to embed coaching and mentoring in business and society. As an early provider, the University of Sydney has trained hundreds of coaches and stimulated extensive research. At other Australian universities, there are notable faculties at James Cook University, Queensland University of Technology, University of Wollongong and elsewhere. Coach training organisations are partnering with universities to extend their predominately skills-based programmes to academia. Throughout the region, coaching faculties exist in major cities in China, India and New Zealand. Singapore has an INSEAD Asia campus and the Civil Service College also offers strong coaching expertise.

The thirst for learning is strong in the region. Training can be obtained from virtual, intensive and/or as part of an overall business or psychology master's programme, so the choices are broad throughout the region. Regardless of the training options available, the need for continuous professional development such as supervision and mentoring, peer learning and/or credentialing tends to follow the US, rather than the UK trends. As the buyer becomes more educated and the market increasingly has more options, we see this trend changing.

The shift of focus from one-to-one to group and team coaching. Team coaching within sport is long established, but it is only relatively recently that coaching intact teams within organisations has become widespread. It's important to note that sports teams have significant differences to most work teams, in their structure, purpose and dynamics (Katz, 2001), so drawing close parallels may be misleading.

The term 'team coaching' is also often misapplied to team building, team facilitation or even general consulting. To be considered as team coaching, an intervention must work with the entire team together, rather than individually, and must employ coaching approaches and methods. Mainly confined (for cost reasons) to top teams and high impact project teams, team coaching requires a much wider skill set than one-to-one coaching (Clutterbuck, 2008), but transition courses are now available in some countries. For the most part, team coaches are externally resourced, but there is an emerging trend to equip members of internal coaching pools with team coaching skills.

The shift from one-to-one coach to team coach requires a major upgrade in competence and the acquisition of extensive additional knowledge and skills in managing group dynamics (family therapy is one of many useful disciplines from which team coaching borrows). Team coaching is an order of magnitude more complex and more demanding than individual coaching. For example, in one-to-one coaching, there may be conflict within the client and between the client and third parties. Occasionally, there may be conflict within the coach and between coach and coachee. In team coaching, we have all these dimensions, plus conflict between team members and between sub-groups or alliances within the team, as well as between the team and the team leader. Making the shift to team coaching requires extensive study that covers a wide range of relevant disciplines and, in the authors' view, formal accreditation.

A major obstacle to creating coaching cultures is previous wasted effort, where large sums have been invested in trying to turn line managers into coaches – only for it to have little or no impact. One of the reasons such initiatives fail is that the relationship between line managers and their teams is a complex, adaptive system. Like all such systems, changing one element (sending the manager on a short course to learn to coach) simply creates resistance as the system attempts to restore the previous state. Experiments show that a more effective approach is: a) to educate the entire team about coaching, so they can work together to create a localised coaching culture; b) to give the process time, so that people can absorb different ways of thinking, rather than just a few simple coaching tools; and c) to relate the coaching education process to real issues the team faces and needs to deal with in the course of its day-to-day work.

Choices for the Asia Pacific region

One of the advantages of being relative latecomers to organised, professional coaching and mentoring is having less baggage to hinder progress. The coaching communities within the Asia Pacific region have – if they choose to exercise them – wide choices about the models they wish to adopt, adapt or create.

Use of executive coaches is perhaps less widespread within the region as a whole than in Europe and North America, but Australia and New Zealand appear to have similar levels of use. There is, therefore, a huge opportunity to divert investment that would have gone mainly into external coaching into creating a much better balance between internal and external coaching resources. There may also be the opportunity to build teams and/or cultures where coaching is the primary mode of interworking. This is unlikely to be a threat to effective, competent coaches – anecdotal evidence suggests strongly that organisations, which have good understanding of how to use internal coaching, are better able to recognise and make effective use of high quality external coaches.

One of the ways to become shrewd about using coaches is to develop in-house capabilities to run assessment centres. This allows in-house human resource functions to see for themselves the differences between coaches at different levels of maturity. Some companies now grade internal and external coaches in ways that allow them to align how they use them with their maturity level and what they should pay. Hawkins and Smith (2006) refer to four levels of coaching application, requiring increasing levels of overall competence – skills, performance, behaviour change and transformational – and the four maturity levels (mentioned above) map reasonably well with these. Add to the mix, factors such as the client's level in the organisational hierarchy and relevant experience and it becomes possible to make better-informed judgements about the fee ranges appropriate in each externally resourced coaching assignment.

In thinking about developing coaching and mentoring cultures, Asia Pacific organisations can again establish their own priorities and approaches, which meet their specific needs. The starting point is a strategic plan that addresses the following questions:

- What would a coaching culture look like and feel like in our context? (For example, what behaviours would we see?)
- How can we adapt generic coaching culture surveys to assess where we are on the journey towards achieving a coaching culture?
- What are the critical elements of coaching culture and what priorities do we want to put on them?
- What investments do we want to make in terms of time and money, and over what time period?
- How will we ensure value for money?

Use of mentoring versus internal coaching. In an internal coaching brief, there is often a skills and/or networking brief and consequently this imparting of knowledge is called 'mentoring'. Additionally, this resource is often internal and has been either assigned to or selected by the mentee. However, internal workplace coaches and organisational external coaches can provide the same opportunities. The terminology can sometimes be the sticking point. One key element is that mentors are more likely to act as role models and to make introductions that help the learner build their networks; certainly coaches can and oftentimes do provide similar support. But, a critical differentiator is that while coaching behaviours can be delivered within the line manager – direct report relationship (and, in conditions of high psychological safety, line managers can also be effective internal coaches), developmental mentoring does not appear to work well within the boss–subordinate relationship, partly because of role conflict and partly because line managers find it difficult to give equal quantity and quality of mentoring to all of their direct reports. Both coaching and mentoring may be required by the organisation, and recommended good practice is to integrate the two approaches. It is interesting to note that line manager reluctance to use coaching behaviours can be overcome to a significant extent when they have the opportunity to practise developmental conversations within a mentoring relationship, where there is less at stake for them or their teams if an experiment does not work.

Cultural integration and professionalism is a focus for measurement of maturity. Increasingly the professional coaching bodies have acknowledged that continual professional development and developmental mentoring are associated and overlapping disciplines. Whether this is within existing professional bodies or not depends on how flexible and culturally sensitive those bodies are. Overall, the signs are positive that the leadership of the professional bodies understand the importance and value of such progress – but it may take time to educate the thousands of ordinary member coaches, who do not yet appreciate the richness of a diverse international panorama of coaching.

Supervision is another area, where coaching in Asia Pacific can leapfrog North America. Regularly examining and reflecting upon their coaching practice with a trained and qualified supervisor is the key to continuous increase in coaching quality. Associations of coach supervisors are now established in Australia, Malaysia and Singapore, but coaches in the region also receive supervision from elsewhere and particularly from Europe, where the greatest concentration of supervisors and research into supervision lies. A more extensive indigenous resource would accelerate the development of coaching generally within the region.

Coaching and mentoring applications

New applications of coaching and mentoring keep emerging. For example, when mothers take maternity leave and are absent from the workplace for several months, the transition back into the working environment can be very difficult. First tried in London in the early 1990s, maternity mentoring supports the returning mother in regaining her confidence and sense of self-worth. Maternity coaching is a more recent phenomenon, in which an externally resourced professional coach, who has been through a similar transition elsewhere, gives guidance, advice and emotional support through the first few months of return to work. Maternity mentoring is now undergoing a resurgence, as experience shows that it is more valuable for the returner to have these conversations with someone who understands the nuances of the specific culture and how the unwritten narratives of the organisation have changed during her absence.

Another recent application to emerge is ethical coaching/mentoring. Largely a response to the ethical scandals within every major economy in recent years, the role of an ethical coach-mentor is to be a resource to which people can turn, if they are faced with an ethical dilemma. The ethical coach-mentor is trained in both coaching-mentoring skills and in the basic psychology of ethicality. So they have the competence to help someone think through ethical dilemmas and to develop ethical resilience.

Some coaches and mentors have been trained in the use of psychometrics, which can be helpful in initiating conversations about specific preferences and behaviours. However, those with psychology qualifications tend to be more cautious about using popular instruments, such as Myers-Briggs Type Indicator (MBTI), for a raft of well-founded evidential reasons. Again, the user of coaching is typically not in a position to recognise what is appropriate and valid and needs to trust the coach and their training.

While coaching has tended to remain within its boundaries of sport and business, mentoring has expanded into many more spheres of activity. In the field of justice, for example, mentoring programmes have been highly beneficial in reducing reoffending. Europe and Canada have excellent examples of programmes aimed at helping immigrant populations integrate into their host societies.

There are examples of either coaching or mentoring (or both together) benefiting people at every stage of life and in most environments – from school, to work, to prison. In the world of education, we see examples such as:

- helping students from disadvantaged backgrounds catch up in literacy and numeracy;
- preventing bullying;
- reducing incidence of student absenteeism, poor classroom behaviour, carrying knives;
- supporting disadvantaged or disabled students in accessing higher education and sticking with it; and opening up higher education to young women in communities, where this would normally be discouraged;
- helping teachers at all levels to become more effective;
- supporting university academic staff in achieving tenure.

In the world of work, we see applications at every transition stage of the leadership pipeline from managing self, through managing others, managing managers and so on. The first large-scale mentoring programmes in the workplace were aimed at graduate recruits, but we now observe extensive coaching and mentoring applications focused on:

- supporting equal opportunity and diversity objectives – gender, race, religion, disability, etc.;
- preventing and coping with burnout;
- performance improvement in specific tasks or roles;
- talent management (nurturing and retaining talent);
- major role transitions;
- supporting significant culture shift;
- smoothing merger and acquisition;
- transition to overseas assignments;
- board effectiveness;
- supporting new judges in becoming confident and competent in their roles.

Mentoring and coaching have also been extensively applied in the military. For example, the Royal New Zealand Air Force's mentoring programme has achieved gold award status from the International Standards for Mentoring Programmes in Employment. Coaching and mentoring are also widely used in medicine to support clinical staff, such as doctors, nurses and paramedics, and other staff from cleaners to chief executives. There are also numerous mentoring programmes aimed at entrepreneurs, from microbusinesses in India, Africa and South America, to business start-ups, with some programmes, such as Youth Business International, working with thousands of mentoring pairs in more than 60 countries.

Conclusion

A more accurate title for this chapter might be *A brief history of coaching and mentoring … so far*. Coaching and mentoring as professions and as important tools of corporate management are still at an early stage of development. There are vast holes in our knowledge of both disciplines and there is a lot more evolution to come on the journey to maturity. The infancy years have belonged largely to the United States. The teenage and early adult years have been heavily influenced by European thought and culture. Can Asia Pacific now make its presence felt as coaching and mentoring enter the next, more mature phases of their development?

References

Bachkirova, T., Jackson, P. & Clutterbuck, D. (2011). *Coaching and mentoring supervision: Theory and practice*. Maidenhead, UK: McGraw-Hill.

Clutterbuck, D. (1985, 2013). *Everyone needs a mentor*. Wimbledon, UK: CIPD.

Clutterbuck, D. (2008). *Coaching the team at work*. London: Nicholas Brealey.

Clutterbuck, D., & Megginson, D. (2005). *Making coaching work*. London: CIPD.

Clutterbuck, D., & Megginson, D. (2011). Coach maturity: An emerging concept. In L. Wildflower & Brennan, D. (Eds), *The handbook of knowledge-based coaching: From theory to practice*. London: John Wiley and Sons.

Clutterbuck, D., Whittaker, C. & Lucas, M. (2016). *Coaching supervision: A practical guide for supervisees*. Oxford: Routledge.

de Haan, E (2008). *Relational coaching: Journeys towards mastering one-to-one learning*. Chichester: Wiley.

Fenelon, F. de (1699). *Telemachus, son of Ulysses*. Republished by Cambridge University Press, 1994.

Gallwey, T. (1974). *The inner game of tennis*. London: Jonathan Cape.

Garvey, B. (2011). Researching coaching: An eclectic mix or common ground? A critical perspective. In R. Wegener, A. Fritze & M. Loebbert (Eds), *Coaching entwickeln. Forschung und Praxis im Dialog*. Wiesbaden: VS Research.

Global Coaching Mentoring Alliance (GCMA). (2015, 16 December). Press release. Retrieved 6 August 2017, from www.emccouncil.org/eu/en/gcma.

Grant, A. M. (2017). The third 'generation' of workplace coaching: Creating a culture of quality conversations. *Coaching: An International Journal of Theory, Research and Practice, 10*(1), 37–53.

Hawkins, P., & Shohet, R. (2012). *Supervision in the helping professions*. Maidenhead, UK: McGraw-Hill.

Hawkins, P., & Smith, N. (2006). *Coaching, mentoring and organizational consultancy: Supervision and development*. Maidenhead, UK: McGraw-Hill/Open University Press.

Hofstede, G. (2001). *Culture's consequences: Comparing values, behaviors, institutions, and organizations across nations* (2nd edn). Thousand Oaks, CA: Sage Publications.

Hughes, G. (2003). *Transcendence and history: The search for ultimacy from ancient societies to postmodernity* (Vol. 1). Columbia: University of Missouri Press.

ICF Singapore Website. Retrieved 6 August 2017, from www.icfsingapore.org/research.html.

Katz, N. (2001). Sports teams as a model for workplace teams: Lessons and liabilities. *Academy of Management Executive, 15*(3).

Kegan, R. (1982). *The evolving self.* Cambridge, MA: Harvard University Press.

Kochan, F., & Pascarelli, J. T. (2003). Culture, context, and issues of change related to mentoring programs and relationships. In F. Kochan & J. T. Pascarelli (Eds), *Global perspectives on mentoring: Transforming contexts, communities, and cultures* (pp. 417–428). Greenwich, CT: Information Age.

Kolb, D. (1984). *Experiential learning: Experience as the source of learning and development.* Englewood Cliffs, NJ: Prentice Hall.

Kram, K. (1985). *Mentoring at work: Developmental relationships in organisational life.* Glenview, IL: Scott, Foresman.

Laske, O. (2008). Mentoring a behavioural coach in thinking developmentally: A dialogue. *International Journal of Evidence Based Coaching & Mentoring, 6*(2).

Levinson, D. J. (1978). *The seasons of a man's life.* New York: Ballantine.

McDermott, I., & Jago, W. (2005). *The coaching bible: The essential handbook.* London: Piatkus.

Megginson, D. & Boydell, T. (1979). *A manager's guide to coaching.* London: Kogan Page.

Mezirow, J. (1990). *Fostering critical reflection in adulthood.* San Francisco: Jossey-Bass.

Neenan, M. (2009). Using Socratic questioning in coaching. *Journal of Rational-Emotive & Cognitive-Behavior Therapy, 27*(4), 249–264.

Ruru, D., Sanga, K., Walker, K. & Ralph, E. (2013). Adapting mentorship across the professions: A Fijian view. *International Journal of Evidenced Based Coaching and Mentoring, 11*(2), August.

Standards Australia. (2011). *Coaching in organizations (HB332–2011).* Retrieved 6 August 2017, from https://infostore.saiglobal.com/preview/AS/misc/handbook/HB332-2011.pdf?sku=1465966.

Starr, J. (2002). *The coaching manual: The definitive guide.* Harlow, UK: Pearson Education.

Whitmore, J. (2002). *Coaching for performance: GROWing people, performance and purpose* (3rd edn). London; Naperville, USA: Nicholas Brealey.

Wilson, C. (2007). *Best practice in performance coaching: A handbook for leaders, coaches, HR professionals and organizations.* London: Kogan Page.

Zeus, P. & Skiffington, S. (2000). *The complete guide to coaching at work.* Sydney: McGraw-Hill.

2 Key challenges for coaching and mentoring in Asia Pacific

Derrick Kon and Anna Blackman

This chapter will consider the following key challenges for coaching and mentoring in Asia Pacific:

- Challenge 1: the increased demand for coaches and mentors in Asia Pacific as a result of the talent dynamics and leadership needs in this region.
- Challenge 2: the necessity for cross-cultural coaching and mentoring competence due to the cultural diversity in the Asia Pacific region.
- Challenge 3: the need to build a coaching and mentoring culture in organisations with the rise of millennials in the workforce.
- Challenge 4: the need for more empirical research on coaching and mentoring in the Asia Pacific region to be conducted to provide an evidence base for addressing the challenges outlined.

Challenge 1: rapid demand for coaches and mentors in Asia Pacific

Asia Pacific's position as the growth engine of the world economy has intensified in recent years. While, in 2000, the region accounted for less than 30% of world output, by 2014 this contribution rose to almost 40%. Moreover, Asia Pacific accounted for nearly two-thirds of global growth in 2015 (International Monetary Fund, 2015).

The establishment of the Association of Southeast Asian Nations (ASEAN) Economic Community (AEC) in 2015 was a major milestone in the regional economic integration agenda in ASEAN, offering opportunities in the form of a huge market of US$2.6 trillion and over 622 million people. In 2014, AEC was collectively the third-largest economy in Asia and the seventh largest in the world (AEC, 2015).

The AEC Blueprint 2025 (ASEAN, 2015), adopted by the ASEAN Leaders at the 27th ASEAN Summit on 22 November 2015 in Kuala Lumpur, Malaysia, provides broad directions through strategic measures for the AEC from 2016 to 2025. The AEC Blueprint 2025 will lead towards an ASEAN that is more proactive, having had in place the structure and frameworks to operate as an economic community, cultivating its collective identity and strength to engage with the world, responding to new developments and seizing new opportunities. The new Blueprint will not only ensure that the 10 ASEAN Member States are economically integrated, but are also sustainably and gainfully integrated in the global economy. The ASEAN Economic Community will also establish free movement of talent across the region which will further intensify competition among ASEAN businesses to attract the best leaders. The economic growth of Asia Pacific region implies more talent is needed to be developed to drive the growth of their organisations. The question then is where this talent is going to come from?

Talent shortage in Asia. The 10 ASEAN member states – Brunei, Cambodia, Indonesia, Laos, Malaysia, Myanmar, the Philippines, Singapore, Thailand and Vietnam – are projected to be the fourth-largest global economy by 2050 (Straits Times, 2016). As such, the region will require enormous investment in infrastructure and human capital development to achieve ASEAN's goal of becoming globally competitive in a wide range of industries.

Talent shortage is particularly acute in Asia, where Western multinationals and local companies compete to attract and retain top talent. According to the 2015 Talent Shortage Survey by the Manpower Group (Man, 2015), in APAC, Japan faces the largest talent shortage at 83%, followed by Hong Kong at 65% and India in third place with 58%. Taiwan (57%) and New Zealand (51%) came in fourth and fifth respectively, while Singapore (40%) came in seventh place after Australia (42%). As the ASEAN community moves toward greater integration, the competition for talent in Asia Pacific including ASEAN will intensify.

Accelerating the developing of Asia Pacific leaders. When Asia Pacific growth is coupled with the talent shortage in Asia, companies are looking at ways to accelerate the talent development of their leaders, managers and hi-potentials.

In a study on accelerating the leadership development in Asia Pacific by The Conference Board (2013), the following findings were highlighted based on numerous interviews and a survey of 210 executive-level human capital professionals in Asia:

- Only 7.2% of survey respondents believed their company's leaders are "very prepared" to address business challenges over the next one to two years and 45% said their leaders are not prepared or only marginally prepared.
- 11% of respondents have been very successful in identifying and accelerating leadership talent. Few have an adequate pipeline: almost 74% report being only somewhat successful at this endeavour, while 15% have been unsuccessful.
- This situation is exacerbated by significantly higher levels of turnover in Asia, particularly among high performers.

The findings concluded the following four programmes would have the greatest impact on developing leaders in Asia:

1   Action learning
2   International assignments
3   Rotational programmes
4   Executive coaching/mentoring.

In terms of investment, the two largest costs are found in action learning (e.g. business challenges and simulations) and executive coaching/mentoring. There is a rise in demand for coaches or mentors in the Asia Pacific region.

Challenge 2: cross-cultural coaching and mentoring in Asia Pacific

Geert Hofstede (1984), who established the most widely used system of studying cultural variables, defined culture as "the collective programming of the human mind that distinguishes the members of one human group from those of another" (p. 21). In essence, culture is that complex whole which includes shared characteristics (e.g. language, religion, heritage and values) that distinguish the members of one group of people from those of another.

There is no common 'Asian' culture or approach to business. The Asia Pacific region consists of many, widely diverse cultures with long histories and very little in common between them. While there may be some overt similarities in the way some things are valued (such as education and personal relationships), what is learned as being appropriate in one part of the region is not automatically the same elsewhere. Minkov and Blagoev (2014) highlighted the fact that there is no one single Asian management culture that distinguishes the Asian countries from those of the rest of the world. Cultural differences include national-level differences in behaviours, attitudes and values collectively (Caligiuri, Lepack & Bonache, 2010). Thus, it is important to better understand the role of culture in work (Peterson, 2007) in order to be effective in coaching and mentoring across cultures. Nicholas and Twaddell (2010) highlighted that cultural factors to look at in coaching could include 'losing face', directness versus reticence in different cultures, the dominant/submissive behaviours of specific cultures and that a troubling issue to some may not be perceived as a problem at all in other cultures.

Coaching across cultures means increasing one's self-awareness so that one is aware of one's own beliefs and becomes more open to those of the clients: "If we understand the dynamics of culture, we will be less likely to be puzzled, irritated, and anxious when we encounter the unfamiliar and seemingly irrational behavior of people in organizations" (Schein, 2010, p. 9). Self-aware coaches can help clients consider and leverage new possibilities that fit their own needs, leveraging new possibilities from two seemingly contradictory perspectives (Rosinski, 2003). Leveraging possibilities must also be coupled with nuanced coaching wisdom and skills such as knowing when and what change a client is ready for. With cultural differences comes the diversity of coaching practices discussed in Passmore (2009).

In the 2010 CIPD Learning and Development Survey (CIPD, 2010), international organisations highlighted that, to meet business goals, organisations mentioned that their staff need to develop management and leadership skills first (42%), followed by intercultural skills to help raise awareness of other cultures (40%) and then people management skills (32%). That is, leaders and managers, who could be internal coaches or mentors, would benefit from reflecting on their identity, cultural preferences and abilities to bridge the cultural differences in their working environment. By recognising our own cultural conditioning and that of the coachee or mentee, our cross-cultural coaching or mentoring can assist to provide context, compassion and connection.

Vignettes 1 and 2 show the importance of cross-cultural awareness to coaching and mentoring.

Vignette 1

Will That Cross-Cultural Coach Really Help Your Team?

By Andy Molinsky and Christian Höferle (https://hbr.org/2015/04/will-that-cross-cultural-coach-really-help-your-team)

Yes, cross-cultural coaches can help (assuming you've picked a capable one). But you need to keep in mind that the coaching relationship is not culturally neutral and it's prone to the same cultural issues that you're trying to address in the business ... So how can organizations and coaches make sure that the coaching doesn't fall prey to these difficulties?

First, the coaches themselves need to be attuned to the fact that the very cultural differences they're helping their clients with can also interfere with the coaching process. Too often coaches are so focused on the 'external' – on what the client might be struggling with in his or her work environment – that the dynamics within the coaching relationship gets overlooked.

Second, use the coaching process as an arena for noticing and working with cultural differences. If a client struggles with authority, see how that plays out in the relationship. If the problem is making small talk, use the session as an opportunity to do that as well. The point is that the coaching session itself can and should be an opportunity to both point out cultural differences and to practice developing global dexterity.

Third, make sure that the coaching process itself is understood as valid and legitimate. For some, especially those from Western cultures, there are obvious benefits to the idea of personal skill building. But that's not necessarily the case for others who may feel that it's inappropriate or self-indulgent to focus so directly on enhancing one's own personal welfare.

Vignette 2

Discussing the Cultural Differences in a Mentoring Relationship in *Management Mentors* (2011). (www.management-mentors.com/about/corporate-mentoring-matters-blog/bid/66333/Discussing-the-Cultural-Differences-in-a-Mentoring-Relationship)

As technology enables us to reach across the globe, we are increasingly seeing mentoring relationships that are cross-cultural in ways never thought possible. American companies will often have someone in America mentoring someone long-distance in Europe or Asia. This requires a sensitivity to the cultural differences that exist so as to avoid derailing a relationship.

These kinds of challenges can be minimised or avoided if one begins by having a cultural discussion around expectations. In addition, taking the time to learn about each other's culture and background is very effective. This helps to build a relationship and in some cultures, it's only after a relationship is established that feedback can be received from a mentor or coach without it being perceived as offensive.

Cultural differences are not limited to international areas but also within a given country or district. In our own country we have differences based upon geography as well as ethnic differences. One of my earliest experiences as a consultant was to go from Boston to a client in the South. I learned in that experience that being direct is not always perceived as positive. A certain gentility in expression was expected and got better results.

Therefore, to become more effective in coaching and mentoring across cultures in Asia Pacific, it is helpful to understand culture, cultural frameworks and dimensions and how to better coach and mentor in this region.

Cultural competence for coaching and mentoring across cultures

Jenkins (2006) highlighted that, to perform effectively, we need to know how to leverage development of cultural competence. It is importance for coaches and mentors to be alert in ensuring that their interactions with their clients are neutral and without cultural bias and stereotyping. Therefore, coaches and mentors should engage in self-discovery to develop cultural awareness and cultural competence. That is, a good cross-cultural coach or mentor should assume there is always more going on than meets the eye and therefore, they need to be aware of cultural distinctions to become familiar with the various ways people can differ. There are a number of cross-cultural models that could assist us to raise our cultural awareness and level of competence.

Hofstede's Cultural Dimensions model. The work of Hofstede (1980) on the national dimensions of culture is perhaps still the most referenced in the workplace. He used a values survey that had been distributed to IBM employees in over 50 countries across the globe. His analysis provided six cultural dimensions used to compare cultural differences.

The cultural dimensions are:

1   Individualism versus Collectivism. Individualism measures the extent to which a culture expects people to take care of themselves and/or where individuals believe they are masters of their own destiny. Countries which are more individualistic are the USA, Australia, the UK and Canada. Collectivism measures the tendency for group members to focus on the common welfare and feel group loyalty. Countries which tend to be more collectivist include Columbia, Peru and China where the culture places greater value on the success or well-being of the group versus the individual.

2   Masculinity versus Femininity. A masculine society, such as Japan, Italy, the USA and the UK puts emphasis on competition, earnings, achievement of tasks and advancement. Cultures which are feminine in orientation, such as Denmark, Sweden, Norway and the Netherlands, tend to emphasise relationships with managers and co-workers, co-operation among members in a work group and benevolence.

3   Power distance index. This measures the degree to which influence and control are unequally distributed among individuals within a particular culture. Singapore, Hong Kong and Mexico, for example, will have more authoritarian (i.e. more accepted power distance) organisations, whereas in the case for New Zealand, Australia and Ireland these countries tend to have organisations with more open relationships among the levels within their organisations.

4   Uncertainty Avoidance index. This measures the degree to which individuals or societies attempt to avoid ambiguity, risk and the uncertainty of the future. Those scoring high on the Uncertainty Avoidance Indicator (UAI) tend to view difference as dangerous and will adhere to rules and stay committed to employers longer (e.g. Japan, Belgium or France). Those scoring low in Uncertainty Avoidance tend to view differences as interesting. Low UAI societies, such as Hong Kong, Singapore and Sweden feel comfortable with ambiguity and consequently are able to influence their own lives and those of their superiors or authorities.

5   Long-term orientation versus Short-term orientation. Long-term orientation measures the degree to which a culture emphasises values associated with the future, such as thrift and persistence. Short-term orientation measures the degree a culture emphasises values that focus largely on the present.

6   Indulgence versus Restraint. Indulgence societies allow relatively free gratification of basic and natural human drives related to enjoying life and having fun. Restraint societies suppress gratification of needs and regulate it by means of strict social norms.

Knowing one's own cultural profile will assist coaches and mentors in better understanding others when coaching and mentoring.

Trompenaars and Hampden-Turner's seven dimensions of culture. The seven dimensions of culture (Trompenaars & Hampden-Turner, 1998) looks at seven value differences, or dimensions, which help explain national cultural differences. The seven dimensions are:

1   Universalism versus Particularism
    (What is more important, the rules or exceptions based on relationships?)
2   Individualism versus communitarianism
    (Do we function in a group or as individuals?)
3   Neutral versus affective
    (How do we express our emotion?)
4   Specific versus diffuse
    (How separate do we keep our private and working lives?)
5   Achievement versus ascription
    (Do we have to prove ourselves to receive status, or is it given to us?)
6   Past, present, future
    (Do we focus on our heritage, the present day or what will come tomorrow?)
7   Internal versus external control
    (Do we control our environment or are we controlled by it?)

Again, the model helps to increase the awareness of one's own cultural assumptions and that of the cultural perspectives of others. Trompenaars and Hampden-Turner (2012) in their later study highlighted that it is not enough to just be aware of cultural differences but one must work towards reconciling cultural differences. They proposed a 4R process (Recognise, Respect, Reconcile and Resolve) for working with their seven dimensions.

Rosinski's Cultural Orientations Framework. Rosinski's (2003) definition of culture includes visible elements such as behaviours, language and artefacts, as well as invisible ones such as values, beliefs and norms. He proposed the following steps to deal with cultural differences:

1   Recognise and accept differences
2   Adapt to differences
3   Integrate differences
4   Leverage differences.

Rosinski (2003) subsequently developed a Cultural Orientations Framework (COF) as a conceptual framework and primary assessment tool particularly designed for coaches to have coaching conversations that facilitate leveraging cultural differences and creating new possibilities. The COF may be used for various purposes such as assessing cultural differences, discovering new cultural choices, bridging between different cultures, envisioning a desired culture and leveraging cultural diversity (Rosinski, 2003, pp. 50–51). The COF is an online self-report assessment tool that takes approximately 15 minutes to complete. The COF asks questions regarding seven cultural categories that include 17 cultural dimensions.

Plaister-Ten's Cross-Cultural Kaleidoscope™. A systems approach helps clients accommodate the multiple perspectives in a cross-cultural environment (Plaister-Ten, 2013). Raising culturally bound awareness and building culturally appropriate responsibility constitute the essence of good intercultural coaching practice. Plaister-Ten (2013) developed the Cross-Cultural Kaleidoscope™ to navigate in a cross-cultural landscape which will facilitate this awareness and responsibility building. The Cross-Cultural Kaleidoscope™ is a model that examines both the internal meanings of individual cultural values, whilst offering a set of lenses through which to examine the external influences that may affect emotions, thoughts, decisions and behaviours. Plaister-Ten's Cross-Cultural Kaleidoscope™ is discussed in a later chapter.

Livermore's Cultural Intelligence. The cultural intelligence model of David Livermore (2015) is rooted in a four-factor framework that synthesizes the volumes of material and perspectives on intelligence and cross-cultural leadership. Cultural intelligence (CQ) is composed of four qualitatively different capabilities: CQ Drive; CQ Knowledge, CQ Strategy and CQ Action. Together, these four capabilities make up a person's overall cultural intelligence quotient. A high cultural intelligence doesn't come automatically, but anyone can develop it. Of the four CQ capabilities, improving CQ Knowledge is most straightforward as we can take the time to learn more about cultural differences.

From the above descriptions, we can see that for cross-cultural coaching and mentoring to be effective, we need to be aware of our own cultural orientations as well as learning as much as we can about the cultures that influence our clients. As there is a risk of stereotyping cultures, it is important to develop intercultural sensitivity, by paying attention to how behaviours/ approaches resonate (or not) with the coachee or mentee, as that will provide feedback of sorts.

Bennett (1993) has proposed a Developmental Model of Intercultural Sensitivity (DMIS) to gain enhanced cultural sensitivity. DMIS's six stages provide a structure for understanding how people experience cultural difference and they describe how a person sees, thinks about and interprets events happening around them from an intercultural-difference perspective. Bennett's stages of intercultural sensitivity are denial, defence, minimisation, acceptance, adaptation and integration. Adapting to the other person does not mean forsaking our own beliefs and behaviours but, instead, tweaking our actions to help our coachee or mentee feel comfortable. In essence, the coach or mentor should progress through the different phases of cultural sensitivity, ranging from ethnocentrism (denial, defence and minimisation) to ethnorelativism (acceptance, adaptation and integration) to generate greater intercultural sensitivity and, thereby, increase their own intercultural competence.

Challenge 3: building a coaching and mentoring culture

By 2020, millennials (those born between the early 1980s and the early 2000s) will form 50% of the global workforce, and by 2025 millennials will form 75% of the workplace according to studies by PwC (2011) and Deloitte (2016). More importantly, 'The Millennial Age' has come to Asia, that is by 2020 Asia will have 60% of the world's millennial population so millennials are the future of Asia's workforce.

Coaching and mentoring will be a key engagement process in working with them as, according to a report by Meister and Willyerd (2010), millennials have clear ideas of what they want from their boss – which include mentoring and coaching.

In another study by the Intelligence Group (2014), 72% of millennials would like to be their own boss, but if they have to work for a boss, 79% would want that boss to serve more as a coach or a mentor. The study also shows that 88% of millennials prefer a collaborative culture over a competitive culture and they are looking to make a difference in their professional lives. Autonomy, and the ability to work through challenges, are more desirable to millennials than being told how to do things. They want to be inspired by leaders rather than be micro-managed. It is no surprise, therefore, that millennials prefer to be coached and mentored rather than supervised.

Mentorship has become one of the single best ways to promote effective intergenerational relationships in the workplace of today. In leading Asian organisations including companies such as Proctor & Gamble both the mentor and the mentee realised that both have something to learn and gain from the relationship. But, what is a coaching and mentoring culture?

A coaching and mentoring culture expands coaching and mentoring to a broader scope, impacting the entire organisational structure and energising all employees at all levels of an organisation hierarchy. A coaching culture is defined by Hawkins (2012, p. 21):

> A coaching culture exists in an organization when a coaching approach is a key aspect of how the leaders, managers and staff engage and develop all their people and engage their stakeholders, in ways that create increased individual, team, and organization performance and shared value for all stakeholders.

Peak performance can be achieved by an organisation that integrates the coaching culture. Each employee can take ownership and accountability of their work thereby raising the effectiveness of individuals and their managers and leaders. With a strong coaching culture, we will see high levels of employee engagement, productivity and customer satisfaction all contributing to an organisation in reaching its strategic and financial goals at a greatly increased success rate. According to a study by Bersin & Associates (2011), organisations that have a strong senior leader and cultural support of coaching have superior results. For example, organisations in which senior leaders 'very frequently' coach had 21% higher business results. Further, organisations with 'excellent' cultural support for coaching had 13% stronger business results and 39% stronger employee results. Another study by the International Coach Federation (ICF, 2015) and the Human Capital Institute (HCI) showed that with organisations with a strong coaching culture, employees were more engaged, and the businesses produced stronger financial results. Vignette 3 further highlights this.

Vignette 3

The Benefits of a Coaching Culture – MIT Sloan Management Review (2007)

http://sloanreview.mit.edu/article/the-benefits-of-a-coaching-culture/
Three researchers Ritu Agarwal and Corey M. Angst, professor of information systems and research assistant professor, respectively, at the Robert H. Smith School of Business at the University of Maryland, along with Massimo Magni, assistant professor of organisation and MIS at Bocconi University, found that instilling a coaching culture in the sales organisation paid dividends. That is, those salespeople who reported more intense coaching from their sales managers reported real performance improvements over the time period.

   Thus, Agarwal concludes, "You will get a significant boost in productivity and performance when your supervisor employs a coaching culture." In fact, the differences in coaching represented 36% of the differences in reported performance among surveyed salespeople. "I wouldn't go so far as to say that means there would be a 36% [boost in productivity]," adds Agarwal.

While we recognise that the building of a coaching and mentoring culture is important, its implementation can be a challenge (Forman, Joyce & McMahon, 2013; Hawkins 2012). For coaching to be successful, it cannot be a sporadic event that is scheduled occasionally but rather a coaching practice infused in an organisation. Everyone in an organisation should adopt a coaching mindset which requires us to give up the notion that we need to have all the answers and our way is the best or the only way; that is we need to have the attitude and confidence to help others work things out for themselves. The requirements for a successful coaching culture are included in Table 2.1 below.

Suggestions for building a coaching and mentoring culture in organisations

In essence, for a coaching and mentoring culture to happen, both coaching and mentoring practices have to be cascaded and entrenched throughout the organisation. Megginson and Clutterbuck (2006) identified four stages in

Table 2.1 Requirements for a successful coaching culture

Requirement	Description
A focus on both organisational and employee success	Managers are clear on the mission and vision of the organisation and how their team's priorities fit in. They also understand that even when they are coaching to a specific performance or productivity issue, they also must strive for the employee's increased job satisfaction and long-term engagement. Likewise, career or personal development coaching always has a relevant business context.
A belief in coaching and a backbone (the practices and systems to encourage and reward it)	The organisation, starting with its senior leaders, has an established belief that coaching by managers is important – not only to workforce development or to a solid leadership pipeline but also to the achievement of current business priorities. Without this belief leaders would say, "I've got too much work to do; no time to coach!" Systems and practices (e.g. recruiting, competencies, performance management, promotions and compensation) align with espoused beliefs. Managers who coach are held up as role models.
Individualised partnerships	Managers establish unique coaching partnerships with their team members based on an understanding of each employee's motivators, skills and preferences about being coached. Employees share accountability for successful coaching. This personalised approach enables managers to be more strategic, effective and efficient coaches.
Coaching essentials	Managers build strong relationships by establishing trust, building confidence and unleashing potential. This isn't done through feedback or specific coaching conversation skills. Managers get to know each team member, have regular, honest conversations and create a supportive, encouraging environment through a variety of leadership actions. This foundation enables them to weave coaching seamlessly into their employee interactions.
Skills	Managers seek coaching moments to coach informally in addition to conducting more formal check-ins. They use skills appropriately (given the individualised partnerships they've established) to address specific situations and employee requests.

Source: Blessingwhite (2008).

developing a coaching culture which serve as a useful guide to help organisations identify how far they are on the journey towards developing a coaching culture as noted below:

- The Nascent stage, where an organisation has little or no commitment to creating a 'coaching culture', where some coaching may happen and it's highly inconsistent in both frequency and quality.
- The Tactical stage, where the organisation has recognised the value of establishing a coaching culture, but there is little understanding of what this means, or what's involved. There is a broad understanding of coaching within departments and managers can see the benefits although it may be considered an HR function.
- The Strategic stage, where there has been considerable effort to educate managers and employees in the value of coaching and give people the competence to coach in a variety of situations. This can only have a flourishing effect on the safety culture. Senior management appreciate the need to demonstrate good safe practices in all areas of the business.
- The Embedded stage, where people at all levels are engaged in coaching, both formally and informally, this then becomes part of 'how we do things around here' and is an integral part of day-to-day activities, like quality, etc.

In a later study by Clutterbuck (2014), through interviews with hundreds of HR professionals responsible for coaching and mentoring, he noticed that successful organisations tend to focus on four main areas when strategising to cultivate a coaching and mentoring culture:

- accessibility and relevance: creating or increasing access to an appropriate and relevant coaching or mentoring modality;
- support and reinforcement: building and sustaining the momentum for coaching and mentoring in the organisation;
- integration: making coaching part of the way 'we do business around here';
- measurement: evaluating progress and effectiveness of coaching.

Barbara Greene's (2012) phases (Plan, Learn and Apply, and Sustain) is another useful tool to build a coaching and mentoring culture. Each phase builds upon the other for a comprehensive approach. In 'Plan', the organisation must plan to create awareness and engagement. In 'Learn and Apply', the objective is to have everyone learn what coaching and mentoring is and the differences. The 'Sustain' phase is critical to the coaching and mentoring culture's long-term success. To flourish, the coaching and mentoring approach needs to be fully integrated in all talent, leadership development and other organisation initiatives such as strategy and innovation. Other coaching models include the GROW model (Whitmore, 2009) and solution-focused coaching (Berg and Szabo, 2005) and, according to Lindbom (2007), a mix of regular, frequent, formal and informal coaching (coaching on the fly) conversations becomes self-reinforcing. As Govindarajan (2005) highlighted, unlike a strategy consultant who may push a generic model of competition on an organisation, the strategy coach works with the organisation to build a strategy from within.

Thus, coaching and mentoring should no longer be stand-alone initiatives but integral to the organisation's way of life. The organisation must recognise and reward coaching and mentoring culture behaviours and continue to develop coaching and mentoring skills so that individuals become more confident in using them. Processes need to be in place to ensure there is constant feedback and review of progress and managers and leaders should take the opportunity to highlight successes and note any tangible returns on investments because of the coaching and mentoring culture in place.

Challenge 4: the need for more empirical research on coaching and mentoring in the Asia Pacific region

The final challenge we have come across is the lack of empirical research on coaching and mentoring with examples from or on the region of Asia Pacific. This is not an isolated incidence, the depth of research on coaching and mentoring is limited in all areas across the globe. This is changing, however, and there has been an increase in the academic literature over the past decade on coaching and mentoring.

A number of reasons can be put forward to explain the lack of progress in the coaching research. First, there are practical barriers. Many studies are conducted by coach practitioners in real-world settings making it difficult and often unethical to randomly assign participants to different experimental and control conditions. Even where quasi-experimental designs can be developed, they are likely to involve longer time frames and the employer organisations may be reluctant to fund coaching programmes in these situations. The current state of coaching reflects a continuing concern among researchers involved with establishing coaching as a legitimate human resource development activity and with the development of coaches as professionals. To mature as a field, the research needs to move beyond these concerns and focus on developing sound theoretical models based on more sophisticated research.

It would be easy to suggest that despite a significant increase in the number of empirical studies, little actual progress has been made in demonstrating the effectiveness of coaching or providing guidelines for coaching practice. Alternatively, it could be argued that the growth in studies that evaluate coaching programmes in a number of sectors and locations suggest that coaching has now established itself as a legitimate HR development tool and that coaching programmes can be positively evaluated by a variety of participants and methods. The present challenge for researchers in this area is to accept this conclusion and begin to examine coaching in more detail and with a more critical approach. While there is an increase in studies on coaching in general, there is still a nearly non-existent base of coaching and mentoring literature focused specifically on the region of Asia Pacific.

Conclusion

This chapter has explored the challenges of coaching and mentoring in Asia Pacific. We first looked at the talent and leadership demands in Asia Pacific which sees coaching and mentoring being embraced more and more in this region. This led to the challenge of the increased demand for coaches and mentors in Asia Pacific.

Next, we discussed coaching and mentoring in this culture-rich Asia Pacific region which led to the challenge that organisations will need to increasingly seek coaches and mentors with intercultural competence. We have briefly reviewed the concept of culture and key cross-cultural models with the intent to raise the awareness of national cultural differences and dimensions. The key point is that any coach/mentor working with a coachee/mentee from another cultural background should be aware that we are inclined to interpret an answer or a behaviour of the coachee/mentee according to our own perspective, based on our own values. As such, we need to move from ethnocentric thinking to an ethnorelative perspective so as to increase our cultural awareness. While being effective in coaching and mentoring across cultures is not an easy task, we are convinced that developing cultural intelligence and cultural sensitivity will enhance our intercultural competence. With this, coaches and mentors can become more effective and impactful in their coaching or mentoring engagements.

With the millennials becoming a major proportion of the workforce, the third challenge we see is for Asia Pacific organisations to recognise the need to work on building and sustaining a coaching and mentoring culture in their workplace. The intergenerational workplace of today and the rise of the millennials in Asia Pacific with its preference for coaching and mentoring must be taken seriously and not be viewed as just a novel concept. Organisations that develop a coaching and mentoring culture will create and build a competitive workforce which will lead to higher organisational performance and eventually stakeholder benefits.

The final challenge we discussed was around the lack of research on coaching and mentoring with specific reference to countries in Asia Pacific. While there is growth in empirical research on coaching and mentoring, most of the examples provided or research conducted is in the western world without consideration of how it may be implemented in the east.

References

AEC. (2015). *Factsheet on ASEAN Economic Community (AEC)*. Singapore: Association of Southeast Asian Nations.

ASEAN. (2015). *ASEAN Economic Community blueprint 2025*. Jakarta: Association of Southeast Asian Nations.

Bennett, M. J. (1993). Towards a developmental model of intercultural sensitivity. In R. M. Paige (Ed.), *Education for the intercultural experience*. Yarmouth, ME: Intercultural Press.

Berg, I. K., & Szabo, P. (2005). *Brief coaching for lasting solutions*. New York: Norton.

Bersin & Associates. (2011). *High-impact performance management*. California: Maximizing Performance Coaching.

Blessingwhite. (2008). *The Coaching Conundrum 2009 global executive summary*. Princeton, NJ: Blessingwhite-Inc.

Caligiuri, P., Lepak, D. & Bonache, J. (2010). *Managing the global workforce*. Chichester, UK: John Wiley & Sons.

CIPD. (2010). *Learning and talent development: Annual survey report*. UK: Chartered Institute of Personnel and Development.

Clutterbuck, D. (2014). *What every HR director should know about coaching and mentoring strategy*. www.davidclutterbuckpartnership.com/what-every-hr-director-should-know-about-coaching-and-mentoring-strategy/.

Deloitte. (2016). *The 2016 Millennial Survey: Winning the next generation of leaders*. Retrieved 17 August 2017, from www2.deloitte.com/content/dam/Deloitte/global/Documents/About-Deloitte/gx-millenial-survey-2016-exec-summary.pdf.

Forman, D., Joyce, M. & McMahon, G. (2013). *Creating a coaching culture for managers in your organisation*. London: Routledge.

Govindarajan, V. (2005). Coaching for strategic thinking capability, strategy coaching. In H. Morgan, P. Harkins & M. Goldsmith (Eds), *The art and practice of leadership coaching* (pp. 196–199): Hoboken, NJ: John Wiley.

Greene, B. A. F. (2012). *The power of a coaching culture on organizational performance*. Retrieved 17 August 2017, from www.executivecoachglobal.com/the-power-of-a-coaching-culture-on-organizational-performance/.

Hawkins, P. (2012). *Creating a coaching culture*. Maidenhead, UK: Open University Press, McGraw-Hill.

Hofstede, G. (1984). *Culture's consequences: International differences in work related values*. Beverly Hills, CA: Sage.

ICF. (2015). Building a coaching culture for increased employee engagement. USA: International Coach Federation.

International Monetary Fund. (2015). *Regional economic outlook: Asia and Pacific*. Washington, DC: IMF.

Jenkins, H. (2006). *Convergence culture: Where old and new media collide*. New York: New York University Press.

Lindbom, D. (2007). A culture of coaching: The challenge of managing performance for long term results. *Organization Development Journal*, *25*(2), 101–106.

Livermore, D. (2015). *Leading with cultural intelligence: The real secret to success*. New York: Amacom.

Man. (2015). *ManpowerGroup 2015 Talent Shortage Survey*. USA.

Megginson, D., & Clutterbuck, D. (2006). Creating a coaching culture. *Industrial and Commercial Training, 38*(5), 232–237.

Meister, J. C., & Willyerd, K. (2010). Mentoring millennials. *Harvard Business Review*, May.

Minkov, M., & Blagoev, V. (2014). Is there a distinct Asian management culture? *Asia PacifiBusiness Review, 20*(2), 209–215.

Nicholas, J., & Twaddell, K. (2010). Group executive coaching in Asia: Same same but different. In D. Wright, A. Leong, K. E. Webb & S. Chia (Eds), *Coaching in Asia: The first decade*. Singapore: Candid Creation Publishing.

Passmore, J. (2009). *Diversity in coaching*. London: Kogan Page.

Peterson, D. (2007). Executive coaching in a cross-cultural context. *Consulting Psychology Journal: Practice and Research, 59*(4), 261–271.

Plaister-Ten, J. (2013). Raising culturally-derived awareness and building culturally appropriate responsibility: The development of the Cross-Cultural Kaleidoscope. *International Journal of Evidence Based Coaching and Mentoring, 11*(2), August.

PwC. (2011). *Millennials at work, reshaping the workplace*. Retrieved 17 August 2018, from www.pwc.com/m1/en/services/consulting/documents/millennials-at-work.pdf.

Rosinski, P. (2003). *Coaching across cultures: New tools for leveraging national, corporate and professional differences*. London: Nicholas Brealey.

Schein, E. H. (2010). *Organizational culture and leadership*. San Francisco: Jossey-Bass.

Straits Times. (2016). *Asean – the new growth frontier*. Retrieved 17 August 2017, from www.straitstimes.com/business/asean-the-new-growth-frontier.

The Conference Board. (2013). *Fast track: Accelerating the leadership development of high potentials in Asia*. New York.

The Intelligence Group. (2014). *The Cassandra report: Global issue*. Summer/Fall. New York.

Trompenaars, F., & Hampden-Turner, C. (1998). *Riding the waves of culture: Understanding diversity in global business* (2nd edn). New York: McGraw-Hill.

Trompenaars, F., & Hampden-Turner, C. (2012). *Riding the waves of culture: Understanding diversity in global business* (3rd edn). New York: McGraw-Hill.

Whitmore, J. (2009). *Coaching for performance: GROWing human potential and purpose – the principles and practice of coaching and leadership* (4th edn). London: Nicholas Brealey.

3 What does good practice look like?

Anna Blackman and David Clutterbuck

A coach is said to be someone who establishes options, introduces challenges and initiates alternative behaviours (Witherspoon & White, 1996). According to Eggers and Clark (2000) and Evers, Brouwers and Tomic (2006) a coach is someone who is able to prompt the coachee (the person being coached) with questions so that they are able to discover the answers themselves. The role of an executive coach is to provide feedback about the executive's behaviour and the impact that behaviour is having on others both within and outside the organisation (O'Neill, 2000; Witherspoon & White, 1996). It is argued that with this feedback executives are able to gain an increase in their performance and that of their team with an increased sense of self-awareness, self-esteem and better communication with their work colleagues (Kilburg, 1996). In turn this should lead to increased morale, productivity and higher profits (Kampa-Kokesch & Anderson, 2001; Smith, 1993).

Although much of the organisational coaching literature uses the term 'executive coaching', we use 'coaching' as a more inclusive description, incorporating all forms of coaching (including executive, management, team, line manager and leadership coaching) taking place in business. Coaching can be conducted by either external coaches or internal line managers or human resource management and development staff (Brandl, Madsen, & Madsen, 2009; Teague & Roche, 2011). Although internal coaching is recognised within human resource management and development as a critical skill for all managers to have as part of their repertoire of human resource tools (Swart & Kinnie, 2010), there are several different approaches to coaching, and any one coaching programme can include a range of techniques and activities. Coaching programmes can also vary in terms of the number, variety and types of techniques that are used within the programme, the length of the programme and the type of consultant employed as the coach (Blackman, 2006).

This is all well and good; everyone can agree on these principles. Any coach (or coachee, for that matter) will say that is what a coach does. But that is the end product; how do we get there? What are the elements on good coaching that make the coaching experience a success? What does good practice look like?

Not to, but with

Research identifies a long list of potential barriers to effective coaching by line managers, from being seen to have their own agenda to finding it hard to break out of parent-child behaviours. All of these can be overcome, if the line manager and the team have clear expectations about the nature and purpose of coaching. One of the big mindshifts needed is from the assumption that the line manager will do coaching to team members, to the recognition that their role is to create the environment, where coaching happens. (The coach may be another team member or someone from outside, as well as the manager.)

Teams focused on delivering demanding targets don't have a lot of time for the abstract and theoretical. They do want to know what the benefits of achieving a coaching culture will be (both individually and collectively) but, for the most part, they want to see how what they are learning can be applied to practical and relatively immediate issues the team faces in delivering what is expected of it (for further reading see Clutterbuck, 2015b).

As Clutterbuck has said, there is a general, if often implicit, assumption that coaching is something done to direct reports, rather than with them. When that happens, it is indistinguishable from line management. But, when the coaching process is owned by both coach and coachee and both take accountability for making it work, then the coachee helps the coach help them. Working with each other, they coach each other. When teams demonstrate a coaching culture, the role of the manager is not to do coaching but to create the environment, where coaching happens. So, team members also coach each other and, in many cases, coach their boss.

Coaching is not merely the passing on of a skill or process but it is a relationship. Skills can be passed on and learned quickly; relationships require time. It takes time but also humble collaboration on the part of all concerned. It requires months of collaborative practice to build competence and confidence (for further reading see Clutterbuck, 2014).

Reflection before action

Acquiring the coaching mindset takes time. Coaching is both a mindset and a skill set. A concentrated workshop can provide basic knowledge, skills and some opportunities to practise in a safe environment outside the team. But the impact of coaching typically happens between coaching conversations, when the learner reflects on insights, ideas, issues and intentions. It seems that learning to coach and be coached is most effective when broken up into relatively small chunks, with sufficient space (at least a couple of weeks) to reflect, absorb and practise using what has been learned.

Good coaching practice provides opportunity and space for the coachee or team to think things through. Ethical coaching/mentoring helps people (for further reading see Clutterbuck, 2013b) think through situations so that they become aware of potential value conflicts, ethical dilemmas and the factors that may impact on their own and others' careers and personal identity. Good practice requires the ability to disentangle intent and impact, means and ends; to dig out apposite lessons from complex and highly charged situations; to help people rediscover their belief in their own potential to be principled and to influence their environment for good.

Good coaches and mentors need to have a deep insight into their own thinking processes, in relation to their own behaviour and their own decision-making. They need strong skills in questioning and challenging – both of themselves and of others. They need to be able to help other people step back and critique their values, judgements and actions; yet the coach/mentor cannot be judgemental themselves. So, before action, the outcome of the coaching/mentoring is reflection-for-action, a solution or approach that fits the well-thought-out circumstances and values of the situation.

Reflection allows the opportunity to run through different scenarios and their strengths and weaknesses. It allows a measured understanding of what's possible and what's not. It allows space, both time and psychic space, to work through different options and responsibilities.

One of the most intractable issues for top teams is how to translate bland statements of values into heart and soul commitment amongst the wider workforce – especially when there is little difference between the values statements of one company and the next. Genuine engagement with shared values can only happen through conversations that allow people to reflect on experience, to build strong connections between their personal values and organisational values and to explore with others how values work out in practice. In particular, people need frequent conversations that explore how values conflict and they need practice in how to reconcile values conflicts in ways that are self-honest and less influenced by self-interest than might be the norm.

Mentoring and coaching as whole-of-organisation practice

To reiterate what was said above, coaching and mentoring are not things done to people but ways of working with others. Therefore, it should not be just one or two people in an organisation who are coached or mentored (which may happen when an individual is not up to the job) but good coaching and mentoring should be embedded practices in the whole organisation (Clutterbuck, 2017b).

Within the team, developing an environment of psychological safety is closely correlated with speed of acquiring a coaching culture. At the same time, teams progress more confidently if they feel that their learning journey is supported from outside, for example, by senior management. External support may take the form of a specialist team coach or facilitator – an outsider with the skills to help the team deal with issues such as unsurfaced conflict or clarifying the team purpose.

But, if you are going to change the system, you have to change the whole system. Change one part and the system will resist. Change the whole and you have a high chance of making the change stick. In the team context, it is critically important to engage the whole team – manager and all his or her direct reports – in understanding and supporting the change to a coaching culture. An analogy with just training the line manager is ballroom dancing. If only one partner knows how to tango, a couple is not going to do well! In a team with a coaching culture, everyone understands the basics of coaching and can coach everyone else. (That includes, on occasion, the line manager being coached by a direct report!) Equally, everyone needs to know how to be coached, so they can help the coach help them (Clutterbuck, 2015b).

Good practice will, therefore, require a new mindset from managers and staff. As well, organisations may want to create internal coach and mentor positions within the organisation to ensure a whole-of-organisation response. Some key characteristics would include:

- A designated mentoring programme manager. Increasingly, these individuals have received specialized training for the role (the European Mentoring and Coaching Council is considering accrediting programme manager training programmes, for example). They tend to be responsible for promoting and supporting mentoring in general, rather than just managing a single initiative.
- High-level engagement from top management.
- Ensuring that both mentors and mentees are trained and that both are supported over the life of the supported relationship.
- Continuous development and supervision.

This is already happening. In recent round-table discussions with HR professionals around the world, responsible for mentoring, a number of themes have emerged:

- Greater integration between different mentoring programmes in the same organisation. For example, cascade mentoring takes the perspective that people who receive mentoring should also become mentors, in a chain of giving. So, a number of European organisations are exploring programmes, in which graduate recruits are mentored by junior and middle managers and, in return, they mentor disadvantaged persons from the wider community. One of the benefits of this approach is that it links employee development and corporate social responsibility agendas.
- Clarifying the different interpretations of mentoring within the same organisation. For example, IBM has identified four types of mentoring, aimed at different audiences and for different purposes. Central resources support all of these types of mentoring, but interpretation and programme management are customised.

- Taking greater account of the differences in expectations of mentoring from diverse cultures. Companies, such as Shell, have learned that it is important to make these different expectations overt and to enable mentors and mentees to address them at the level of the individual relationship.
- Social media hold the potential to change radically how mentoring is delivered. Many multinationals now regularly conduct both one-to-one and group mentoring through social media. However, a key issue now emerging for such companies is the extent to which employees (and particularly talented employees) can be supported in developing dynamic networks of mentors. In these networks, there may be one or two close mentoring relationships, focused on medium- to long-term career development, several medium-term relationships focused on development of specific (leadership) competencies and ad hoc short-term relationships, focused on transfer of skills or knowledge. Intrinsic to these mentor networks is that the traditional senior to junior hierarchy of relationships is often irrelevant – it is the learning exchange that is important and peer and reverse mentoring will play an increased role.

The bottom line of all these changing perceptions of mentoring is that current approaches both offer and demand a lot more flexibility from organisations and from participants. At the same time, it creates the potential for both organisations and participants to gain a great deal more from their investments in this powerful form of co-learning.

Team coaching

Team coaching is another area that is still a relatively new kid on the block. There is only limited academic literature and not much practitioner literature to draw upon. And much of what is described as team coaching fails on one or both of the two key acid tests:

- Does it address issues from the perspective of the team as a whole (rather than involve a series of interventions with individual members of a team)?
- Does it apply coaching principles and methodologies (as opposed to facilitation, team building and so on)?

In short, team coaching is at a similar point to where executive coaching was 15 years ago. Many of the trends we see in team coaching reflect this stage in its evolution. Among these are:

Movement towards standards and professionalisation. We don't have reliable data about what proportion of people claiming to be team coaches have appropriate training in the role, nor at what level. Being an effective one-to-one coach may bring a coaching mindset, but it doesn't prepare a coach for the complex dynamics of teams. Moreover, the potential for unprepared coaches to break the golden rule of 'do no harm' is much higher when working with teams than when working with individuals.

From discussions with other people active in promoting quality of team coaching, there appears to be a consensus that the minimum preparation consists of at least 120 hours of study, practice, reflection and supervision at postgraduate certificate level. The team coach needs, in addition to high expertise in coaching method, a solid understanding – at a minimum – of:

- group and team psychology;
- team facilitation skills;
- systemic thinking and theory;
- group dynamics;
- roots and causes of team dysfunction;
- a wide range of team diagnostic tools;
- how to work in the moment with group diversity, conflict and sub-groups.

Useful questions to consider, when comparing different options for training as a team coach, include:

- How well grounded is this course in the evidence-based literature?
- What have the course tutors contributed to the development of the field of team coaching (for example, through research, publications or development of standards)?
- How eclectic is the knowledge base? (Is it mainly based on one specific methodology or does it give me what I need to build my own philosophy and approach?)

The General Council for Mentoring and Coaching (the coordination body for the European Mentoring and Coaching Council, the International Coach Federation and the Association for Coaching) has already begun to look at team coaching competencies and standards. The Association of Coaching Supervisors is exploring the issue of supervision for team coaches. A critical issue here is that supervisors of one-to-one coaches don't necessarily have experience in or a sufficient body of relevant knowledge in team coaching. Fortunately, we are beginning to see a consensus about the role and quality of supervision in this context.

Increased clarity about what team coaching is for. In terms of the competencies required of coaches and the impact of coaching, the scale proposed by Hawkins and Smith (2014) (skills, performance, behavioural, transformational) strikes a chord with that part of the coaching community which looks to an evidence base as the foundation of their practice. Perhaps driven by market forces, team coaching's early days were marked by an emphasis on achieving relatively short-term performance goals. As buyers slowly become more knowledgeable and as more coaches working mainly in behavioural and transformational contexts move into the field, there has been a visible shift. Team coaching is now much more about helping a team achieve greater capability, from which results are likely to flow. Those results are likely to be much wider and typically less subject to simplistic measurement. One way to describe the purpose of team coaching is 'to enable the team to better coach itself'. This inevitably involves the creation of some level of coaching culture.

One of the ways to depict coaching – and by extension, team coaching – is that it helps people achieve greater understanding of both their inner world and their outer world and to have the conversations that use those under-standings to achieve better decisions and act upon them. So, the role of the team coach is, first, to offer ways in which the team can increase its under-standing of internal and external contexts; and, second, to support the team in having the open, purposeful and effective conversations it needs to make use of its insights.

The systemic dimensions. In research on coach maturity, one of the core characteristics identified in the most mature coaches was that they focused as much on the systems, of which the client is a part, as the presented issues. Indeed, it is probably not possible to bring about deep, lasting change without addressing those systems. When team coaches work with teams to resolve specific issues, they can easily end up as consultants, unless they recognise and have the skills to explore the systemic dimensions. Systems may be internal to the team, external or across the internal-external boundary. Working with team systems – especially those that operate across the team's boundaries with the outside world – requires courage, flexibility and a strong dose of intu-ition! However, this has now become a core part of the leading-edge team coaching training programmes.

Internalization of team coaching. There is a clear trend, internationally, for organisations to bring in-house much of the coaching that used to be delivered by external professional coaches. A pragmatic approach to building coaching capability includes:

- Having clear and evidence-driven approaches to ensure the quality of externally resourced executive coaches. Assessment centre data indicate that approximately 70% of coaches acquired through non-evidence-based processes – and a similar proportion of coaches provided by coach pools – are not up to the task of coaching the C-suite.
- Building a cadre of internal professional coaches. Contrary to popular opinion, there is no credible evidence that internal coaches are less com-petent overall than externals. A negative factor may be that they can be less able to challenge power structures within the organisation; but a positive factor is that they understand and can better work within the corporate politics.
- Enabling and supporting coaching within work teams. This is not about sending line managers off on short 'sheep-dip' coaching courses – which

has very little positive impact. It is much more about creating a coaching culture within a work team. Key factors here are that everyone in the team knows how to coach and be coached; that they take collective responsibility for their own and each other's learning; and that coaching skills are developed over time, by working on shared, current issues, which the team needs to address.

Some organisations, which have relatively advanced coaching cultures, are already developing internal cadres of team coaches, drawn from the senior ranks of either or both HR and executives in line management roles. These may work either on specific issues – such as supporting a new project team to move rapidly through forming, storming and norming to performing – or more generally to support a team at any level to create its own coaching culture.

All of these trends are likely to gather momentum. The volume of qualified (trained and academically accredited) team coaches is likely to increase, for several reasons. First, coaches, who have dabbled in team coaching will – if they are serious about the practice – want to take advantage of the opportunities to test, ground and upgrade their practice. Second, for many experienced one-to-one coaches, team coaching is a natural evolution of their practice. However, the market for team coaching shows no immediate signs of developing as rapidly as the supply. Educating corporate buyers will be the challenge (for further reading see Clutterbuck, 2017a).

Diversity is a process not just an objective

Diversity mentoring seems to work best when (Kochan, 2012):

1   It is one of a suite of initiatives that support a clear diversity objective. Mentoring on its own cannot deliver for women or any other minority group.
2   It is a well-designed programme where the mentee is working to enhance their individual capacity for success.
3   Programme goals, whatever they are, are made clear to everyone, to avoid misunderstandings and to minimise resentment amongst those that are excluded.
4   Someone is a champion for the programme – ideally a steering committee is appointed so that the programme can be sustained after original champions move on.
5   Pairs are well-matched. Matching across or within the diversity group depends on whether it is important for members of the majority group to learn about the diversity issues, or whether it would be beneficial for the mentee to learn coping strategies from a mentor of the same diversity group.
6   Mentors and mentees are well trained and their expectations are aligned.
7   Programmes are tracked and evaluated (Richardson & Clutterbuck, 2017).

Studies by two professors at French business schools (Hae-Jung & Doz, 2013) identify seven characteristics of a multicultural manager:

1　Sensitivity to one's own and other cultures
2　Cultural awareness and curiosity
3　Cultural empathy
4　Multilingual skills
5　Contextual understanding and sensitivity
6　Semantic awareness
7　Ability to switch among cultural frames of reference and communication modes.

It is logical that relationships are likely to have higher rapport and greater intensity of learning, if mentors are able to recognise and value the cultural perspectives that mentees bring to the mentoring conversation, to empathise with different ways of interpreting events and to recognise when linguistic differences may lead to divergent interpretations of meaning.

The qualities identified in the French study can be described as *multicultural intelligence*. This is valuable in any organisation that encompasses a variety of cultures. Even where the language is the same – for example, US and UK English – lack of cross-cultural awareness can be a barrier to effective operations. There are numerous examples of instances of communication failure, where US and UK nationals have taken radically different and, in some cases, opposite meanings from the same words or phrases. (For example, 'put an issue on the table', which may mean deal with an issue now or park it, according to your cultural upbringing!)

The problem is that only a small proportion of coaches and mentors within companies typically have high levels of multicultural intelligence. Even among people who have spent considerable periods as expatriates, multicultural intelligence can be relatively low – especially in multinationals, where expatriates live in relative isolation from their host cultures.

Some of the general steps that organisations can take to support coaches and mentors in developing multicultural intelligence include:

• Basic cultural awareness training – certainly not a complete solution, but a useful starting point! At the minimum, this should include an understanding of cultural dimensions, differences in body language and cultural values. (The work of Philippe Rosinski on coaching across cultures is a valuable resource for coaches and mentors.)
• Using managers, who have high multicultural intelligence to coach and mentor peers.
• Reading anthropological literature about specific cultures *and one's own culture* – for example, the book *Watching the English*, by Kate Fox, raises awareness on how perspectives and behaviours that are considered normal by English natives can be confusing to people from other cultures.

- Encouraging coaches and mentors to develop at least conversational competence in languages other than their own. Bilingual and trilingual people frequently think differently in each language, because each evokes different patterns of association.
- Companies should also be prepared to hold an assessment centre for external coaches – in Europe 70% of those assessed fail to meet the basic standard required.
- Use the same principles to build an internal cadre of coaches – this is a major trend internationally.
- Integrate coaching and mentoring. Train both mentors and mentees, coaches and coachees – if people understand how to be coached or mentored the relationship is much more productive and effective.
- Incorporate team coaching into the resources available, to ensure that key teams become high performing teams.
- Make sure coaches and mentors are supported (ideally through supervision, but at a minimum through online resources).

Within the coaching or mentoring relationship, coaches and mentors can be proactive in developing their own multicultural intelligence. Based on the seven characteristics from the French study, they can, for example:

- *Take opportunities to explore and appreciate the culture of the coachee/mentee and how it differs from their own.* For example, they can explore issues such as:
  - What is a typical day in their traditional environment?
  - What values do they hold most dearly and why?
  - What are the most vivid stories they tell to their children? (Myths and parables are invaluable for understanding concepts of relationships, social exchange, duty and so on.)
  - What does the coachee/mentee find strange about the culture of the coach/mentor?

- *Cultivate cultural curiosity.* If one looks for them, there are multiple opportunities to learn about other cultures at work and in other environments, such as on holiday. At work, people tend to sit for lunch with people from their own culture – that's a habit that can easily be broken with forethought. On holiday, we tend to have very shallow interactions with locals, but taking an interest in their culture is almost always rewarded with a warm response. Ask the coachee/mentee to recommend a few books, which have been translated from their language into yours and read them with an eye to what you can learn about that culture.
- *Practice cultural empathy.* This requires moving beyond intellectual curiosity to engaging with and appreciating the richness of the other culture. Ask oneself the question, "If I had grown up in that culture, how would I be looking at this issue?"

- *Use the coaching mentoring conversations as an opportunity to learn some basics of the other person's language.* This is not just about being able to say please and thank you, when visiting their part of the world. Conducting the session entirely in the coach's or mentor's language is a subtle indicator of power in the relationship. Learning some of the other person's language helps to counterbalance this and emphasises the two-way learning nature of the relationship.
- *Create opportunities to view issues through the lens of the coachee's or mentee's culture.* Whenever they seem to be making less progress than they should, the coach/mentor should consider the possibility that there is a culturally based barrier. This is a time to dig deeply into how they make sense of the situation, what real or imagined constraints they perceive and what values they perceive to be strengthened or undermined by the options available to them.
- *Seize opportunities to discuss the subtleties of language* – how the meaning of words or phrases changes slightly in translation. For example, there may be one word for something in English, but two or three, with subtly different meanings, in the other language – and vice versa. These discussions can provide some of the most valuable opportunities to identify different patterns of thinking. Similarly, it is helpful to develop sensitivity to the meaning of metaphors in different languages and cultures. For example, in much of Europe, the owl is the symbol of wisdom and intelligence, being closely associated with Athena, the Greek goddess of wisdom. In Hindu mythology, the owl is associated with (among other things) transition, because it accompanies the soul of the departed into the next world. In North American Indian mythology, it is a malevolent harbinger of doom.
- *Develop the habit of thinking about how people from a different culture would approach issues.* Use your coachee/mentee to help you develop this ability. Ask them, "How would people in your culture typically go about this?" Experiment with different speeds of talking. Identify the limitations of typical styles of thinking in your own culture and practise applying alternative modes from other cultures. For example, a manager from a Western culture, used to applying linear, cause and effect logic, might consider an issue instead from a ying and yang perspective, in which opposites can co-exist.

While it is ideal for coaches and mentors to have developed these skills before they enter into a cross-cultural learning alliance, for most the relationship is their opportunity to acquire multicultural intelligence in a relatively safe environment, where experimentation is both accepted and a reinforcement for the rapport between them and their coachee/mentee. The coach/mentor is therefore strongly recommended to create and share with the coachee/mentee a personal development plan built around their increasing multicultural intelligence (for further reading see Clutterbuck, 2013a).

Fee and Gray (2013) found that international volunteers' learning incidents differ in terms of their context, process and outcomes. The results also highlight the transformational nature of international volunteer placements, and in particular the role of culture in triggering this transformation. Volunteers' transformational learning occurred in a variety of contexts and across a range of learning outcomes. However, much of this was underpinned by the vast cultural differences that infused aspects of the volunteers' work and non-work learning. These cultural differences contributed to the bulk of the transformational learning triggers (mistakes, incorrect expectations) and provided the platform for the novelty and challenge that shaped the learning outcomes reported. While the volunteers' learning was not exclusively culture-driven, transformational change tended to emerge from the radically different cultural milieu. Given the 12-month study period, it remains unclear whether the influence of cultural difference on volunteers' learning is sustained once they acculturate or whether its patterns and impact are distinct during the cultural adjustment process (e.g. Black, Mendenhall & Oddou, 1991).

Challenging accepted wisdom

In recent years Clutterbuck and colleagues (Clutterbuck, 2015a) have been taking a critical perspective on the related and heavily overlapping discipline of coaching. Here are eight of the common assumptions, which are being questioned, together with alternative perspectives from observations and evidence-gathering:

1   Coaches need to set clear goals at the start of an assignment. Consider the contrary evidence: a Harvard study of 200 coaches found that, for almost all of them, the original goal morphed into something different as the client better understood their values and their environment. Over-focusing on narrow goals blinds people to other possibilities, encourages riskier behaviour and is associated with lower performance in, for example, career progression. Coaching is often about helping the client work out what they want to do. Having achieved that, they are often smart enough not to need a coach to help them do it. Most models of coaching place goal-setting as a middle step, after understanding context.
2   Coaching needs to be solutions focused. The need to find a solution within the session often comes from the coach (wanting to feel useful) rather than from the client, who may simply want to get his or her head around an issue, so they can take their time working out the right solution. A clear danger in solutions focus (which, of course, does have many uses) is that the client agrees to a solution before they are ready to do so.
3   Coaching is non-directive, mentoring is directive. Professional mentors often say exactly the opposite. Neither statement stands up to scrutiny. There are actually many approaches to both coaching and mentoring, with varying levels of directiveness, but the mainstream of both is

non-directive. John Leary-Joyce describes mentoring as 'coaching plus' – the pluses being having contextually specific knowledge and/or experience, being a role model and a greater influence on networking. Mentors use their wisdom to help another person develop wisdom of their own – telling people what to do isn't part of the skill set or role.

4   Coaches shouldn't take copious notes. If you do, you cannot be attending fully to the client. Neuroscience tells us that we cannibalise the bits of the brain we need for active listening when we try to capture words on paper or screen. Pausing every now and then (having captured one word notes from time to time) and asking the client "What would you like to capture from what we have just been saying?" is far more effective. It's also more client-centred – are your notes really more valid or important than theirs?

5   A good coach can coach anyone in anything. A contrary view is that coaches need to have enough contextual knowledge to frame really insightful and empathetic questions and to ensure the safety of the client and themselves. As an example, a coach ignorant of insider dealing rules working with a bank employee was implicitly colluding with unethical and potentially illegal behaviour, because he lacked appropriate subject knowledge. There's also the matter of credibility. Whether we like it or not, very senior executives often expect their coaches to have experienced what it is like to work at their level in a business. One of the clear lessons of The Leadership Pipeline is that people have to go through a significant mindshift at each stage from managing self, through managing others, managing managers, managing functions and so on.

6   Coaching is a process. The research into coach maturity tells us that coaches also go through radical mindshifts about their professional practice. One of the key transitions is from thinking of coaching as something you do to something you are. Coaches at the third level of maturity integrate immense personal learning and reflection into a personal philosophy that aligns with their sense of being.

7   Number of hours of coaching is a good guide to coach efficacy. Actually, the results from coach assessment centres, involving hundreds of coaches, indicate that there is no significant correlation. There is even less correlation between coach competence and level of fees charged!

8   The client is the focus for coaching. It is increasingly apparent (though we lack good empirical evidence) that coaching someone without paying attention to the systems, of which they are a part and which influence their behaviour, is less effective than working through the client to change the systems as well. This isn't always possible, of course, but focusing too much on the client alone creates a self-limiting belief on the part of the coach and this is likely to be played out through the client.

As coaching matures, it's gratifying to see all the three main professional bodies taking a more evidence-based approach to coaching practice, though it is arguable that Europe is in the vanguard compared with the USA (as it is in the use of supervision).

As individual coaches, we can enhance our own practice by identifying assumptions we make about how we coach and what good coaching looks like – then asking ourselves the questions:

- What evidence do we have for this assumption?
- Is this assumption always true, or just sometimes true?
- What are the contexts and situations when it might not be true?
- Is the evidence in support of this assumption itself based on other assumptions, which might be questioned?

We can also open ourselves up to other perspectives – for example, by selecting supervisors who come from a discipline we are relatively unfamiliar with; or by developing a portfolio of memberships of organisations or social networks that will direct us toward different ways of looking at the familiar.

References

Black, J. S., Mendenhall, M. & Oddou, G. (1991). Toward a comprehensive model of international adjustment: An integration of multiple theoretical perspectives. *Academy of Management Review, 16*(2), 291–317.

Blackman, A. (2006). Factors that contribute to the effectiveness of business coaching: The coachees perspective. *The Business Review, Cambridge, 5*(1), 98–104.

Brandl, J., Madsen, M. & Madsen, H. (2009). The perceived importance of HR duties to Danish line managers. *Human Resource Management Journal, 19*, 194–210.

Clutterbuck, D. (2013a). *Skills of a multicultural mentor.* Retrieved from www.coaching andmentoringinternational.org.

Clutterbuck, D. (2013b). *Step forward the ethical mentor.* Retrieved from www.coaching andmentoringinternational.org.

Clutterbuck, D. (2014). *Why line manager coaching often doesn't work and what to do about it.* Retrieved from www.coachingandmentoringinternational.org.

Clutterbuck, D. (2015a). *Eight coaching myths and misconceptions.* Retrieved from www. coachingandmentoringinternational.org.

Clutterbuck, D. (2015b). *How to build a coaching culture in work teams.* Retrieved from www.coachingandmentoringinternational.org website.

Clutterbuck, D. (2017a). *Emerging and developing themes in team coaching.* Retrieved from www.coachingandmentoringinternational.org.

Clutterbuck, D. (2017b). *Second wave mentoring.* Retrieved from www.coachingand mentoringinternational.org website.

Eggers, J., & Clark, D. (2000). Executive coaching that wins. *Ivey Business Journal, 65*(1), 66–71.

Evers, W., Brouwers, A. & Tomic, W. (2006). A quasi-experimental study on management coaching effectiveness. *Consulting Psychology Journal: Practice and Research, 58*(3), 174–182.

Fee, A., & Gray, S. J. (2013). Transformational learning experiences of international development volunteers in the Asia Pacific: The case of a multinational NGO. *Journal of World Business, 48*, 196–208.

Hae-Jung Hong, Rouen, & Yves Doz. (2013). L'Oreal masters multiculturalism. *Harvard Business Review*, June, 114–119.

Hawkins, P., & Smith, N. (2014). *Transformational coaching*. In E. Cox, T. Bachkirova & D. Clutterbuck (Eds), *The complete handbook of coaching* (2nd edn, pp. 228–243). London: Sage.

Kampa-Kokesch, S., & Anderson, M. (2001). Executive coaching: A comprehensive review of literature. *Consulting Psychology Journal: Practice and Research, 53*(4), 205–228.

Kilburg, R. (1996). Toward a conceptual understanding and definition of executive coaching. *Consulting Psychology Journal: Practice and Research, 48*(2), 134–144.

Kochan, F. (2012). A comprehensive view of mentoring programs for diversity. In D. Clutterbuck, K. Poulsen & F. Kochan (Eds), *Developing successful diversity mentoring programmes*. Berkshire: Open University Press.

O'Neill, M. (2000). *Executive coaching with backbone and heart: A systems approach to engaging leaders with their challenges*. San Francisco: Jossey-Bass.

Richardson, M. & Clutterbuck, D. (2017). *Mentoring and sponsorship: Rivals or bedfellows?* Retrieved from www.horizonsunlimited.com.au website.

Smith, L. (1993). The executive's new coach. *Fortune, 128*(16), 126–132.

Swart, J., & Kinnie, N. (2010). Organisational learning, knowledge assets and HR practices in professional service firms. *Human Resource Management Journal, 20*(1), 64–79.

Teague, P., & Roche, W. (2011). Line managers and the management of workplace conflict: Evidence from Ireland. *Human Resource Management Journal, 21*(1), 1–17.

Witherspoon, R., & White, R. (1996). Executive coaching: What's in it for you? *Training and Development, 50*(3), 14–15.

4 Role and future of coaching supervision in Asia Pacific

Vimala Suppiah

Who coaches the coaches?

Coaching supervision is a bold and unfamiliar terrain for coaches and the coaching profession in Asia Pacific. Although a small community of accredited coach supervisors work in this region, generally there is a lack of awareness about what coaching supervision is and the benefits it can bring, both for the coach's continuous professional development and for the clients we serve.

It still amuses me to relate the story as to how I discovered coaching supervision at the bottom of a glass of chardonnay! As a novice ICF certified coach in Kuala Lumpur, Malaysia, I was chosen to provide a six-month coaching assignment to turn around Branch Managers of a global leader company providing workforce solutions whose subsidiaries are based in Kuala Lumpur. Although my past work experience working in the UK's National Health Service in a strategic role to implement diversity initiatives gave me the confidence to take on this assignment, needless to say, in the course of my work I came across some interesting challenges. Specifically, one was when I was coaching a very intelligent and articulate senior manager who related all the things that were not right in the company but was totally unaware that his own ineffective performance as a Branch Manager was the issue. After the coaching sessions with this manager, I would drive back with many questions running through my head and feeling challenged. As I began to experience and explore reflective thinking and reviewing my own practice, I began to question and doubt the depth and breadth of my own coaching interventions. The question "am I on the right track?" led me to research the subject matter of how and from where coaches get support and wise counsel when they meet road blocks. This opened a new world called coaching supervision. My curiosity led me to ask the questions within my own coaching fraternity if they were aware of coaching supervision. Most of the time I was met with a blank stare which led me to explore a little bit further and I discovered that there was very little discussion or awareness of what coaching supervision is.

Most of us, from time to time, can hit a road block, experience some challenges and blind spots and come across ethical dilemmas during the course of the work we do. Coaching is an intense, people-centred process where the work with clients can be on a one-to-one basis or within a team and under-taken by either externally commissioned coaches or internally trained coaches. Coaching has both an observable and an unobserved element built into its process. The observable part of the coaching process is the first meeting, securing the coaching work, doing an assessment such as 360 degree, building trust and rapport, contracting with the coachee on the coaching agenda, undertaking inquiry, designing and delivering the coaching assignment. The unobserved aspect of the coaching work is what a coach experiences while at work, such as moments of jubilation as a breakthrough is achieved or some self-doubt as we get embroiled in boundary issues, blind spots, challenges and sometimes we may even go through burnout. There are also moments when a coach needs someone more experienced to guide him or her through a tough assignment or to be a sounding board or to be a mentor to broaden the scope of their work and share the latest developments in the field of coaching.

Asia Pacific is well served by a growing body of coach training providers throughout the region. Consequently, coaches in this region have ample opportunities to gain knowledge and practical guidance on how to do the observable part of coaching. But there is very little evidenced-based data or research as to how coaches in this region undertake continuous professional development (CPD) or how they are supported through some form of super-vision. Additionally, there is not much evidence for how coaches are engag-ing in interactive reflection on the many aspects of the work they undertake. In fact, there is little to demonstrate how the work of coaches is being moni-tored to assess the effectiveness of what they do. There are locally trained coaches and coaches from other parts of the world undertaking work in this diverse multi-ethnic and culturally defined region. Yet, there is little awareness or documentation of the impact or the role of culture within the coach-client system. Of course, in the matter of continuous professional development, there are coaching networks such as the International Coach-ing Federation Chapters that provide fellowship, opportunities to network and monthly educational inputs towards enhancing their learning. But there is no evidence of a well-thought-out quality controlled mechanism to ensure quality of practice that meets set standards.

In the field of behavioural science, professionals such as counsellors, psychotherapists, nurses and social workers have ongoing supervision as a developmental pathway to quality control their own work. But, coaching, which is an emerging profession in Asia Pacific, is lagging behind in getting to grips with the relevance of coaching supervision, let alone quality control the work they undertake. Added to this, there is little evidence of any mean-ingful dialogue on how coaching supervision can be beneficial for the indi-vidual, the client and for the profession. Within this context, this chapter attempts to outline four things: coaching supervision and its benefits, a snap-shot of the coaching industry in Asia Pacific, coaching supervision in this region and a way forward.

Coaching supervision and its benefits

"The fish is the last one to see the sea." While the art and science of coaching is a truly complex intervention that can transform individuals, teams and organizations, the coach can experience many blind spots and doubts as he/she experiences the doing of coaching. Supervision, therefore, is that space for a coach to check-in with an experienced coach who is qualified to provide a safety net for a supervisee's professional development and to support the supervisee through challenges and ethical dilemmas or boundary issues. But, what is coaching supervision?

In a one-day workshop (August 2015) conducted in Kuala Lumpur, Malaysia, and organized in partnership with the Association of Coaching Supervisors and Mentors (ACSM) and conducted by the UK's Coaching Supervision Academy (CSA), 13 experienced and curious Malaysian coaches came together to take the green shoots of coaching supervision to the next level. The definition of coaching supervision formalized on that day is:

> Coaching supervision is a co-created learning relationship that supports the supervisee in his or her development, both personally and professionally, and seeks to support him or her in providing best practice to his or her clients.

> (CSA, 2015)

Hawkins and Schwenk (2006, p. 2) define supervision as

> A structured formal process for coaches, with the help of a coaching supervisor, to attend to improving better the quality of their coaching, grow their coaching capacity and support themselves and their practice. Supervision should also be a source of organizational learning.

Another definition by Bluckert (2005, p. 102) is

> Supervision sessions are a place for the coach to reflect on the work they are under taking with another more experienced coach. It has the dual purpose of supporting the continued learning and development of the coach as well as giving a degree of protection to the person being coached.

In his book, Machon (2010, p. 110) explains that the work of a coach is

> to expand [the] client's awareness and vision, to cultivate super-vision and thus offer the potentiality for growth. Similarly, supervision is to help the coach practitioner to step back and reflect on their practice in order to return to their work, with greater awareness and considered and informed interventions that may best serve their clients.

Within the context of these definitions, it is also pertinent to ask how to ensure that quality control mechanisms of coaching practice are embraced in the overall discussion on coaching supervision. In an article written by de Haan and Birch (2010), they highlight the benefit of coaching supervision in relation to ensuring the quality and professionalism of the work undertaken by executive coaches in organizations. They go on to define coaching supervision as an essential prerequisite to maintaining the quality, competence and professionalism of an executive coach. Quality control for coaching supervision improves the coaching experience for both coach and coachee.

The quality control element has relevance for Asia Pacific as there is a lack of research studies on how coaches who work in this region are quality controlled given the current increasing growth and potential growth of coaching in this region. The desire to chase the dollar (as some coaches are able to demand high fees) versus the need or requirement to work within an ethical framework can be seen as that window of opportunity to launch a meaningful dialogue on the relevance of coaching supervision. There are also ample opportunities to commission work to promote quality assurance processes to benefit clients and to map out good practices. Many of these kinds of work are not yet thought through in this region but will, very soon, become essential.

The benefits and the developmental growth in having coaching supervision (and I include myself in this) is, indeed, an eye opener. While in supervision, it provides the coach practitioner with an opportunity to question: What am I learning? What might I be missing? How can I serve my client better? Where can I grow? Through this self-reflection, the coach is constantly seeking to raise their awareness, to fine tune his/her practice to serve the client better. Similarly, the supervisor also takes the coach on a journey of self-reflection, deeper awareness and discovery, learning and expanding their vision to enrich their coaching. Who could argue with this? The feedback from coaches on the benefits they gain via supervision is that it works!

The coaching industry in Asia Pacific

This region is one of the fastest growing economies and has the most culturally diverse population. The growth in multinational organizations doing business in Japan, Malaysia, Singapore, South Korea, India, China and in Indonesia has seen the introduction of coaching as a developmental tool for executive and business coaches to operate across Asia Pacific. There is growing evidence of many coaching programmes being designed and run by coach training providers. It is predicted that by 2020, 60% of Asia Pacific's workforce will be made up of Millennials, the Gen Ys. Against this backdrop, can coaching play a part to develop the much-needed leadership capabilities and up-skill the young workforce to be groomed, engaged and productive? It is predicted that the demand for leadership, executive and business coaching is set to rise in Asia Pacific. In that context, the coaching industry is well placed to provide both coaching education and coaching services.

Bresser's (2009) study found

> South Eastern Asia to be one of the world's largest and most dynamic
> coaching regions, with coaching in many ways in its early stages, but
> growing fast. Coaching is clearly on the rise and in the process of becom-
> ing more mature.

With the current economic and business growth in this region, indicators
point to a rising presence of multinational corporations (MNCs) in Asia
Pacific. But, what are the key challenges for these MNCs working with a
local workforce? The main one is the talent pool in this region. In his article,
Braithwaite (2015), the managing director of Odgers Berndtson in Asia, conducted one-to-one interviews with more than 60 large European and US-
owned multinationals and says that "the difference of Asia is all about people.
It's about finding people so we can deliver business."

The other challenge is around communication and the culture gap
between a western-led management style and practices versus the 'home
grown' work environment, work ethics, attitudes and socio-cultural norms
which get meshed into the world of work. And, set within a somewhat
rigid hierarchical Asian corporate culture where it is the norm for the Asian
workforce to look up to senior management with high regard and with
micro-management style being the order of the day, the effort to introduce
a coaching culture is an uphill struggle. When managers are sent for training, it is mainly to acquire work-based skills. Even when management
training in soft skills and leadership is rolled out, the transactional cultural
dimension in the workplace environment is not conducive to facilitating
real change to be internalized following such training experiences. Against
this backdrop, where is coaching as a profession and as an industry in this
region? And also, how are the rapidly mushrooming coach training providers contributing (if any) to the growth and developments of the professionals? Added to these questions, where is coaching supervision as part of
the continuous professional development for the coaches who are here providing a service?

In this talent-gap and culture-gap environment, the concerns to talent
build and develop leaders are some of the top concerns affecting MNCs both
for today and in the future. In the midst of these concerns, there is evidence
of a growing body of executive, leadership and business coaches working in
this region. It appears that both mentoring and coaching are mainly driven
within and by the multinational clients who value the benefits of coaching
and mentoring. Similarly, the need and urgency for Asia Pacific organizations,
SMIs, SMEs and the public sector to embrace coaching as a developmental
tool is now growing, but slowly. These major initiatives are encouraged and
supported by management gurus like Marshall Goldsmith who are advocating
for coaching to be aggressively embedded in business environments of the
future (Goldsmith, 2006). These are encouraging and welcoming signs to

re-enforce the benefits of coaching. And as these developmental initiatives begin to raise the awareness of coaching, the need to have coaching supervision to be firmly grounded in the coaching landscape is crucial.

Where is coaching supervision in Asia Pacific?

Coaching supervision is a relatively new and growing field and many coaches are often under the misguided belief that it is only useful when they are in training or if a problem arises with a client. However, this is far from the case. The link between theory learned in a classroom environment from a coach training provider and the actual doing of the coaching work is like a new driver starting to drive after passing the driving test. The learning curve is steep and scary in both cases! The Chartered Institute of Personnel and Development Report (2009), stated that, "Coaches see the main benefits of supervision as developing coaching capability (88%) and assuring the quality of their coaching (86%)." While the scenario in the western hemisphere on coaching supervision is in its early stages of development, here in Asia Pacific, it is in the gestation period. There are promising ripples as coaches are enrolling into the training to become coach supervisors and this is increasing the awareness about supervision in this region. The Coaching Supervision Academy (CSA) which was founded in 2001 by Edna Murdoch and Miriam Orriss is one of several training bodies that provide an accredited programme on coaching supervision in this region. The CSA trained coach supervisors are in a position to offer coaching supervision, but how actively they offer their services and how productive they are as coach supervisors is not certain. Since the inception of the one-day workshop in Kuala Lumpur on 15 August 2015, the Association of Coaching Supervisors and Mentors (ACSM) have worked diligently to raise awareness of the relevance of supervision to a coach's practice. Supported by ACSM, the first cohort of coaches are training with the Coaching Supervision Academy (CSA) and will become accredited coach supervisors in mid-2018.

However, there is still some confusion and conflicting views about coaching supervision versus mentor coaching, the latter of which ICF promotes widely for the purpose of ICF Credentialing. In that context, the Mentor Coaching process sets clear guidelines on the development of coaching skills and in attaining a level of coaching competency for the purpose of credentialing. Brett (2015) states that,

> another common misconception is that coaching supervision is just very high coaching ability and that no additional training/experience is required to serve as a supervisor. The awareness that specialized training is needed is gaining interest but not yet fully embraced by all wishing to serve in this role. Identifying the unique qualifications, traits, and skills of a coaching supervisor and defining how to train coaches to serve in this role will be important in clarifying this misconception.

The European Mentoring and Coaching Council (EMCC) holds a firm position on coaching supervision and has it as a requirement in its Code of Ethics for all members to be in regular supervision. It has set out guidelines on a definition and recommends steps to finding a supervisor. However, though coaching supervision is not yet in the DNA of the International Coaching Federation (ICF), at the July 2014 Board meeting it approved the formation of a task force to develop and publish more specific guidelines, compare the standards of other coaching bodies and to make recommendations for future policies on coaching supervision. Further to this, ICF has set up work groups to define and set out their position on coaching supervision and the discussions have been held within its Credentialing Committee and among its subject matter experts. There are plans, following the work of the Credentialing Committee, to submit their findings to the ICF Board for further consideration.

In Europe, the United Kingdom and the USA, there is evidence that coaching supervision is not only a requirement for the coach, but buyers of coaching services are now asking for evidence of a coach being in supervision as part of their hiring criteria. But in Asia Pacific and as discussed earlier in this chapter, there are some complex issues in raising awareness and gaining clarity on what coaching supervision is and is not. There is a certain amount of scepticism and fear that one's work is under scrutiny and that supervision is not needed. One well-established coach training provider admits that it will take at least two years for coaching supervision to be an acceptable intervention as coaches in Asia Pacific are not yet out of the woods. Currently, coaching supervision seems to be practised among a few enlightened coaches but any meaningful developmental work remains in the background. Apart from some coaches who have gone on to achieve the Diploma in Coaching Supervision, there is little evidence that the coaching community in Asia Pacific has initiated a dialogue on the relevance of coaching supervision for the integrity of the profession.

A way forward

What defines good coaching practice in Asia Pacific? As in coaching, the work on supervision has many opportunities for coaches and the coaching profession in this region to undertake some ground-breaking work to promote excellence and raise coaches to the best ethical and professional standards. But, the initial work should focus on raising awareness of what coaching supervision is and the distinctive differences between coaching supervision, mentor coaching, peer coaching and reciprocal coaching. Following are some recommendations.

1   Develop a framework for continuous professional development specifically on reflective practice and promote an environment of learning through case presentations. Documenting evidence-based practices would

contribute to making the professional element of the small community of accredited coach supervisors who are offering coaching more acceptable.

2 Initiate a dialogue session or round-table. Those of us who are actively engaged in executive, leadership and business coaching or in organizational development work can initiate a dialogue session among the existing cohort of supervision as part of their work.

3 Research. With support from interested parties and with the small community of accredited coach supervisors who are offering supervision as part of their work, small studies and research can be commissioned to study the relevance and benefits of coaching supervision in this region.

4 Culture, coaching and supervision. The work on the cultural impact of coaching is an interesting area of work and further exploratory work on this would also be useful. It would be valuable to gather data from coaches if they bring this into coaching and into supervision. And, also, further test out the need for cultural sensitivity and coaching models.

5 Standards. There is a need to set standards to benchmark the work of the coach, against which new coaches can judge the quality of their work. Training providers are also stakeholders in this process and should be raising the bar in training student coaches and complying with accepted standards of coaching delivery. Setting standards and guidelines is not easy as coaching still remains an unregulated industry. There is no need to re-invent the wheel, as much work has been done by the European Mentoring Coaching Council (EMCC) and the International Coach Guild (ICG).

6 Raising buyer awareness. There is a need to keep buyers of coaching services in that stakeholder loop and raise their awareness as well.

In conclusion, I make a humble request for working alliances to form among the small group of Accredited Coach Supervisors who are working in this region, to share thoughts and mutual expectations of the future role of coaching supervision for the betterment of coaching in this region. An Asia Pacific-wide network can be brought about by the Association of Coaching Supervisors and Mentors (ACSM), the Association of Coaching Supervisors and similar bodies to gather data, commission work and hold seminars.

References

Bluckert, P. (2005). Non-directive supervision of coaching. In J. Passmore (Ed.), *Supervision in coaching: Supervision, ethics and continuous professional development* (Chapter 7). London: Kogan Page.

Braithwaite, M. (2015, 5 January). *Rising to the challenge: Why multinational corporations must better prepare for doing business in Asia*. Retrieved 17 August 2017, from www.odgersberndtson.com/en-au/insights/rising-to-the-challenge-in-asia.

Bresser, F. (2009). *Full report: The state of coaching across the globe – results of the Global Coaching Survey 2008/2009*. Frank Bresser Consulting. www.frank-bresser-consulting.com, August.

Brett, C. (2015). Coaching Development Ltd. www.coachingdevelopment.com/.

The Chartered Institute of Personnel and Development Report (2009). *Annual Survey Report 2009: Recruitment, retention and turnover.* Retrieved 17 August 2017, from www2.cipd.co.uk/NR/rdonlyres/41225039-A846-4D2D-9057-E02CDB6BFC0B/0/recruitment_retention_turnover_annual_survey_2009.pdf.

Coaching Supervision Academy. (2015). One Day Experiential Coaching Supervision Workshop held on 15 August 2015, Kuala Lumpur, Malaysia.

de Haan, E., & Birch, D. (2010). *Quality control for coaching.* Ashridge Business School. www.ashridge.org.uk/Media-Library/Ashridge/PDFs/Publications/Quality ControlForCoaching.pdf.

Goldsmith, M. (2006). Cited in *Coaching: A global study of successful practices*, American Management Association, 2008: Retrieved 17 August 2017, from www.opm.gov/WIKI/uploads/docs/Wiki/OPM/training/i4cp-coaching.pdf (p. 6).

Hawkins, P., & Schwenk, G. (2006). *Coaching supervision.* London: CIPD Change Agenda.

Machon, A. (2010). *The coaching secret: How to be an exceptional coach.* UK: Pearson Education Limited.

Part II

Coaching cases

5 Coaching in Thailand

Chérie Carter-Scott

In October, 1974, I started coaching with my first official paid coaching client. After a successful coaching assignment, he shared his amazing results with everyone he encountered and my coaching practice was launched. Since 1974, I have coached in the US, in Europe and in Asia. I have also trained coaches across the globe and I have learned that to be an effective coach, I need to understand the culture and be culturally sensitive. To put it precisely, American culture isn't universally applicable. One of my biggest lessons was to stretch out of my comfort zone to learn about others rather than expecting others to conform to the paradigms of North America's melting pot of cultures. My repeated lesson in life is that confidence coupled with humility works!

The purpose of this chapter is to focus specifically on coaching in Thailand (formerly known as Siam). I will present information on the relationship between Thai culture and executive coaching in Thailand. I will focus on how to conduct coaching taking into consideration the culture and on building on what is possible.

I first visited Thailand in 2005 as a tourist and returned to Thailand as a medical tourist. I came back to Thailand to purchase a home in the South, on the Andaman Sea. In 2010, I was invited to teach leadership, management and coaching at Webster University Thailand. At that time, my husband and I started to live in Thailand. Numerous opportunities were presented to us to coach in multinational companies. The focus of our coaching has been to bridge cultural gaps between Westerners and Thai nationals. As foreigners in this beautiful and fascinating country, we rapidly became students of the language and the culture. The more we learned, the hungrier we became to understand the subtleties and nuances that we didn't quite understand in Thai culture.

Culture

It is important to define what we mean when we use the word 'culture'. Culture is the collection of values, learned beliefs and behavioural dictates that are shared within a group of people that is self-sustaining and transfers these paradigms from generation to generation. Culture is typically defined as the ways of living, behavioural norms and expectations, language and linguistic expressions, styles of communication, patterns of thinking, beliefs and values of a particular group. A culture may include shared language, folklore, ideas, thinking patterns, concepts held in common, communication styles and accepted 'truths' held sacred by members of the group. In addition, members of a culture have similar expectations of life itself. Culture serves as a road map for both perceiving and interacting with the world. Another way we can define culture is to say that culture is the behavioural software that 'programs' us to conform to the expectations of the larger group.

Frequently, culture plays a greater role in determining communication behaviour than race, ethnicity or other diversity factors and can create conflicts because of differences in perception, orientation, beliefs and communication styles associated with those cultures. Some facts are:

- culture determines attitudes and behaviours;
- most cultural norms and rules are assumed and not formally written down;
- people's behaviours are interpreted through each person's cultural filter;
- no human being is 'culture-exempt'.

Cultural differences in a global economy have become increasingly important to multinational corporations, to expats and to those desiring to respect, honour and mesh with another culture.

The usefulness of coaching

As defined by the International Coach Federation (ICF), "Coaching is partnering with clients in a thought-provoking and creative process that inspires them to maximize their personal and professional potential." The ICF has stipulated Core Competencies to standardize the practice of coaching in order to increase the professionalism in the industry. Coaching has proved to be a valuable tool and when you are sensitive to the culture, the results can be absolutely profound and permanent.

Professions come into existence when there is a need; they die out when that need has been replaced with a new invention, a new process, a new innovation or technology that causes the old profession to become obsolete. In our fast-paced, intense and ever-changing world, coaching helps unearth vision and passion, focuses motivation, develops gravitas and facilitates successful transitions.

We live in complex times. We are bombarded by more stimulation than ever before in the history of the world. We need to make more choices in one day than previous generations made in their entire lives. In addition, the world in which we live is constantly changing. The changes include and are not limited to: environmental, technological, political, economic, scientific and global changes. As well, we also must contend with task-saturated lives in which responses are expected in nanoseconds and there is less and less time available to process information and data. In short, there appears to be less time, higher expectations and a plethora of electronic devices that demand immediate attention and instantaneous responses to a variety of questions and challenges leaving little to no time to reflect.

When a person is juggling multiple tasks, attempting to achieve more than seems humanly possible and s/he is faced with decisions they don't feel confident making, they may feel alone. This scenario is more the norm in this century rather than the exception. The pressure to make the right decisions and choices weigh heavily on executives wrestling with M&A, expansion and reorganisation opportunities. This is one of the conditions that has given rise to the profession of executive coaching.

Another area for the application of coaching is the transition from manager to leader. Some of the conventional judgements in this area are: managers have their eye on the bottom line, whereas leaders have their eye on the horizon; managers look at how and when, while leaders look at what and why; managers maintain the status quo, while leaders challenge the status quo; managers do things right, while leaders do the right thing. As an executive coach, I realize that this transition, like many others, requires awareness, discussion, a shift in behaviours and experimentation with new ways of relating to people, systems, priorities and tasks. It is with a coach that this transition can be explored and deployed.

Corporations and individuals seek out a professional coach for the following reasons:

- to sort out options and determine the most preferable direction;
- to uncover one's underlying preference and receive support;
- to manage the gap between where you are presently and your desired future;
- to assist in overcoming obstacles and breaking through blocks;
- to have support in the achievement of career goals;
- to help articulate capabilities, direction, new visions, vistas and ventures;
- to help process disappointment, dismissal or disillusionment;
- to learn to believe in oneself;
- to find the building blocks between your current perception of yourself and the desired future identity;
- to build needed skills to provide upward mobility, i.e. 'gravitas'.

It is less expensive to hire a coach to support an existing executive, than to replace that valuable resource with a new one. Corporations want to employ coaches for a variety of reasons:

- to enhance performance;
- to increase effectiveness on the job;
- to help executives develop 'people-soft skills';

- to augment gaps in their professional development;
- to prepare leaders for dealing with increasing demands when they are promoted;
- to develop a variety of skills in preparation for leadership;
- to help executives become more self-confident and able to receive feedback;
- to become smarter with time and task management.

The types of situations that are coachable include circumstances

- to assist cultural integration in mergers and acquisitions;
- to eliminate gaps between the present and the transitional future;
- to break through obstacles (as in the film *The King's Speech*);
- to address confidential and sensitive situations;
- to support relocation and orientation;
- to assist transitions between assignments or careers;
- to formulate visions, goals and strategies;
- to overcome challenges with personalities on the job (or off);
- to facilitate choice-making from an inner-directed place.

Buddhist culture

One of the most important cultural influences in Thai culture is Buddhism. Nearly 95% of the population is Theravada Buddhist. This form of Buddhism is supported and overseen by the government, with monks receiving a number of governmental benefits. A major focus of the daily life of Thai people and rooted in ancient Siamese culture is the promotion of that which is refined and avoids coarseness. As a deeply Buddhist people, Thais place great emphasis on the outward forms of courtesy; being self-effacing, modest, not embarrassing or intruding on others are an essential part of Thai culture.

A serene disposition is deeply valued; conflict and sudden displays of anger are shunned in Thai culture. For these reasons, coaches should do their best to avoid conflict or outwardly display anger. Disagreements or disputes should ideally be handled with a smile and blame should be avoided whenever possible. In everyday life in Thailand, there is a strong emphasis on the concept of *sanuk*, meaning fun. The idea that is omnipresent is that everyday life should be fun. Because of this, Thais can be quite playful at work and during day-to-day activities, which can be interpreted as 'playing on the job' by those who are not familiar with the culture. Displaying positive emotions in social interactions is also important in Thai culture.

This concept of *sanuk* fits nicely with the coaching premise that you can have a life that is satisfying, fulfilling, financially rewarding and fun. *Sanuk* can then be seen as a connector between Thai culture and coaching. For example, one automotive expat executive was focused on results and one day was encouraged to have more *sanuk*, which shocked her. She brought this up in our coaching conversation as a problem: "how can I be results-driven and have more fun at the same time?" The outcome of the session was her determination to assess each situation and sort into three virtual baskets: 'urgent', 'important' and 'when time permits'. She discovered that she had been reacting to every situation with her 'urgent' response mechanism and making this adjustment made her more aware, shifted her mindset and enabled her to have more fun on the job.

Often, Thais will deal with disagreements, minor mistakes or misfortunes by using the phrase '*mai benrai*', translated as 'no worries'. The consistent use of this phrase throughout Thailand reflects a disposition minimizing conflict, disagreements or complaints. A smile and the sentence '*mai pen rai*' communicates that the incident is not important and therefore there is no conflict or shame involved. This also flows over into the social expectation that nothing is so important that you would outwardly display negative emotions like anger in public. When people are publicly angry, Thai people either think of them as not having the proper upbringing or bringing shame on their family from their behaviour. This is rather different from the Western work ethic and requires heightened awareness from the manager. When coaching expats in Thailand who are results-driven, it is useful for the coach to understand how the foreigner's behaviour may be perceived and to shed some light on cultural differences and perceptions.

Thai culture

Respect for hierarchy is deeply ingrained in this paternalistic culture. The king of Thailand and the royal family are venerated and loved by Thai people and many Thai people claim they would willingly die for their king. Thais are very proud of their monarchy and the royal family is held in such high regard that to make a derogatory comment is literally punishable by imprisonment.

Since the Thais are supportive of hierarchies and respect all forms of authority, decisions are generally made by senior management with minimal or no consultation with middle or junior management. The eldest person historically has always had the most respect although things are changing now and younger people can receive similar respect if they have exceptionally more talent and experience than their peers. For example, a young adult who has been coached for several years will garner more respect because of their investment of time, energy and experience in this new industry. An older executive, coached by a younger Thai, would normally act in a superior manner unless the younger person had proven their capability and competence. This superior attitude would only be relinquished in the coaching relationship.

I will now present various aspects of Thai culture as they relate specifically to coaching. There are certain concepts, words and expressions that are deeply embedded in Thai culture, are known and understood by Thai people in their family circle, yet not addressed in the workplace. For example, concepts such as *thii tam thii soong*, *phradet*, *prakhun* and *katanyu rookhun* are common knowledge and specifically not addressed.

Thii tam thii soong means that people should behave and treat other people according to their own and other people's status. The words literally mean low place (class) or high place (class) and pertain to age and family background. It can be a challenge for younger people to coach older or more senior people. Senior people look to their peers or even more senior advisors and coaches. Younger coaches often feel intimidated by the seniority of a person with stature, experience or a significant title on his or her business card. This is a part of the culture that must be addressed if a young coach is to grow his or her coaching practice. When the newly graduated coach walks into the HR department and states that s/he is ready to coach the executives, the response may be a raised eyebrow coupled with disbelief. This doesn't mean that anyone in their 20s cannot coach someone older; what it does mean is that this is a delicate situation that must be addressed with sensitivity and appropriateness.

Knowing your place and liking it. This is one of the qualities of Buddhism that permeates all aspects of Thai culture. As a visitor to Thailand, it appears as if people are content with their lot in life and bear no resentment toward others who have more resources at their disposal. This can create conflict in a coaching relationship when the coach is encouraging the client to look at their ideal desired future. The Thai executive may experience tension between their cultural dictates which state, "Know your place and like it!" which also means "Be grateful for what you have!" versus look deep within and see what you really want. The difference in mindset is important to address since accepting your lot in life is antithetical to going for what you really want.

Sam ruam is related to the Buddhist concept of moderation, 'to travel the middle path'. *Sam ruam* is about striving to exercise restraint, to maintain composure in stressful situations and to avoid extreme displays of emotion. This principle could conflict with a coaching relationship. There are times in the coaching relationship where the coach is encouraging the client to stand up, speak up and express his or her feelings. On the contrary, with the concept of *sam ruam*, the important value is restraint not full self-expression. The conflict in this situation would result in the client being non-responsive and caught between two separate value systems: the traditional Thai behavioural expectations and the urging of the present-day coach.

Sam ruam is also valued because it represents class. The higher the class one has, the more the person should restrain from showing extreme emotions. The example is derived from the royal family who rarely show any emotions in public. The coaching client who has been let go from his job and feels hurt, angry, confused and lost is reluctant to express his feelings since that would not be *sam ruam* or exercising restraint. His tendency is to keep it all inside of him, thinking rather than feeling or expressing his feelings.

Unfortunately, matters like this don't always get sorted out with just thinking. They often require the exploration of associated feelings to move on to the next opportunity. When coaching a terminated Thai, you can encourage him or her to share feelings; but remember to keep in mind that *sam ruam* may reinforce their cognitive orientation rather than eagerly exploring their affective realm.

Building relationships is essential for doing business. There is a complex expectation of respect and building relationships *before* conducting business; this patience along with practicing emotional restraint are values that coaches are likely to encounter when they begin coaching in Thailand.

Business relationships develop slowly in Thailand and require time and patience. Establishing a coaching contract may take several meetings with the sponsor or with the sponsor and the client together over weeks or even months to create a successful business understanding about the purpose and potential outcomes of a coaching relationship. Building long-term relationships is essential in Thailand and there is a required etiquette. Here are some requirements.

When you make an appointment, arrive early and know that face-to-face meetings are usually preferred, even though the Thai executive will be fully booked and will most often arrive late. The senior person should always be introduced first. Decisions will never be finalised in the initial meeting and establishing the anticipated price-point is essential in order for negotiations to commence. Therefore, comparative research for the appropriate fee to charge for your coaching credentials is strongly advised prior to your meeting with a corporate sponsor.

Knowing (something of) the Thai language. Jai means heart, mind or spirit. There are literally 743 '*jai*' words in the Thai language. The word *jai* is combined with other words to create the feeling of an emotion; words that describe emotions or feelings generally end with *jai*. Through the *jai* words, one can perceive how consciousness is shaped along with the range of Thai states of mind and emotions. Below are five '*jai*' words with reference to coaching.

Nam jai refers to genuine acts of kindness and the desire to help someone. *Nam* means water and *jai* means heart. Therefore, *nam jai* is literally translated as water from the heart. *Nam jai* is a value that requires a person to demonstrate consideration for another and even that they are willing to make sacrifices for another. This is essential in the coaching relationship and should be embodied and referenced as a way to build cultural bridges. *Nam jai* is in alignment with coaching practice since coaching is an act of kindness supporting another in getting what they truly want.

Hen jai is empathy, understanding, the willingness to listen, to be flexible and humane. *Hen* means to see. So, the literal translation of *hen jai* is to see into another's heart. *Hen jai* goes beyond empathy and demonstrates the willingness and flexibility to accommodate another. In coaching, *hen jai* is essential since empathy is required in coaching and should be addressed as a way to build relationships and especially cultural bridges between the coach and the Thai culture. Demonstrating *hen jai* enhances the coaching relationship.

Wai jai means starting to trust someone. In the past, there may have been issues that created reticence or doubt. That reluctance has now been replaced with trust, which is absolutely fundamental in coaching. If your coaching client says they have *wai jai* with you, it means that they believe you have their best interests in your heart. *Wai jai* is a wonderful compliment, so when you hear it accept it graciously.

Mun jai means that you have self-confidence and self-trust. You believe in your own capabilities, self-worth and competence. Helping the client to develop *mun jai* is an important aspect in the coaching contract and helps them feel deserving and capable to plan a desirable future.

Greng jai refers to a person restraining his intentions if there is the potential for discomfort, inconvenience or conflict with another. The word *greng* means fear. In this context, the fear is about making another uncomfortable. *Greng jai* is deeply embedded in the Thai culture. You need to know about *greng jai* because it could be a block to supportive direct questioning and interpreted as confrontation, thereby creating discomfort. Asking powerful questions encourages the client to go deeper and look at his or her preferences, choices, attitude and behaviour patterns in relation to their desired future.

Greng jai has many interpretations. For example, the hesitation to ask questions when you haven't understood someone, the reluctance to provide feedback for another especially when it's not positive or encouraging your client to stand up for him/herself when it might inconvenience or cause another discomfort. All of these examples of *greng jai* might create a disconnect between coach and client. *Greng jai* can make coaching more challenging since many of the *greng jai* behaviours are antithetical to the expectations in the coaching relationship. When you are meeting with a new client, it is best to address *greng jai* upfront and discuss how it might impact your coaching relationship and, if it does, encourage your client to say, "Remember we discussed *greng jai*? I'm not sure how to best address it?"

Thai concepts practised in business

The following are some Thai concepts that are useful to know if you will be conducting coaching sessions with Thai executives.

Hai kiad means to give honour and respect. Honour and respect are important in the coaching relationship since the coach needs to respect and honour the client. This principle is in complete alignment with core coaching competencies like building trust and intimacy, partnering with the client and active listening. Therefore, *hai kiad* is fundamental to the coaching relationship in Thailand. You can discuss it in your initial session. You could say that it is your intention for both of you to experience *hai kiad* with each other. This is a great first step to approach your potential client with a reference from Thai culture.

Phradet is the traditional Thai model of effective leadership based on the exercise of authority and toughness. *Phradet* is legitimate power to harm or punish another. *Phradet* is the exercise of authority and toughness. Delegating and demanding are two main functions of *phradet*. In coaching, if the client's boss has *phradet* and s/he is dealing with a tough Theory 'X' leader s/he can anticipate conflicts if the worker is not totally compliant.

In this model when superiors designate tasks, the authority to complete the tasks is not delegated, but remains with the superior. Loyalty and hard work are demanded, discipline and punishments are administered, policies are formulated and firmness is exercised along with introducing potential improvements. In traditional Western business theories, this could loosely be compared with Douglas McGregor's Theory 'X' which proposes that people don't like to work, must be forced to work and are unwilling to assume any responsibility. When coaching a Thai executive who is working under a boss practicing *phradet*, you need to understand the risks involved with the misinterpretation of the client's intentions. For example, if your client is sitting in his office, contemplating a complex problem in manufacturing and his *phradet* boss sees him looking at the ceiling, he may be perceived as a slacker rather than a hard worker. Therefore, managing perceptions becomes more important in this environment than in more Theory 'Y' environments where the model assumes that people like to work, they self-manage well and they easily take responsibility. This concept can also be seen as 'tough love' in the Western sense.

Phrakhun is the traditional Thai system of patronization. This comes from the benevolent king, the ultimate father, who cares for those in need. Men of means in Thailand are expected to follow the example of the king and provide assistance for those less fortunate. This includes giving money, shelter, food and clothing to those who lack the essentials, caring for the sick and needy in a crisis, providing protection to outsiders, sponsoring education, marriage, ordination, funerals, rewards, lending prestige, conferring status and, in general, demonstrating both care and concern. It is one of the reasons that all companies listed on the Thai Stock Exchange have a non-profit charitable foundation to ensure that the *prakhun* of the organization is properly administered. If your coaching client is interested in humanitarian/ non-profit activities, you, as the coach, can invite him or her to research the non-profit side of these organizations as a potential homework assignment.

Bunkhun is a psychological bond that emphasizes the indebted goodness towards another who out of kindness and sincerity gave what was needed at an important time and the recipient remembered the goodness and is always ready to reciprocate the kindness. In the relationship with Thai parents, *bunkhun* or indebtedness extends until death. There are two aspects of *bunkhun*: *katanyu rookhun* and *mettaa karunaa*.

Katanyu rookhun translates into gratitude and indebtedness. The executive holds this obligation or duty toward his/her parents, guardians, teachers, caretakers, mentors and bosses. *Katanyu rookhun* identifies relationships that are organized around general rate of exchange for mutual benefit. The recipient of the kindness does his or her best to reciprocate the received generosity, which is held as a responsibility and duty. Therefore, Thai people will give gifts that appear to be random, but are, in fact, *katanyu rookhun*.

In business relationships, this can be interpreted as the 'store of goodwill'. In a coaching relationship, the client may state, "This is what will please my parents", or "This is what will make my parents proud when they tell their friends about my career." Since part of the *katanyu rookhun* is attributed directly to the parents, there is a deep desire to please them with all of the choices and decisions that the adult-child makes. The conflict may arise between the expectations of the Thai executive who has *katanyu rookhun* as their first priority, meaning attending to the needs of their parents which may also mean ignoring their own wishes or preferences. This conflict is seen as a double bind. In Thai culture, the question is, "Can I please my parents (since I owe them *katanyu rookhun*) and at the same time honour my preferences?"

In a session with a young banker, he shared with me that he had been offered three banking jobs in different banks. I asked how he felt about these opportunities and he said, "Bored. I am totally bored with banking!" I asked what he would like to do with his feeling of boredom. He thought and replied,

> My parents are so proud of me being a banker ... they tell all their friends that their son is a banker and they are impressed. I don't think I could disappoint them after all they have done for me!

I asked if pleasing his parents was more important than pleasing himself and he nodded his head and gave a clear, "Yes, it is!" At that moment, I was educated about *katanyu rookhun*. Ultimately, as a coach, you can open the door of possibilities and the person has a choice whether to walk through to a new dimension or to stay with their cultural dictates.

The second aspect of *bunkhun* is *mettaa karunaa* which is the quality of being merciful and kind. This is especially pertinent where the superior/stronger person behaves in a benevolent manner towards the subordinate, especially when an error or mistake has been made. It comes from a Buddhist teaching stating that we should be kind towards all living creatures. In coaching conversations, an objective might involve an employee not living up to the expectations of their boss and, as a result, feeling guilt or shame. As a coach, you can reference *mettaa karunaa*, when appropriate, in dealings with bosses and/or parents. When the executive feels embarrassment, guilt or shame for having disappointed, let down or failed a key person held in high respect, the question would be, "Is it possible for your boss to extend *mettaa karunaa* toward you?" Since this is a reference point in Thai culture, it is appropriate that you know the term and know how and when to address it.

Baramee is the exercise of influence that a leader possesses that commands obedience and loyalty from others. It is the power and strength derived from respect and loyalty. When a leader has *baramee*, it will be difficult for the Thai executive to express any wish that may not be in alignment with his or her leader. When a leader has developed sufficient *bunkhun* over the years, s/he would then possess *baramee*, which translates into a deep and trusting relationship with his/her subordinates (Holmes and Tangtongtavy, 1997).

A useful summary of these concepts is in Table A5.1.

Relationships in Thai culture

In Thai culture, there are three circles of relationships that have an influence on coaching:

1   *The family circle* is the innermost circle, intertwined with the fortunes of other family members. This circle includes mutual rights, duties, respect, informality and free flow of communication. In coaching, the Thai client may want to please his or her parents so much that he or she is reluctant to look at what they want in their own life. They may repeatedly respond, "I don't know!" At a certain point the coach needs to draw out the expectations of family, friends and even peers. Asking powerful, supportive, empathetic questions will help draw out the hidden conflicts such as "Who might know the right thing to do? Would you like to ask them? Would that be helpful?" This way you can obtain either agreement or reaction from the executive who can give you more to work with than, "I don't know!"

2   *The cautious circle* are those whom the Thai person relies on regularly and includes work colleagues, doctors, tailors, market vendors, their child's teachers. To this group of people, behaviour is courteous, deferential, friendly and somewhat formal. Thai people depend on these support people for their day-to-day survival and well-being. In coaching, the Thai client might want to be so cautious around his or her work associates, including you as their coach, that they appear inauthentic, seem to hold back or are politically motivated rather than accessing their true self. The coach could easily be grouped into this cautious circle and the Thai client might be motivated to say what he or she deemed was appropriate or expected rather than the truth.

3   *The selfish circle* is the outside world whom the Thai person may encounter once and never again and with whom s/he has no real relationship with at all. In this anonymous circle, the Thai person can do whatever s/he pleases including spitting, littering, pushing, riding motorcycles on the sidewalk, without any adverse consequences.

Knowledge of all three of these circles is helpful when coaching Thai executives, since it is part of the fabric of the culture that is rarely addressed. In a non-confrontational patriarchal society, any attempt to criticize others publicly or be openly angry amounts to an unpardonable loss of face. In such a culture, the smile is the most useful non-verbal tool and disarms as well as hides a large variety of emotions and reactions.

The 13 smiles of Thai people

In Western cultures, people don't necessarily differentiate between different types of smiles, however in Thailand they do! Therefore, when you are coaching a Thai executive, notice the smile and be sure to ask what it means if you are unsure. Never assume. This core competency is specified under Active Listening as: "Distinguishes between the words, the tone of voice, and the body language of the client."

Thailand is known as the Land of Smiles, which indicates a good deal of relaxation and a friendly attitude but might not always be entirely positive. An Australian director of a team of Thai managers was given a present by one of the managers. He said his daughter made it to remind the director to smile. The director looked surprised. The manager said, "We always know what type of mood you are in by the look on your face. Try smiling more and people will approach you more often." This information was illuminating to him. He never thought that a facial expression was so important. He realized that the people around him noticed his expression and demeanour much more than he could have imagined. He decided in our coaching to include the awareness of his expressions, body language and his intention to become more approachable in all aspects of his demeanour. I shared with him the 13 smiles of Thai people. He was very grateful.

1 The "I'm so happy I'm crying" smile.
2 The polite smile for someone you barely know.
3 The "I admire you" smile.
4 The stiff smile, also known as the "I should laugh at the joke though it's not funny to me" smile.
5 The smile which masks something wicked in his mind.
6 The teasing, or "I told you so!" smile.
7 The "I know things look pretty bad but there's no point crying over spilt milk" smile.
8 The sad smile.
9 The dry smile, also known as the "I know I owe you the money but I don't have it!" smile.
10 The "I disagree with you" smile, also known as the "you can go ahead and propose it but your idea is no good" smile.
11 The "I am the winner" smile, the smile given to a losing competitor.
12 The "smile in the face of an impossible struggle" smile.
13 The "I'm trying to smile but I can't" smile.

In all my years of coaching, I have never encountered so many sessions with the focus on smiling. It is interesting to me to realize how important the smile is to Thai people and their culture.

Coaching Thai clients

Some objectives that clients have formulated in coaching with me are:

1 Overcoming shyness.
2 Finding the courage to speak up in meetings.
3 How to work effectively with foreigners.
4 Preparing to work abroad.
5 How to make the shift from manager to leader.
6 Reconciling cultural discrepancies from the family to the corporate environment.
7 Work/family balance.
8 How to deal with and manage conflict in the work environment.
9 How to deal with politics, especially Thai workers in a multinational corporation.
10 How to work effectively with diverse cultures when the expectations, style of management, work ethic and capacity to work are extremely different.

Managing inner conflict. While western cultures are known to emphasize individuality, the Thai culture, like many other Asian cultures, is a collectivist one. Thais are raised to naturally focus outwardly – to always think about how one is expected to behave in others' eyes in certain situations. When asked "what do you want to do", the client may answer from the place of "wanting to do what is expected in order to be deemed appropriate and kind". With cultural understanding and respect, a coach can empathetically understand that desire to please and gently encourage the client to find his or her own voice and preferences. In a corporate context, the transition from Manager to Leader is also about finding one's true voice and not simply doing what one is told to do. Khun A wanted to excel, but all his cultural dictates advised him to blend in and harmonize. When his father approached him about heading up the family business, he basically held his breath. He envisioned accommodating 40 individuals with differing agendas and being caught in the middle of every decision. He felt very uncomfortable but found that he couldn't speak. The pressure was overwhelming and his guilt of even thinking that he didn't want to do this was enormous. The inner conflict was the focus of our coaching sessions. His specific objective was how can I communicate my wishes to my father in such a way that he understands what I want, supports my wishes and my choices. This is not an easy objective for any Thai to tackle.

Finding the courage to talk. Khun S is from a Chinese-Thai family. He works for an American multinational automotive manufacturing company based in Thailand. Because he showed promise as a manager, his boss recommended that he spend time with an external coach with extensive experience. In a group session, Khun S was exposed to several executive coaches and he chose the one he felt most comfortable with. His objectives for the coaching process were:

- how to work effectively with diverse cultures;
- how to be engaged with talkative extroverts;
- how to behave like Senior Management does;
- how to comfortably talk more (Boss feedback);
- reconcile contradictory messages from family and boss.

We had a total of six sessions in which we focused on his objectives and, since he had been briefed on the expectations of coaching, he was well prepared and ready to utilize coaching to his advantage. He expressed his concerns like this,

> Sometimes I feel like I am not present with the foreigners. I understand what they are saying, but it takes me so much time to communicate my thoughts in English and I don't want to be the person who slows down the meetings. I am also a bit perfectionistic and when my English is not up to my standards, I become shy, hold back and appear as if I am not interested or engaged. I need to overcome this tendency because it is holding me back in my career development. In addition, when I agree with someone, I say very little, because I agree and there seems to be no point in speaking. When I disagree, I hold back because I don't want to risk conflict with others on the team. Therefore, I rarely speak at all. I need to find my voice, learn how to express myself, when I agree and when I disagree, and find the courage to participate when I am not a perfect communicator.

Khun S shared with me that his Chinese background was a block to speaking up at meetings. In his family of origin, he only spoke when a senior family member addressed him. He automatically transferred this familiar behaviour to the corporate environment. He saw clearly that this ingrained behaviour had to be overcome. In our sessions, we addressed the Thai concepts of *nam jai*, *hen jai* and *greng jai* as they related to our coaching relationship.

Throughout our coaching sessions, Khun S was ready, willing and able to start experimenting with new behaviours. In each session, he explored new steps to branch out of his comfort zone. He saw that he needed to reframe speaking up at meetings to 'adding value'. He started to see himself, not as a manager who was required to attend a meeting, but as a leader whose thoughts, opinions and innovative ideas could make a difference to the team and the overall company. He started to accumulate evidence of his leadership and the positive reinforcement he received; he was visibly blossoming. He noticed it and those around him were observing the changes as well.

My final session with Khun S was extremely gratifying. He enthusiastically recounted his progress, his breakthroughs and the feedback from management, which included a promotion. He proved that, even though there were challenges to overcome, his commitment was stronger than all the obstacles.

Doing the difficult thing. Khun M is a manager for a European manufacturing company in Thailand. Her main objectives were related to learning
how to deal with the inconsistent work ethics in the corporation. She noticed
a manager who was taking advantage of the corporation. He said he was
taking leave to care for his mother, yet my client saw him later that day in the
mall, not at the hospital. He said he needed to attend to a friend in need, yet
my client saw him running errands. She repeatedly observed him abusing the
kindness of the organization that employed both of them.

She asked me, "What should I do?". I asked, "What is your feeling?". She
replied, "Angry because he steals from the company that has given us all so
much!". I asked, "What do you want to do?". She said,

> I am torn inside. Part of me wants to expose him, but I also feel bad. Part
> of me wants to let it go, but I simply cannot. Part of me wants *karma* to
> be served so I won't have to do anything at all. I think what he is doing
> is wrong, but I don't want to be the one to say so.

She told me that her ethics were different from her co-worker's. She shared
that she wanted to ask her mentor about proper action in Thai corporate
society. I encouraged her to do so. This guidance helped her to know what
to do in the future. It was a difficult situation, but ultimately, if she were to
continue to work in that company, where she felt such deep loyalty, she
would have to find the courage to speak up in a manner that would not sabotage her future. Together we mapped out a plan whereby she would explore
the company policies, procedures and the consequences of abusing them.
When she obtained a template for addressing such situations, she could then
comfortably and appropriately address ethical differences.

She wanted to lead and she knew in her heart that she had to do the difficult thing. Finding her truth, sharing it with the right person and standing up
for what she believed was right action is the definition of true leadership in
any culture.

In conclusion

When you coach in Thailand, it is important to understand how to use the
culture as a connector for coaching, and to know when the coaching principles may conflict with Thai concepts. Putting assumptions, cultural
norms and expectations on the table helps open up the conversation to go
to a deeper and more authentic level. Thailand is in the early stages of
development when it comes to coaching; however, with experienced
coaches who understand and utilize cultural sensitivities, leaders will be
successfully developed. Helping Thai people develop into effective leaders
is a mission for many coaches living in Thailand. Cultural sensitivity is
always recommended when coaching an executive from a culture different
from your own.

Table A5.1 Western coaching assumptions versus Thai coaching perspectives.

Western coaching assumptions	Thai coaching perspective
Your answers are inside of you	Your parents know what is best for you
You have the power to cause desired results	Power may be outside your control
You can have what you want	You must think of your parents' needs first
Willing to take a risk	Concerned about saving 'face'
Ask powerful questions	*Greng jai*: don't create discomfort
Ask to coach in sensitive areas	*Greng jai*: avoid confrontation
Younger people are accepted as coaches	Older people are more respected as coaches
Focus on individualism	Focus on collectivism and hierarchy
Expression of emotions is encouraged	Expression of emotions is discouraged
Everyone deserves respect	*Thii tam thii soong*: behave according to your class and place in society
Stand up for yourself	*Sam ruam*: practise restraint and modesty
Theory 'Y' benevolent leadership, 'tough love'	*Phradet*: leadership authority and toughness in Western terms, Theory 'X'
Non-profit endeavours are an option, not a requirement in this individualistic culture	*prakhun*: caring for those less fortunate is a requirement in Thai culture
The leader may have strong relationship	*Baramee*: the leader has a deep and trusting relationship with subordinates and commands obedience and loyalty
Don't bite the hand that fed you!	*Bunkhun*: indebted goodness, to be repaid
Entitlement based on family name/status	*Katanyu rookhun*: gratitude and indebtedness to parents
Three mistakes and you are out!	*Mettaa karunaa*: merciful and kind when a mistake has been made by one less fortunate
Repayment of favours applies to some, but it is bought into by all in the culture	*Katanyu katawethi*: loving indebtedness not expressed through loving behaviours
Do the right thing	*Karma*: what goes around, comes around
Get the job done, and do it now!	Build good relationships, which may take time
Question: What do you want?	Question: What should I do?
Find your voice and speak up, become heard!	Harmonize, blend in, no need for attention

Source: Persons (2016).

Reference

Holmes, H. and Tangtongtavy, S., (1997). *Working with the Thais: A guide to managing in Thailand*. Bangkok: White Lotus.

Persons, L. S. (2016). *The way Thais lead*. Chiang Mai, Thailand: Silkworm Books.

6 The Cross-Cultural Kaleidoscope™ model

A systems approach to coaching in the Asia Pacific region

Jenny Plaister-Ten

High stakes, high stress

The global company was engaged in the research and testing of a new source of energy. If found, it would be a scientific breakthrough. The company was on a limited timeline with limited budgets; the stakes were high. There were many stakeholders, including financiers and governmental bodies from around the world. The world's smartest scientists were being recruited.

The company was a quasi-private/public institution and at times it was difficult to establish where the centre of power lay. With input from many sources, this became political. As a result, several CEOs had resigned, frustrated by their lack of control in the situation. Team spirit and trust were low and individual motivation was weak. At the same time, stress levels were high due to the time imperative and the risk of funding drying up. Personal and national reputations were at stake.

The company had not used coaching or mentoring before as an intervention. It did not have a human relations department or policy, but management from the US and the UK wanted to offer coaching to key players as a show of support for their development. However, they also saw coaching as a route to remove certain problems in behaviour that were causing slower than expected progress. Therefore, the programme was in part remedial and in part developmental.

A meeting was called to define coaching objectives. Notably the coachees in question were not present at the first meeting but were subsequently invited to comment on the coaching objectives already set for them – at my insistence. This subsequently illuminated surface level 'acceptance' from the coachees that was not necessarily indicative of a motivation to change.

The challenges

The Chief Scientific Officer (CSO), a Chinese National, was sent to coaching by his Australian boss in order to become more assertive. He needed to exert more influence on the external stakeholders, in particular one from South Africa. These stakeholders were highly influential from both advisory and financial standpoints. The CSO led a multicultural team but was not great at delegating. Furthermore, he did not have a good relationship with his peers, particularly the Chief Operations Officer (COO), who was from Hong Kong. The COO was also sent to coaching because of his dictatorial approach. Individual sessions were set up on a monthly basis. In addition to the individual coaching, senior team coaching also took place on a bi-monthly basis, in order to guide the multicultural team through a transition to a new Chief Executive Officer (CEO), a Singaporean National.

Several challenges emerged during the course of the coaching programme that extended over one year. They were as follows:

Challenge number one. In exploring the issue of his perceived lack of assertiveness, it occurred to me to ask the CSO, "What does assertiveness mean to you?". He said he did not know. His English-language skills being challenged, he looked in the dictionary. As he had been working in Japan most recently and had a better grasp of Japanese than English he was trying to find meaning for one word: assertiveness in three languages. He could not find a translation in any language that made any sense to him; there did not appear to be a direct word for assertiveness in the Chinese language. So effectively, his management were asking him to become something he had no understanding of, and did not even have a word for.

Challenge number two. The CSO kept referring to "you taught me", "what I learned from you". Yet, when I challenged him to describe what he was doing differently back at his workplace, as a result of this learning, he struggled to describe a scenario where he had implemented any changes. His management had highlighted this type of behaviour during the tri-partite meeting. It seemed that he said one thing and then did as he pleased thereafter. Management perceived this as a lack of 'follow-through'. This behaviour was also causing him problems with his peers who did not trust him to keep agreements. He presented with signs of stress and did not appear to have any coping mechanisms or an ability to delegate well. Despite my attempt to keep a non-directional stance in the coaching engagement, the CSO seemed to treat me as if I were his superior.

Challenge number three. The COO was very unpopular with his peers due to his dictatorial approach, particularly around health and safety issues. He issued many imperatives and rules without communicating the consequences of a lack of adherence. He was brusque and rude and presented for coaching with many 'shoulds' and 'oughts' about how others needed to behave. Since he saw his role as dealing with life and death matters, he was very clear about the unacceptability of a lack of adherence to rules. This had the effect of alienating others and certain members of staff even went so far as to sabotage any efforts he made to provide for a safe environment.

Challenge number four. Team trust was low. Co-operation across departments was minimal and silos were being created based upon functional expertise or nationality. There was very little communication amongst the senior leadership team. There were also deep-rooted fears that the new CEO may halt the project and seek an alliance with a third party in another part of the world or that the stakeholders would pull the plug on the financing of the project.

Introducing the model

The Cross-Cultural Kaleidoscope™ model provides the coach with a tool that enables the users to reflect upon an intercultural situation. In my intercultural work it often transpires that the values and beliefs that are culturally constructed, either during socialisation or during adult life, may be completely subconscious. This is because our cultural values and beliefs are 'below the waterline' as explained in the well-known 'cultural iceberg' metaphor. Yet, it is below the surface of the water that most cultural clashes have their origins.

The Cross-Cultural Kaleidoscope™ model provides for both a macro and a micro view of the factors contributing to the values and beliefs that drive behaviours and contribute to decisions in a corporate environment. It moves away from linear goal-oriented approaches, such as GROW (Goal, Reality, Options, Will), and towards a more contextual approach, suitable for both 'Western' and 'Eastern' mindsets. Yet, our mindsets may be hardwired in the past and no longer serve us. It is therefore incumbent on the coach or facilitator of the Kaleidoscope model to reflect this back to the coachee/mentee and to facilitate 'unlearning'. Thereafter, changes in habits or perpetual thought patterns may be initiated where practicable.

The cross-cultural kaleidoscope™ A systems approach

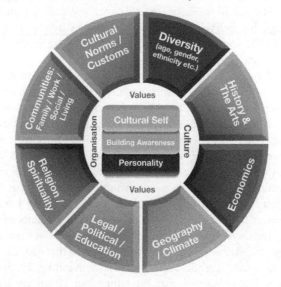

Figure 6.1 The Cross-Cultural Kaleidoscope™ model.
Source: 10 Consulting, 2016.

The Kaleidoscope may be utilised in several different ways, depending on how the coach intuits that it will have the most impact upon learning for the coachee. There are no hard and fast rules or step-by-step process to follow; intuition is key.

Scenario one: I was signposted through my intuition to the education lens of the Kaleidoscope. In China, rote learning appears to be the norm and consequently students have not generally been taught to speak up for themselves. This translates to the workplace where it could cause a loss of face to speak up, for fear of being wrong. This is particularly evident in the presence of elders or those with more seniority. This is completely different to learning styles in 'the West' where speaking up for oneself and one's ideas is considered good practice. Furthermore, conventional education practices in 'the West' consider that a mistake represents a learning opportunity. It should be noted, however, that the situation in China is changing amongst the younger generations and with those that have been educated in Western universities or learning styles.

Scenario two: I was signposted, again through intuition, to the cultural norms lens in conjunction with the education lens of the Kaleidoscope. I realised that my coachee was behaving like a grade-A student. Teachers in Asian societies hold one of the most respected positions and students remain deferent and subordinate to them. Although our relationship deepened in trust and respect, I could never be sure that he was changing his behaviour even though I was using role-plays, perceptual positions and other techniques to embed the learning. Eventually I realised that I was his teacher, not his coach. He did not want to cause me a loss of face by appearing not to be learning. He could not, or would not, assume responsibility for needing to change his behaviour. He was so driven by the fear of failure and therefore possible loss of face. As a result, all that he learned remained in the cognitive zone.

Scenario three: When working with the COO, I considered the situation through the legal and cultural norms lenses along with the impact thereafter on the cultural self (the inner lens). His behaviour was consistent with the fact that he was older than his peers and he considered his position to be of the highest order. This was because he was not only responsible for implementing the systems according to a set of rules, but it often concerned matters of health and safety. He had decided to implement a set of rules based on UK health and safety in an environment where these rules were not taken as seriously. In hierarchical societies (such as Hong Kong, China, or Singapore) respect for elders in a position of authority results in a deferent workforce. Yet, the COO was not being given this level of respect because the workforce was distributed around the world. This had the effect of making him even more authoritarian, almost demanding compliance. In working with him I also learned that his father had a military background and this also informed his view of himself as a person with lots of right and wrong ways to do things. His 'cultural self' started to accept this and to review whether or not this was appropriate in the current context. His 'unlearning journey' had begun.

Scenario four. When coaching the leadership team I used the Kaleidoscope model as a team building tool. Here I invited each member to talk about his or herself from the point of view of the history lens. This illuminated rich perspectives from the past. I then invited each person to explain how that past might be impacting the present, and in particular in their work role.

One of the main differences that the team discovered was in the relative use of the words 'I' and 'We'. In collective societies (such as China, Hong Kong or Singapore) the imperative is viewed from the point of view of 'we'. Someone from Hong Kong may be less collective in orientation than someone from China and more collective than someone from Australia, for example. In individualistic countries such as Australia, the USA or the UK the imperative is more typically viewed from the point of view of 'I'. This meant that when coaching the team it was important to realise that ideas of responsibility might have different meanings: from responsibility to myself, my family, my team, my company, my neighbours, my country. Once all meanings had been elicited and shared, trust could be built. This took some time but thereafter, communication started to flow. This subsequently demanded an enquiry into communication patterns. Hall's (1976) work on high-context and low-context communication patterns provided a vehicle to explore communication style patterns and preferences that show up in the cultural norms of the Kaleidoscope. This, and the use of metaphor, elicited a group identity and purpose.

Exploring meanings and patterns

This case is a good example of the coach's role in exploring meanings, going way beyond the scope of the tripartite agreements set at the beginning of the assignment. It reveals how important it is to have common understandings when working with people whose first language is not the same as the lingua franca. It illuminates how easily we can assume that others share our mental map of the world. Whilst this case reinforces our role as coaches as '*pattern excavators*', it may be unusual in that it highlights the need to consider *both* cultural patterns and personal patterns.

The example also suggests that, through a deep level of trust and a willingness to use creative solutions, coaching can be effective beyond language. It explains how, through using the Cross-Cultural Kaleidoscope™ model, deeply engrained patterns may be revealed to both the coach and the coachee. Furthermore, the patterns may be from a culture with which the coach has no experience or knowledge of. It is therefore also incumbent on the coach to be aware of his or her own cultural patterns and to bracket those before engaging in the coaching relationship, as otherwise this would be tantamount to projection and is clearly inappropriate.

Outcomes

The use of the Kaleidoscope during the coaching programme delivered positive outcomes at several levels:

- The CSO began to trust me and wanted to do his best to learn in the sessions. He was being very conformant, but did not make the time to transfer the learning back to his job. He needed much more time than the contract provided for.
- The COO successfully developed a repertoire of behavioural styles and began to develop better relationships with his co-workers as a result.
- The leadership team was more cohesive and communicated better. Trust improved.
- The external stakeholders became more supportive.
- Stress levels improved at several levels in the organisation.
- The new CEO went on to lead a team with a greater commercial awareness than before.

Lessons learnt

- 'Western' coaching processes do not always translate to those cultures that are either deferent in nature, have experienced a different education system, or do not have the same choices and options as in other countries.
- There do not appear to be any ethical or boundary restrictions to coaching several people from the same organisation at the same time as each case is different. It does mean however, that contracting and confidentiality must be strictly adhered to.
- Those sent to coaching (as opposed to self-selecting) can still be coachable but it often takes more time and requires more patience.
- Understandings can vary for words such as 'assertive', 'responsibility' or 'coaching' when coaching someone of a different background.
- Coaching people who are not familiar with the 'Western' concept of coaching takes time and requires a lot of patience from the coach.
- People from different cultures view success differently, leading to different emphases about preferred outcomes.

In summary, a systemic approach to coaching and mentoring across cultures provides for both the breadth and depth required to practice interculturally. The Cross-Cultural Kaleidoscope™ model is a tool to assist with this.

Editorial note

- Coaching and mentoring are used interchangeably throughout.
- The 'West' and 'East' are used to assist with explanation rather than to categorise or polarise.

- All references to nationality are simply to assist with understanding the cultural norms inherent within that group of people. No sweeping generalisations are intended. It is fully acknowledged that every single person, regardless of origin is unique.

Reference

Hall, T. E. (1976). *Beyond culture*. New York: Anchor.

7   Asia's unique leadership challenges

Tony Mathers

Goldminer's mentality

In any coaching assignment, there are two initial aspects to consider. First, the case conceptualisation of the assignment in which a coach will consider the coachee and relevant data inputs received from the coaching programme sponsor to establish a preferred coaching approach. Second, and just as important, is the mindset the coach brings to the assignment.

At the Institute of Executive Coaching and Leadership (IECL) we describe a coach's ideal mindset as having a 'goldminer's mentality'. When you are mining for gold, what do you find more of: gold or dirt? It's dirt of course, but the goldminer continues to sift through mountains of dirt knowing that the gold is there. Without a conviction that the gold is within the dirt, the goldminer wouldn't persist.

An organisational coach needs to have the same conviction; that their coaching counterpart has within themselves the gold, that is, that the counterpart is resourceful. The coach believes their counterpart has within themselves everything they need to succeed, untapped potential and the ability to bring forth that potential to increase their performance in the workplace. A coach that is problem-focused (who focuses on just the dirt, not the gold) will only find more dirt and the counterpart will not experience a positive change in performance.

From our experience, it is critical to take a holistic approach when coaching individuals. We need to deal with the whole person within the organisational context in which they work and the parameters of the coaching mandate. For this reason, IECL coaches use the Integral Model – adapted from Ken Wilber's integral theory (1996, 2000). Using this model, our coaches take into account the four quadrants illustrated below:

- the individual's internal beliefs, attitudes and values;
- the individual's external behaviours, actions and performance;
- the organisation's systems and structures;
- the organisational culture.

In using a whole systems philosophy, IECL utilises the systems landscape to map the context in which the manager/leader is operating and which in

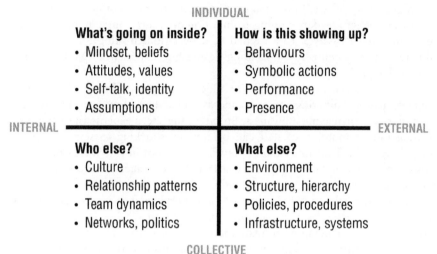

Figure 7.1 Whole system organisational coaching.

turn influences their team and stakeholder 'encounters'. Its strength is to recognise the importance of 'outsight' as well as 'insight' (Armstrong, 2008). Four domains of knowledge/action: personal, behavioural, interpersonal/cultural and social system/environment are considered and conversations are structured around questions that explore these domains.

While it may be desirable to imagine that a coach establishes in advance the best coaching approach for a given coaching mandate and client, the practicalities of coaching senior executives entail a coach being sufficiently nimble in dialogue, presence and knowledge to work with a variety of coaching styles in pursuit of the optimal outcome for the coaching client and their organisation. There is a vast array of skilful techniques and a variety of coaching approaches that executive coaches can access and apply in a coaching environment.

Asia's unique challenges

Leadership positions in Asia throw up different dimensions and opportunities relative to a home-based role. Officially there are 48 countries in Asia but when one considers what is commonly referred to as Asia, it amounts to a little over 20 countries: that's a lot of diversity of cultures, language and mindsets.

Fresh challenges for leaders in Asia can emanate from multiple areas, such as the prevalence of expat executives, either in leadership positions or members of teams led by local executives. This introduces dynamics and cross-cultural influences not always experienced in more generic market leadership environments.

While many of Asia's financial centres are melting pots of race, life experiences and beliefs, leaders coming from a home-country single point of reference may need to adapt to a myriad of expectations making for an entirely different and potentially demanding leadership experience. Mid-America meets Shanghai, anyone?

Cost structures, the availability or indeed non-availability of eligible and suitable people, differing safety standards and expectations can add to the complexity of managing a business. So often, the sheer expense of or the surprising instant mobility of staff can be initially shocking to someone from outside Asia. Staff turnover rates at levels unheard of in the West can be the norm in China or South East Asia; a fact that can alter how one manages people quite significantly.

In the same vein, mature businesses can experience start-up-like conditions in Asia as markets open or consumer consumption reaches critical mass, as Australia is experiencing with many food-based products. The style of leadership required may once again tip off-balance an unsuspecting newcomer.

Four case studies

The first example is that of John, a finance executive with experience in France, Belgium and the UK, who came to Singapore to be the regional CFO for a UK-based manufacturing company with 13 factories spread across a number of Asian countries and numerous points of sales representation. John is ambitious and a hard driving executive who, still in his early 30s, has had swift progression in the company. He is now faced with an opportunity to take the commercial executive lead for the region. Will his style and approach work in this environment?

John has good values and appreciates what motivational leadership should look like but believes there is little appetite in this company and from head office for anything other than getting him to deliver on hefty budget goals (that are a real stretch for him) at all costs. Assessment data were provided that showed a passionate, driven and analytical executive who came across as impatient, brusque in style and defensive in the face of feedback. He got results but it was questionable as to whether his was a promotable style.

The coaching challenge was to encourage and create the environment that would allow John to experiment with leading from a different space, role modelling a different set of values than those that his staff were used to seeing from him. Central to this was for John to believe that he could indeed act differently with authenticity and achieve the same or better results in his new role. John's career history was one of varied corporate environments and, overwhelmingly, he had experienced a command and control leadership style in his career to date. Intuitively, he believed that a more constructive style was the way to be, but there was significant internal doubt that it would either work or that it would be acceptable to the head office leadership. Interestingly, but apparently not particularly relevant for John, was that his current leader was a softly spoken, highly supportive leader.

It was his current leader, the managing director for Asia, who suggested a need for John to display less ego, more humility and a style that is more open and questioning and encouraging of team effectiveness. Without doubt, John's manager felt this change was necessary for his success in an Asian environment.

Initially, our work consisted of trawling through the feedback data and understanding the path that had brought John to where he found himself. His history of rapid advancement, self-taught leadership and role models demonstrating significant controlling behaviour provided great insight as to why John felt comfortable in his certain style and approach. Much discussion as to whether this was a scalable and promotable leadership style in a commercial management setting eventually led John to appreciate that he and his new team would benefit from a radically different approach based on building a tight, well-functioning and focused team.

At an offsite meeting, John surprised his team, his peers and his manager by devoting a quarter of the available time to a deep discussion on what values were required to best execute their strategy and encouraged the adoption of a consultative approach to client relationship management.

At the end of our work together, John found that he had been able to make the shift from a driven, controlling style to one that was eminently more scalable, authentic to his desired self-image and at least as effective as before, but rather more motivational to his people.

The second example is that of Claire, a Malaysian national working in Singapore as the Chief Operating Officer of an international financial services company with a considerable number of expatriates in the senior management layer. She had different objectives: how to transition into the new role and influence her peers to achieve an ambitious strategic plan.

Coming from a finance background, Claire found leading local staff straightforward enough although the recipients may have felt her leadership somewhat authoritarian. Claire's challenge came when she endeavoured to command the respect and engagement from the largely expatriate regional management team. In this more senior context, she became less self-assured and was perceived to be reticent to engage in robust debate with her senior leadership team peers.

Based on assessment data and 360 interviews, desirable coaching goals were constructed and agreed on. The first priority was to ensure that her approach and process around the role of COO was sufficiently defined and disciplined, while the second was to develop into a key long-term Asian management team member with the ultimate personal goal of running a financial organisation herself. While Claire wanted to lead, it was not her strong suit. Her task was to show more leadership, less doing.

As with many COO roles, the job itself varies from organisation to organisation and the strengths and weaknesses of the managing director. On this occasion, Claire had two managing directors within a short space of time whose requirements were quite different. For the purposes of this chapter, I will focus on the second period in which the core requirement of the role was to develop a regional strategy and to lead the eventual implementation plan.

The incoming managing director evidenced a style and expectation that had the role of the COO materially involved in running the organisation on a day-to-day basis, while she focused on long-term strategic growth and top-tier client relationships.

A mixed bag of coaching approaches was necessary for this assignment, starting with some behavioural work, some disciplined performance coaching which, when combined, eventually led to the counterpart being able to transform their long held default patterns at work (and likely in life too).

We first processed the data from present and even past 360s to establish the prevailing perceptions and, especially, to understand development needs or unhelpful traits that had become persistent over time. There was an imperative for Claire to shift her horizon further out, to focus only on the few important issues that were essential to success and to develop increased accountability within her own team and with other leaders to take responsibility for the multitude of tasks and challenges on Claire's plate. For some, leadership comes easily; for others, there's a science and process that can facilitate their leadership style and perceived success. Claire fell into the latter category and she benefited strongly from systematic changes to the way she went about her role.

Over time, Claire became a respected leader of the senior team, albeit in a challenging global and Asian economic environment. Recently, she moved to become the chief executive officer for Asia for a smaller financial services organisation, achieving her ultimate personal goal.

The third example is that of Stefan. As Asia has emerged as an engine of strong economic activity and financial strength, there have been occasions for global and regional companies to build businesses rapidly and sometimes very profitably. It has taken management conviction, the ability to move swiftly, confidently and, depending on the industry or segment, a significant investment commitment. In short, companies can be presented with the chance to make great returns in Asia from an otherwise mature business.

Stefan was the right person in the right place to capitalise on an opportunity although it wasn't altogether identified or supported by his peers and geographic management. He did, however, have the undivided support of his global product leader. Progress was not linear and Stefan's impatient, hard driving style didn't endear him to everyone he dealt with in that time. In his favour, Stefan was the most strategically insightful client I had come across and possibly still is. He was able to envision the future accurately and had the personal confidence to back his judgement and plan to move forward.

The term 'alpha male' jumps to mind when thinking of Stefan. He would never take a simple 'no' as a signal to stop trying to achieve his objective. Successful people with strong personalities take some convincing that their behaviour is not serving their reputation and ability to succeed in the work place. As part of the coaching assignment, a 360 survey was arranged and debriefed with some harsh messages for Stefan regarding his leadership style versus the majority of the norming group for that particular diagnostic. Reflective questions were asked and a general understanding achieved but not lasting change. Further interviews were held with a range of stakeholders with the same results and the same reaction and this was followed up with yet another personality diagnostic that placed Stefan clearly in the dominant quadrant. The challenge for the coach was clear; what to do now?

In my experience, people with strong personalities may take time to accept that what they are being told repetitively, backed by evidence and anecdotes, actually holds merit. More than once, I have found that perseverance, consistency of message and a willingness to keep the mirror up in the face of resistance will break through eventually. It was during our fifth session together that I noticed that Stefan had made a noticeable change since our last meeting. There was an understanding that a collaborative and influencing style was likely going to be more persuasive than any amount of heavy handedness – an acceptance that he had been overusing his natural strengths.

In a three-year period, Stefan continued to grow his business in the region at a rapid rate, completely unforeseen by many of his seasoned Asia executive peers. Stefan uncovered this opportunity to fill a void in the region unseen by others through visionary and courageous leadership. Stefan continues to think big and will always look to a medium-term vision that others cannot see.

The last example is Julian. Here was a highly competent, experienced and inspirational leader parachuted from another continent to stabilise and grow a specialised construction business. His work force numbered 8,000 and was spread across substantial infrastructure projects in an undeveloped and inaccessible country. One of his divisional managers frequently needed to take two flights, a boat journey and a four-wheel drive into ancient forest to visit one of their projects. Julian's challenge was as much about clear, strategic thinking in the absence of peers to debate issues with as it was about maintaining basic leadership and management principles in a developing market.

Julian had a latent talent to lead, a strong but benevolent presence and an ambition to succeed in his role and into the future. A coach surveying available data points might wonder what the coaching goals might be. I had my own moment reflecting on what I might offer someone who presented so strongly.

As always in the coaching world, just ask. There is research that suggests the most beneficial coaching outcomes can come from working with the best executives, polishing a well-cut diamond. Julian was relatively new to the company and the nature of his previous roles, in inhospitable places, hadn't lent itself to copious amounts of professional development. Well educated, he was self-taught in leadership and had little in the way of a company network. Julian's greatest desire was to have quality conversations with someone who was able to offer independent insight and reflections back to him by various means, thereby clarifying his own outlook, thoughts and decisions.

We met in-country and at opportunity elsewhere in Asia. He always came with his own topics and went away with his own solutions. It wasn't strictly coaching but then at senior levels, it rarely is straightforward.

Testing the best

These thumbnails of coaching assignments highlight just a few of the unique challenges that Asia can present to mature businesses and executives alike. From the diversity of the work place and work forces, difficulties with JV partners and over regulation to start-up like challenges producing super-profits, Asia is able to test the best.

References

Armstrong, H. (2009). Integral coaching: Cultivating a cultural sensibility through executive coaching. In M. C. Moral & G. N. Abbott (Eds), *The Routledge companion to international business coaching*. London: Routledge.

Wilber, K. (1996). *A brief history of everything*. Boston: Shambhala Publications.

Wilber, K. (2000). *Integral psychology*. Boston: Shambhala Publications.

8 Transitioning the new CEO while embedding a merger

How coaching supported a newly appointed CEO based in Malaysia who was appointed to lead a newly merged technology company across Asia

Padraig O'Sullivan

Integrating merged companies

Seek is a market-leading employment job board technology company listed on the Australian Stock Exchange. International growth has come through acquisitions of in-country technology companies that Seek then, post-acquisition, develops to home market dominance with home market CEOs. This strategy has been successful in South America, China and more recently in Asia. In 2014/2015 Seek took a controlling interest in Jobs DB and Jobs Street. These companies were competitors based in Malaysia and Hong Kong. Once regulatory approval for the merger was given, the organisation set about merging the entities and laying the foundations for long-term growth. An Australian-based executive led the initial merger and integration. The plan was to hand over the leadership reins to a locally based executive as per their traditional strategy.

My relationship with Seek had been well established at this point, having worked with many of their executives in Australia and South America. I was asked to support an executive called Suresh, the COO of the joint entity, in his efforts to integrate the two organisations and assist him in getting ready to take the CEO role, if he was to be offered that position. Suresh had been the long-term COO of the Malaysian organisation, reporting to the founding CEO who had departed when his company was acquired by Seek.

Leadership transitions, described as a leader moving from one level of leadership to a higher level of leadership, are often fraught with complexity leading to many leadership mistakes and the failure of between 25 and 40% of senior executive leadership transitions (O'Sullivan, 2015). When the transition is at CEO level there is an increased level of complexity involved. A coach supporting the CEO executive needs to take an integrated coaching approach that is informed by a range of evidence bases as one modality is unlikely to satisfy all situations. The coach needs to have an overarching framework to guide the case conceptualisations and coaching intervention choices.

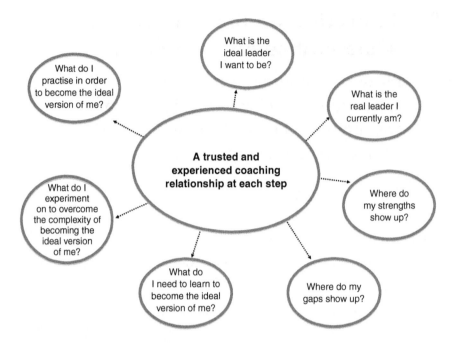

Figure 8.1 Individual development model.

Source: adapted from Boyatzis's intentional change theory.

My practice in supporting transitioning executives utilises two main models or frameworks that naturally complement each other. The initial model is called the Individual Development Model, adapted from Boyatzis's intentional change theory (Boyatzis, 2006). It is a circular, non-linear framework that starts with an ideal leadership frame. In practice, a preceding question often is: "What does this new role require of you as the leader?".

The second framework is the PALDER framework that supports all senior leaders in transition, particularly to executive positions and in expatriate leadership roles. It is a time-based framework that assists leaders in deciding what they most need to focus on at different points of their transition (O'Sullivan, 2015).

The coaching brief was couched in three parts.

1   Assist the COO in post-merger integration activities.
2   Assist him in managing cross-cultural relationships between the various Asian offices and head office in Melbourne, Australia.
3   Support his learning as the COO to maximise his potential as the preferred candidate for a CEO appointment.

Mergers have a high failure rate (Canina, 2009; Cuza, 2011) with the predesigned outcomes rarely being realised. A well-managed cultural integration

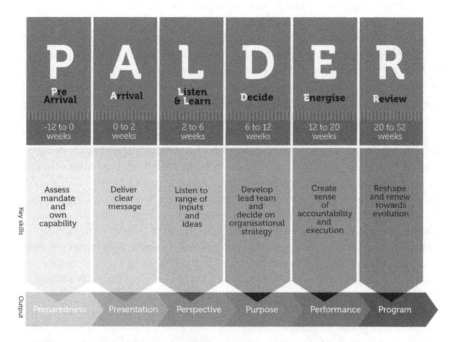

Figure 8.2 The PALDER framework.

Source: taken from the *Foreigner in Charge* book series and used with permission.

or culture optimisation programme put in place post integration can increase the post-merger success rate by 26% (KPMG, 1999, cited in Bertoncelj & Kovac, 2007). The difficulty for a new leader is in understanding what to include in that programme and how best to implement one. The added difficulties of cross-cultural hierarchies that exist between North and South Asian countries such as Hong Kong and Malaysia are made more difficult when the two companies being merged originate in those regions and are used to being market competitors. Neither company had been part of a multinational entity before, both having originated as local start-ups. As a result, there were many complexities in Suresh's situation.

The coaching programme

Coaching is proven to be a useful intervention for leaders in the midst of such complexities. With a skilled coach, individual sessions give a confidential, safe environment to self-examine, explore, develop and compile actions without the fear of judgement or risk of managerial redress if the incorrect decisions are made (Berriman, 2007). During times of complexity such as post-merger or transitioning to more senior levels of leadership, external coaching enables professionals to orchestrate change while maintaining a reflective mindset and stakeholder orientation which will continue to fuel the ongoing changes needed (Hicks & McCracken, 2012).

A carefully designed multi-phased coaching programme was put into place for Suresh. He had never been coached before. His organisation, pre-merger, had placed emphasis on rapid growth in its market sector and little on leader or people development. He expressed positive surprise when Seek offered him coaching support to ensure he succeeded in navigating the multiple transitions upon which he was embarking.

The programme (see Table 8.1) had three distinct phases. The first focused on a successful initial implementation of post-merger strategies and optimisation of employee engagement. This included stakeholder interactions and seeking feedback leading to Suresh undertaking a Leadership Circle 360 assessment. Three-hundred-and-sixty degree instruments can be helpful for leaders to gain insights into the impact they are having as a leader (Dalton, 2005). The choice of instrument was important as Suresh was navigating several transitions and complexities and needed a robust instrument to assist him in understanding his potential reactive tendencies that could negate his leadership competencies. The leadership circle tool is ideal for such a scenario (Anderson & Adams, 2015).

Phase 2 shifted focus for Suresh to raise his awareness of the behaviours, mindsets and habits developed as a COO and how to develop those needed if he were to get the CEO role (Stober, 2008). This involved a high degree of emphasis on behaviour change, internal reflections, stakeholder feedback, feedforward sessions and progress measurement of behaviour change (Anderson & Adams, 2015).

Phase 3 shifted focus again once Suresh was appointed as the Seek Asia CEO in late 2015 to focus on a successful leadership transition. Using the PALDER leadership transition framework (O'Sullivan, 2015) the coaching sessions were planned to ensure each important focus area as a new CEO was considered in the optimal time frame it needed to be.

The programme had a mixture of face-to-face sessions in Kuala Lumpur and Melbourne, supplemented with Skype sessions. Typically, in Phases 1 and 2 we met every 3–4 weeks, with occasional periods of increased frequency if there were situations or concerns that benefited Suresh to have more contact. Preparing for important staff meetings or shareholder presentations are examples of such events. As the programme moved into the latter stage of Phase 3 this naturally moved into a four-week frequency. Currently the programme has been extended and we are meeting every six weeks. Coaching notes called *Reflections and Reminders* were sent after each session by the coach to Suresh as reflective materials and a session record.

Main outcomes

Leadership assessment. The leadership circle 360 assessment was debriefed over two sessions.

Whilst it illustrated strong leadership competencies that had made Suresh a valuable COO during the rapid growth his organisation had experienced, it also illustrated that his desire for control and personal arrogance were potentially going to derail him as a CEO. Hierarchy as a leadership style is common in Asian countries (O'Sullivan, 2016), particularly in Hong, Kong and Malaysia. Yet this style is shunned in Australia (O'Sullivan, 2015). Suresh had to learn to minimise his desire for control and arrogant tendencies if he was to become a successful CEO. This was both from a leadership and cross-cultural perspective.

After digesting his leadership feedback, Suresh did a deep dive into both control and arrogance to understand how these developed for him over his career and how he might minimise both. Originally he grew up in rural Malaysia and his early intellectual talents saw him studying on a scholarship in MIT Boston with many future technology leaders. The desire to be intellectually capable and operationally efficient in a boot-strapped start-up helped Suresh foster both reactive tendencies. He quickly realised that he himself was the potential blocker for a successful integration of both companies and in earnest sought feedback on where he might improve. Using a pulse check process, his stakeholders gave him regular progress reports and suggestions on where he could focus his behaviour change efforts.

Behaviour change. Clearly articulated behaviour goals were identified and shared with his stakeholders for their input and regular feedback. They included:

1   Being less autocratic by trusting and empowering his team mates to make their own decisions and by listening more often than speaking.
2   Being less critical of others by motivating others to over-achieve and not demotivating them or stifling their creativity.
3   Develop humility by being less arrogant or dominant in meetings.
4   Actively help others to grow their capabilities, confidence or scope of work.

Suresh was surprised to find that it wasn't as difficult to change behaviour as he had thought it would be and that the impact of those changes were noticed at home as much as they were at work. His teenage son increasingly and actively involved Suresh in his life, which Suresh appreciated.

Cross-cultural relationships. Suresh identified key stakeholders in both Hong Kong and Melbourne with whom he needed to build relationships. Within the Hong Kong office morale was not as high as the Kuala Lumpur office. He proactively spent fixed periods per month working out of the Hong Kong office to address concerns and to be seen as a leader of 'the Asian business' and not just the Malaysian business. Within Australia he sought to adapt his messaging to the more relaxed style of Australian business etiquette. Having lived in Australia as a student for three months, Suresh had already built up an understanding of Australian standards. Preparing for Board presentations saw Suresh prepare in his natural style and then adapting in accordance with the feedback he received before the meeting.

Table 8.1 Coaching programme

Transition phase	Phase 1	Phase 2	Phase 3
Business imperative	Formation of Seek Asia, leadership and integration team.	Successful acceptance of newly promoted COO into CEO of joint entity.	Re-enrol all employees in the stated vision and strategy. Lead an integrated and empowered leadership team.
Focus/outcomes supported by coaching	Capability alignment to delivery of planned strategic aims and communication plans.	Strong engagement from key employees that Suresh will be the new CEO.	Introduce new leadership team members to their roles and responsibilities.
	Alignment between COO and his respective peers as their future leader.	Successful and early transition into CEO role.	Integration targets and strategies delivered.
Coaching frameworks	**Narrative coaching approach** (Drake, 2007) To assist Suresh in voicing his own story.	**Strengths identification** For Suresh to fully embrace his strengths as a COO and to decide what are the optimal strengths in the future.	**PALDER framework** To guide the transition to CEO from COO using proven methodologies (O'Sullivan, 2015).
	The Leadership Circle 360 assessment To gain insights into his leadership impact and potential (Dalton, 2005).	**Pulse checks** To measure progress over time (and not perfection) (Anderson & Adams, 2015).	**Team development** To identify the optimal ways of setting the environment for top team optimisation (Clutterbuck, 2013).
	Stakeholder involvement Ensuring Suresh engages relevant stakeholders (O'Sullivan, 2015).	**Personality preferences tool** Hays Group.	Virtual team leadership.
			Leading across borders (Curşeu, 2006).

	Integration priorities	Emotional intelligence	Kolb Experiential Learning Model
	Integration planning frameworks to translate business case into tangible actions and time frames.	To understand the range of leadership approaches/inter personal intelligences he might utilise.	(Kolb & Kolb, 2009) A reflective learning process to monitor progress.
	Solution focused approaches To assist in generating a wide range of options and empowerment.		**Journaling** (Stober, 2008) Hyper mindfulness can precede optimal performance.
Expected leadership development as an outcome from those intervention choices	Raise Suresh's awareness on the optimal actions he needed to deploy and the associated risks. Taking a wider consultative approach as opposed to his traditional authoritarian approach. Facilitating the move from old company culture to new joint company culture.	Raise Suresh's awareness of his personal impact as a leader. His leadership style suited his historical company but could be a derailer in the newly merged company. The power of reflection and mindfulness as a regulator of behaviours. Measuring progress rather than perfection.	Suresh to successfully inhabit the role of CEO of the new entity and maintain employee engagement, particularly with employees of the 'other' company. To build stakeholder relationships in the headquarters in Australia. Share and build his (the CEO's) 'teachable point of view', i.e. translation of strategic aims into clear accountabilities and KPIs across the organisation.

Leadership team development. In January 2016 Suresh held his first leadership meeting in his role as CEO. He had been a part of that team for a year earlier as COO. Coaching sessions were spent on preparing for that initial meeting and an offsite meeting later where he and his team clarified their purpose as a team and aligned behind the predetermined strategies (Soudunsaari & Hakanen, 2012). The role of CEO is critical in setting the clarity of direction and pace of change or execution. Suresh was very mindful of his previous reputation for authoritarian-orientated execution and wanted to ensure he stayed open to consultation with inputs from his team.

The coaching then moved to the take-up of the five daily habits of exceptional leaders (Gaster & O'Sullivan, 2014). Using a simple five-question daily reflective process, Suresh took time every morning and evening to take stock on the most important areas of *intentional focus* he needed to have as the CEO. These centred on the work that needed to be done, the people that needed to do that work and how he needed to ensure he was an enabler and not a blocker of that progress.

Ultimately the coaching programme was designed to ensure Suresh was successful in securing and transitioning to the CEO position of Seek Asia. With that he received confirmation of his appointment in December 2015 and commenced in January 2016. His quantitative pulse checks showed on average a 4.7-point improvement (on a 7-point progress scale) suggesting 'very noticeable changes' and 'obvious business impact' improvement from a range of stakeholders against the measured behaviours. Qualitative feedback suggested Suresh has successfully developed competencies in listening, delegating and motivating his team towards achieving shared outcomes. Suresh was afforded the opportunity to have coaching support to assist him navigate these hurdles and he embraced the process. His enthusiasm for learning, reflecting, asking for feedback and being genuine in understanding the suggestions received meant he endeared himself to those around his inner circle who then offered more support.

Coaching for adaptation

Complexities abound during major transitions and leaders find it easy to fail (Watkins, 2003). An organisation undergoing a merger or which has been acquired is a complex system (Curşeu, 2006). The leaders need to be able to straddle both emerging dynamics and provide enabling conditions for stability (Jones & Corner, 2012). A coaching process needs to be adaptable to the situation the clients either find themselves in or ones the coach knows are likely to find the coaching client in the immediate future. Subtly or overtly setting up a multi-phased coaching programme that addresses a range of coaching needs is vital in ensuring the client has the best opportunity to succeed.

Seeking and receiving stakeholder feedback on a regular basis is essential for programme monitoring but also evolution. Based upon his stakeholder inputs some coaching interventions were changed and adapted for Suresh.

Finally, an integrated theoretical and pragmatic approach is vital to assist a leader navigating complex surroundings. Being able to 'pull' from a wide range of theoretical perspectives allows the coaching client to gain greater insight. But framing those insights through a pragmatic lens enabled Suresh to quickly implement actions or options and see the impact they had without delay.

References

Anderson, R., & Adams, W. (2015). *Mastering leadership: An integrated framework for breakthrough performance and extraordinary business results*. New Jersey: Wiley.

Berriman, J. (2007). Can coaching combat stress? *Occupational Health, 59*(1), 27–29.

Bertoncelj, A., & Kovac, D. (2007). An integrated approach for a higher success rate in mergers and acquisitions. *Zb. Rad. Ekon. Fak., 25*(1), 167–188.

Boyatzis, R. E. (2006). An overview of intentional change from a complexity perspective. *Journal of Management Development, 25*(7), 607–623.

Canina, L. (2009). Examining mergers and acquisitions. *Cornell Hospitality Quarterly, 50*(2), 138–141.

Clutterbuck, D. (2013). Time to focus on coaching the team. *Industrial and Commercial Training, 45*(1), 18–22.

Curşeu, P. L. (2006). Emergent states in virtual teams: A complex adaptive systems perspective. *Journal of Information Technology, 21*(4), 249–261.

Cuza, A. I. (2011). Mergers – success or failure. *CES Working Paper, 3*(1), 135–142.

Dalton, F. (2005). Using 360 degree feedback mechanisms. *Occupational Health & Safety, 74*(7), 28–30.

Drake, D. B. (2007). The art of thinking narratively: Implications for coaching psychology and practice. *Australian Psychologist, 42*(4), 283–294.

Gaster, R., & O'Sullivan, P. (2014). *Daily habits of exceptional leaders*. Retrieved 17 August 2017, from http://osullivanfield.com/resources/conference-materials/daily-habits-exceptional-leaders/.

Hicks, R., & McCracken, J. (2012). A coaching blueprint. *Physician Executive, 38*(1), 62–64.

Jones, R., & Corner, J. (2012). Seeing the forest and the trees: A complex adaptive systems lens for mentoring. *Human Relations, 65*(3), 391–411.

Kolb, A. Y., & Kolb, D. A. (2009). The learning way: Meta-cognitive aspects of experiential learning. *Simulation & Gaming, 40*(1).

O'Sullivan, P. (2015). *Foreigner in charge: Success strategies for expat leaders in Australia*. Wollombi, NWS, Australia: Exisle publishing.

O'Sullivan, P. (2016). *Foreigner in charge: Success strategies for expat leaders in Hong Kong*. Sydney, Australia: Exisle publishing.

Soudunsaari, A., & Hakanen, M. (2012). Building trust in high performing teams. *Technology Innovation Management Review*, June.

Stober, D. R. (2008). Making it stick: Coaching as a tool for organizational change. *Coaching: An International Journal of Theory, Research and Practice, 1*(1), 71–80.

Watkins, M. (2003). *The first 90 days: Critical success factors for new leaders*. Boston: Harvard Business School Publishing.

9 Technology leader in Asia

Ram Ramanathan

This case study is of a coaching journey of about six months with a senior executive leader in the Indian subsidiary of a North American technology multinational. This leader headed the company's regional research and development facility in India. The leader was a very experienced senior woman executive who had recently moved to India from North America. The leader faced a challenge for which coaching was suggested by her superiors abroad. She agreed to be coached for the first time.

A common interest in spirituality

Ram (http://coacharya.com) is a leadership coach and trainer, and spiritual wanderer, blending eastern spiritual wisdom with modern psychological and neurobiological knowledge to create mindless awareness. The company HR reached out to me as I am reasonably well known as a coach in India. The reason the client selected me was because we established a connection based on a common interest in spirituality.

The HR manager of the Indian subsidiary invited me to meet the leader at their local office, a 90-minute drive from my home office. While I was happy to talk to her over the phone or at my office, I was reluctant to travel to their office. However, the HR manager was extremely keen that I meet the leader at their office for two reasons: one, that she wanted me to coach her only at the workplace; two, that she had already met two very experienced local male coaches, both of whom she had declined. The HR manager was desperate and said I was her last option and that she did not want to fail in hiring a coach.

A week later, I met with the leader in her office, along with the HR manager who left us after a brief introduction. The HR manager explained that the leader, who was in her mid-forties, was experiencing problems dealing with a couple of her team members causing her emotional distress. When I was alone with the leader, I explained the coaching process to her as one of creating awareness in her to find her own solutions. I then asked about what she really wanted as the outcome of coaching and why it would really be important to her.

"I just want to be left alone to lead my team as the expert and deliver whatever I have promised," she started.

> This is my second job since I moved to India from a very successful career in North America. I was headhunted and picked up for this job two years ago. The first two years were magical. I built a team from scratch and we exceeded all our targets. The last few months have been truly horrible, with rebellious behaviour from two members of my team who seem to be encouraged by the HR management. I have a team of 20 and one of these two is my informal subordinate. She wants to take over from me and is creating trouble. I am not used to this politics and find it very disturbing. I have never been in such a low state in my life. I need to find my emotional balance. I need to find my self-confidence again. This will help me be a successful leader again.

We talked for about 90 minutes, mostly about her successful career thus far, her family she was devoted to, and some of her spiritual values. We found congruence in the area of Hindu philosophy and perhaps this helped build a faster connect to help her agree to work with me.

The problem

Over the next six months we met six times each for two hours, talked on the phone a few times, and emailed several times. We also had two half-day meetings with her team that co-created a new vision and developed specific action plans and commitments. There were two assessments by means of 360-feedback along with these team meetings. By the end of the journey, the leader was heading a well-knit team with her troublesome team members out of the way and three major projects assigned to her unit from HQ that more than tripled her targets and budget.

The first step in the coaching journey was an hour-long conversation with the leader and her line manager as well as the global HR business partner at their HQ. In the company structure, while the R&D Head reported directly to HQ, local HR reported to a regional unit in South East Asia. Based on complaints from two team members, the young inexperienced local HR manager, who was working alone as her experienced boss had moved out, had an audit team sent out by the regional HR group to conduct an enquiry. The leader said that this enquiry was biased against her based on feedback from the local HR manager and that the audit and interventions of the HR manager created a loss of morale with the rest of the team because of the accusing stance of the auditors against her. In a sense, the young HR manager who brought me in was now portrayed as the villain!

In our conversation with the line manager and the global HR business partner along with the leader, it was clear that they believed in the leader and wanted her to succeed as the team leader of the Indian subsidiary, as they had a lot at stake.

First team meeting

With the agreement and commitment of the leader and the HQ team, coaching started with a team meeting of all 20 members of the leader's team. The local HR manager and the site manager, who did not report to the leader, were included in the group. The leader thanked the group for the co-operation she had received from them over the past couple of years and then referred to problems she had been having recently. She addressed the group openly and directly, seeking their help in co-creating a new direction, vision and action, promising her commitment to them.

The team went through a team-building process over an intense five-hour period to come up with a future vision, specific goals for the vision and actions needed to reach the goals. All members of the team wrote down their commitment to a specific action to be implemented within the next six weeks and handed this over to the leader. An anonymous 360-feedback administered to the group during the session showed that only two out of the entire group had negative comments about the leader. Seventeen of the team rated her at the highest level in all areas of people and task orientation as well as leadership capabilities, and three were neutral.

During the discussion, many of the team members mentioned that the leader has too large a team (20) reporting to her. They suggested that at least two people should be designated as team leaders reporting to the leader allowing her to delegate (the leader had, in fact, asked her line manager for this). The team also pointed out that many good practices established by the leader initially were no longer strictly followed, as she was too busy to monitor them. In the anonymous feedback, some members of the team hinted that some team members were falsifying test findings.

The positive feedback and the successful vision to action co-creation boosted the leader's morale. The outcomes of the meeting and the 360-feedback were reported to the leader's line manager and global HR business partner. They immediately allowed her to recruit two senior level deputies, that she had already requested, to support her in managing the team. She had been in dialogue with one and he came in within three weeks and the second in about six weeks.

Professional and cultural differences

Over the next two months, the leader worked on her emotional management and prioritization of her team objectives. The first objective applied to her work-life integration, especially in regard to her teenage children. In the teamwork objective, she took the help of two members who volunteered to monitor progress in the various action plans each of the 20 members had committed to, until her new deputies joined. The two staff reported weekly progress to the leader, the local HR manager and the administrative head of the unit.

As we talked, it became clear the leader's difficulties centred around issues adjusting to the Indian work ethos, which seemed far less professional to her than the US culture she was used to. She viewed the intervention from local and regional HR management as ill-conceived political interventions that encouraged indiscipline and affected performance. Events that unfolded clearly established the incompetence and insubordination of the two members in her team who had complained about her.

What was equally important was the creation of her awareness of these cultural differences and finding ways to address them without being emotionally involved. The leader learnt to deal with people situationally, to be appreciative even in the face of difficult conversations and to be objective and disengaged while still being action oriented. She had excellent leadership qualities and the brief cultural setbacks were soon out of her way.

Second team meeting

We held the second team meeting about 10 weeks after the first. Here too, an anonymous 360-feedback was sought. The feedback was even more positive than the first. The HR manager was not available for this meeting and the two new deputies joined the meeting. Only two participants had negative comments.

In this meeting the focus was on reviewing the process that had been agreed 10 weeks earlier both individually and collectively. Other than the two members who had been critical of the leader, both of whom had performed poorly in this period against actions they had set for themselves, three others too had not performed well. However, in marked contrast to these two who found fault with the system, all others agreed with the system, the process and the support they received and committed themselves to perform better. The proceedings of the meeting were documented and circulated to those involved with their work, both in India and in the USA.

Using the feedback from the two team meetings and documented evidence of incompetence in two members of her team, the leader had these two leave the organization and restructured her team with the two new deputies. In parallel, a senior executive was recruited to head HR.

Blending teamwork into the coaching journey made a crucial, beneficial difference. At one level, it allowed every member of the team to communicate transparently as accountable and responsible members of the organization in co-developing its direction. It helped develop specific actions, that some members volunteered to monitor and report on, which significantly improved performance by setting up a new structure for quality and process control.

Group coaching sessions, when structured well, create emotional bonding within the group and help form the group into a well-oiled team. They allow co-creation through shared views. They also allow individual views to be expressed and resolved, though this aspect needs to be handled with sensitivity. The process we went through was quite similar to what is now termed as systemic coaching.

In between sessions, the leader agreed to work on areas she had committed to and she communicated with me by email and telephone calls both to confirm actions and seek clarification when needed. This allowed her to progress much faster with her desired outcome of self-confidence. In addition, the leader went through a series of Coacharya-specific self-discovery processes that helped her realize her strengths, discover a purpose in life and recreate for herself a long-term vision with near-term goals and actions leading to that vision.

From the leader's perspective, the positive feedback of the team and their proactive approach boosted her confidence in her own abilities and helped her come out of her emotional crisis. The HR manager was extremely surprised after the first team meeting and found it difficult to sustain her negative attitude towards the leader.

The leader benefited from inputs from Emotional Intelligence techniques to create self and social awareness, as well as Appreciative Inquiry principles of co-creation, Neuro-Linguistic Programming interventions of representational systems to build rapport, elements of Positive Psychology to help reframe mind maps and other Coacharya processes to help in time management, delegation and appreciating others' perspectives.

Coaching competencies as defined by credentialing institutions are quite simplistic and need to be significantly enhanced through mentoring capabilities and psychological interventions, which in turn require multi-dimensional coaching using multiple interventions. Defining outcome, creating rapport, communicating well and working towards agreed outcomes are all needed and are common-sense basics in coaching. However, the simple truth is that leaders who seek coaching do so because they are in a disempowered state of mind and desperately seek a solution. Finding a solution in such a mindset is well-nigh impossible. As Einstein said, "No problem can be solved at the same level of consciousness that created it."

The coach needs to empower the leader and create a change of state of mind to create the awareness of underlying issues that leads to leader-created solutions before the leader can start exploring problem issues positively. The wisdom of the coach is useless if the leader is not empowered.

Though the desired outcome of self-confidence was intangible, the leader established several tangible markers to measure increase in her self-confidence and emotional stability. Some of these were: interaction with her team members to monitor performance, ability to deal with them situationally and with emotional intelligence and, eventually, to move towards reconstituting the team harmoniously. The final evidence, from an organizational viewpoint, was the renewed confidence from HQ giving her a larger responsibility with resources.

Learning to reframe

As we reviewed the progress the leader had made during the coaching journey, she felt her biggest achievement to be overcoming her cross-cultural boundary conflict. Though an Indian, the leader had worked in the North American culture for a long time and found it difficult to adjust to the Indian work culture. This is an issue that many have faced several times when coaching senior Indian executives returning home after working abroad for long. Indians tend to personalize the work environment, whereas the typical North American and Anglo Saxon work environment is somewhat depersonalized. While neither is right or wrong, the flexibility to work with either culture to situational resolution requires reframing one's mind map.

It was an internal barrier that the leader needed to overcome. It was her internal view of right and wrong based on her earlier conditioning that made her uncomfortable in the situation in which her team, or at least some of them, required emotional support from the boss and which she could not bring herself to provide, initially. Once she became aware of this need and her ability to provide it, the boundary was crossed.

This cross-cultural boundary issue was further exacerbated by the organization structure, where the HR function reported to the US headquarters through a regional functional centre based in South East Asia, who sent in an audit team to investigate the leader. There was complete cross-cultural chaos.

Other insights the leader had were the renewed confidence in her own leadership skills, understanding that she had the emotional strength to be resilient in facing the odds and the need to have a work-life balance. These were fully addressed during the coaching journey. She felt the self-discovery process and the re-creation of her future were transformational for her and helped cement the work-life integration.

Coach's learning

As a coach, my own significant learning from this assignment was one of how to coach across boundaries, which I could then carry over to other cases.

In this assignment and journey, there were several boundaries for me to cross. At the very beginning, it was one of overcoming judgemental reservation about coaching at the leader's office, which I initially avoided for several practical reasons. At the next level, I was intrigued by the leader's refusal of two other coaches, one of whom I knew well and respected. I wondered if it was a gender issue and saw it as a challenge to accept and work through. As it turned out, neither of these boundaries was difficult to cross.

The boundary of limiting coaching to individuals in one-on-one sessions was always an issue that I liked to challenge. In this case the situation was ideal to blend group and individual coaching, and it worked very well.

About six months from when we started, the client leader called me after a three-week-long trip to North America to say,

> Ram, the company has expanded my unit's role to almost triple its size. Thanks to your coaching, I feel very confident now in handling multiple roles. I don't have the time to continue the coaching. I shall call you whenever I need you!

She hasn't since!

10 Are leaders born or made?

A tale of two executives

Ross Swan

I am a behavioural-based executive coach of some 13 years' experience working in the Asia Pacific region. My services are used either for developmental purposes or for remedial situations. My clients range from Fortune 500 companies to smaller SMEs. The companies used in this case study are/ have been clients for nine years where I have been working with their executives on an individual or team coaching basis.

Using Applied Behaviour Science methodologies (Braksick, 2007), I operate under the premise that nothing changes until behaviour changes. This framework helps me educate my clients as to why people say and do certain things. I focus on what can be directly observed and objectified, utilising a scientific, data-based process that analyses changes and manages behaviours. This then helps me to zero in on a leader's behaviours (Jacobs & colleagues, 2013) and the impact that they have on others.

Applied Behavioural Science truly is the catalyst that helps me develop a leader's strengths and address any barriers to their success.

Are leaders born or made?

I am often asked in my travels as an executive coach whether good leaders are born or made. Of course, we are not talking about the technical skills but the so-called 'soft skills'.

The two cases detailed here answer this question. Both situations discussed here are executives where their employers, Fortune 500 companies, were having issues with their leadership style. The executives discussed are both working in the APAC region with the diversity of employees in their area of responsibility spreading over many cultures. 'Bruce' was from the oil and gas industry while 'John' was from the mining and resources sector. Both were in operational parts of the business with their employers using a robust 360 review system combined with an employee upward feedback session in one case.

The first executive, 'Bruce', was a new employee with the company and was given a senior role working on a project worth many billions. He had always aspired to work for this new employer and wanted to make an impression. He was a touch over 40 and had strong technical abilities and good experience. The issue was, that after a few months on the job, it was evident his leadership skills did not match his technical prowess. This was when I first met Bruce. His new employer took leadership seriously and turned to me to help him.

The feedback the senior management and HR were getting about him was not good at all. People were threatening to leave if something was not done. The feedback was as follows:

- He was using his position to threaten people to get things done.
- He rarely asked people to do things, he just told them what and how to do it and usually in an abrupt manner.
- He micro-managed, showing little trust in his employees.
- He raised his voice often, and being a big man, it was intimidating.
- He focused on his objectives with little focus on other people's goals.

Given the fast pace for the project to deliver and the context of his role, it meant that Bruce didn't have much time to turn things around. Given this dynamic environment I knew we had to do things quickly.

Our first discussion was a positive one because I could see that Bruce genuinely wanted to make things work so he could forge a career within the company. He also didn't deny the behaviours that were evident. He thought that was the way you managed people and just didn't realise the overall impact of what he was doing. A big plus for a positive outcome for both of us.

In our discussion, it was revealed that Bruce's working experience was with a competitor company that had a pronounced autocratic culture and it was not doing as well in the industry as his new employer. Nothing surprising there. He had left a stressful environment with high staff turnover for a company that had a reputation of being good to work for and with relatively sound engagement levels and low staff turnover.

Unfortunately, the culture of his old employer formed Bruce's only leadership frame of reference. That is, to be successful, you need to be an autocratic manager and manage by fear and hierarchical position. He knew little else because he shared with me that his father also had that style which influenced his early years.

He was surprised at the groundswell of feedback asking for his head. Given the culture of his old company, he had never undertaken a 360 before as it was not their practice. He conceded that no one would have been game to speak up anyhow.

The second executive, 'John', was in a similar situation in his new leadership role. He was promoted from a position where he needed little staff, just one assistant, but the new role was high up on his company's leadership ladder with a lot of profile. He was in his mid-40s and had worked for the organisation for over 10 years.

Given his success over many years in his old role, John's reward was to be promoted to head up a different division within the company with some 12,000 staff at his disposal. Like Bruce, the wheels started to fall off after a couple of months. Negative feedback had filtered back to the group CEO who gave me the challenge to help him because, like Bruce's employer, they took leadership effectiveness seriously. I was given six months to work with John. The feedback on John was as follows:

- He was micro-managing.
- He was telling people what to do in an abrupt way.
- He lacked diplomacy in most of his communications.
- He dominated discussions in meetings with his opinions always right.
- He managed with a closed door and only connected with people when it suited him.

Like Bruce, John was similarly surprised with the feedback. It did take more discussion for John to see why he needed to change his ways. He thought his methods were fine as they had served him well thus far. John eventually conceded that in his new role, to make things run smoothly and be a more effective leader, he had to focus on leading people rather than managing a process.

A tale of two leaders

For Bruce, the one thing that drove our discussion in a positive way was that he wanted to be a good leader and work for a successful company. He knew he would have to change his behaviour to stay there. We identified the key behaviours he had to focus on and then mapped out a progress plan for him to start working on. In the interest of brevity, I won't go into the detail of what we decided had to done but it was going to be a challenge.

Within a couple of weeks, we started to see some progress. The one thing that gained him most traction was his humility. He openly apologised at meetings to people he had wronged and asked for their help on his new journey of leadership growth.

People saw his sincerity and responded accordingly. This openness and admission helped them to be more forgiving if he slipped up and plunged into his old ways, something Bruce did often. Slowly he improved. He started to ask people for opinions and decisions and not just tell them, thus displaying a more collaborative leadership style. He found it hard to do, but kept persevering.

He learnt how he could hold people accountable in a non-threatening way which was a major step forward for him. He also learnt that his peers should be treated as allies and not combatants when striving to meet his objectives. Bruce started to see that being more conciliatory towards others not only helped him meet his objectives but helped people achieve theirs as well.

That was 18 months ago and I am proud to say that his 360 feedback is now one to be proud of. In addition, senior management are now saying that he has a good future with the company, not only because of the results he is achieving, but because of the self-actualisation and discovery journey he had undertaken. He is demonstrating signs of true leadership.

With John, after much discussion regarding the feedback we had received, he could see he had to change his leadership style to make his new role work. One of his challenges was letting go of his old ways from his previous job and starting afresh with his new responsibilities. He understood that now his main function was getting things done and having objectives met through others.

After a few weeks there was some improvement and people close to him could see he was trying hard to be a better leader. He showed signs of collaborating with people more and it was obvious that he was working on connecting with people more often. The problem was that he kept reverting all too often into his old habits.

Unlike Bruce, where he would go two steps forward and then one step back, John was only going one step forward and then unfortunately going one back. It was, therefore, time for a frank discussion as to why his progress was stalling.

From my colleagues at Harrison Assessments International (www.harrison assessments.com.au) I have learnt that unless you like doing at least 75% of the things in your job you won't be good at it. This fact has been confirmed in my years as a coach. In John's case, I suspected this to be the root cause. He finally admitted to me that he hated managing people and dealing with their issues. He proceeded to give many reasons why this was so. To summarise, he basically hated dealing with the ambiguity inherent in managing people. He liked to be in control and enjoyed everything when it was clearly either black or white. He hated managing in the grey, that is, the grey areas that people so often created.

Born or made?

So, are leaders born or made? The answer is, simply, it is both.

Let me qualify that explanation. First, whilst some people are born with a DNA that includes the traits needed to be a good leader, they still need to have their God-given talent developed and sharpened. Honing this talent usually comes from an executive's experiences with their development being hastened with quality leadership training and even more importantly with executive coaching and mentoring. So yes, some leaders are born but they still need their skills to be sharpened to be truly great.

The second part of the question is not so simple to answer, but the answer can still be yes. Good leaders can be made but it does take a person's effort and strong desire.

When we reviewed Bruce's case, he was on a fast track towards leadership failure. He needed someone to help him take stock of himself and show him where he was heading in order for him to turn things around. Did he have good leadership traits in his DNA? The answer is obvious, yes he did, but they were just buried deep within.

He did not have the number of traits that came naturally like some of my coachees (working with them in a purely development role), but most traits were there none the less. Given the lack of these natural leadership tendencies he felt challenged and awkward when trying to use them. But what Bruce had that made it work, was a strong desire to succeed. He wanted to be a strong, effective leader and build his career around that.

He therefore pushed through the uncomfortableness he felt and stayed committed to being the leader he wanted to be. As Bruce progressed, the awkwardness slowly began to dissipate. I suspect it may never go completely but his desire to be the best leader he can be will continue to win over his old ways.

John, on the other hand, did not have that desire to push through what he felt were unnatural behaviours to him. He simply wanted to be an engineer which was his profession. Basically, he had left what he loved doing to do something he totally disliked doing: dealing with people's emotions, wants and needs on a day-to-day basis.

He did try hard to change his behaviours but just could not sustain it. The desire to do so was simply not there. The discussion we had on what he truly enjoys doing revealed the truth. The key was – and John was able to admit this to me and, more importantly, to himself – that being a leader of people is something he is just not cut out for. He took his failure in the role on the chin, something I admire in him, and so we asked for him to be moved to another position like his old role.

Sadly, there are still many executives who cannot admit to the simple fact of their unsuitability for leadership and, yet, are still in positions managing people and becoming a major reason for staff disengagement.

With John, the good news is that he contacted me several months later to thank me for bringing the issue to a head because he now is in a role that he loves and is, therefore, successful at.

So, to conclude this tale of two executives, if a manager truly wants to be a good leader and can recognise his/her own shortcomings, then most likely they can.

References

Braksick, L. W. (2007). *Unlock behavior, unleash profits* (2nd edn). New York: McGraw-Hill.

Jacobs, S. & colleagues (2013). *The behavior breakthrough*. Austin, TX: Greenleaf Book Group.

11 Auckland City amalgamation and culture development using the traditional Maori concept of Kaiarahi

Vanessa Fudge

Hakaraia, one of the teachers belonging to that tribe, stood up and said, "The reason you are detained is that we are united by relationship, however, it is the name only of being united that I know, but it will be for you all to express more fully how we are to consider ourselves united. This is all I have to say."

(Maori Dictionary Online)

I have been a coach since 2002, with 10,000+ hours of practical coaching experience. As well as often training and mentoring coaches, I have also served as a university lecturer and international speaker on coaching and mentoring. I am a founder of consulting and coaching firm LeadingWell and a partner at AltusQ.

Two colleagues, Michael Ahie and Ben Marris, whom I have trained and mentored in coaching skills and in running the mentoring programmes as part of the AltusQ coach curriculum, undertook the coaching. This is their story about how they took a coaching approach and integrated it with deep Maori tradition to allow the client to guide them, rather than them guiding the client. With their permission, I now share it with you, as I have with many other coaches, as an example of a client-led, cultural change process relating to values and implemented by volunteers from within an organization, using coaching as the enabler.

The world's most livable city

In 2010, Auckland City amalgamated one regional council and seven territorial authorities with vastly different cultures and purposes to become a single 'super city'. Auckland is home to 1.4 million residents and is the second most culturally diverse city in the world. A city where the Maori, Europe, Pacific and Asia meet.

Auckland City's vision is 'To be the world's most liveable city'. As part of this process, a single stand-alone council organization, Auckland Tourism Events and Economic Development (ATEED), was formed from a variety of separate pre-existing entities. ATEED's role is to lead the successful transformation of Auckland's economy. This includes responsibility for promoting the visitor economy, the city's events portfolio and traditional economic growth activity. ATEED operates with a big mandate but constrained resources. A unified culture was seen as a necessary lever to deliver the outcomes it was seeking to generate.

The new organization also reflected the ethnic diversity of Auckland with over 200 staff from nationalities across the globe. Because of this cultural diversity, the use of language in the group was extremely subject to individual interpretation and to the varying expectations of the many organizations that were merged to form ATEED.

ATEED CEO, Brett O'Reilly, created a brief to build a single culture, internally and organically, by drawing on the Maori concept of Kaiarahi, meaning to guide, escort, conduct, usher or mentor (Maori Dictionary Online). Unlike the standard English meaning of the term mentor (although perhaps characteristic of best practice in mentoring), the word Kaiarahi signifies a form of mentoring where the mentor does as little as possible, operating in a minimal fashion to ensure empowerment for the other(s). Until the Europeans arrived in New Zealand, the Maori largely communicated via a verbal, storytelling culture. It was through this process that O'Reilly wanted to co-create an organization with an aligned purpose and culture.

Creating meaning

Fundamental to the brief was that the organization would use its own guidance from within to create an authentic, organic and aspirational culture representing its own people, generated by its own people. With this clear vision of the outcome, the CEO engaged the coaching team at AltusQ New Zealand to design a process to enable it. This team coaching project set out to combine the essence of Kaiarahi and the storytelling culture to get the organization to create its own meaning.

This was a fundamentally different approach to imposing meaning from the top of the organization or from an external source, but rather in reflecting the Maori tradition of tribal rituals and shared meaning, to have meaning come from within the group and radiate upwards to senior management and outwards to Auckland society.

In 2013, two coaches in New Zealand (Ben Marris, from Western European descent and Michael Ahie, a Maori) began the Kaiarahi Journey. The starting point was to establish a group coaching environment that would set the scene and train internal coaches who would then act as the Kaiarahi (guides) for the organization. The internal coaching team was selected from emerging leaders who were to guide the process and who had already established the credibility to do this.

The CEO made a decision that he and the senior leadership team could only be briefed and could not determine the outcome of this cultural project.

The instructions were "This is your conversation. Go away and have it, then brief us." This high level of trust was integral to establishing the emerging leaders group as the Kaiarahi for the new culture. In a quasi-public service environment, this was no small risk to take for the CEO and the senior leadership team.

The emerging leaders who formed the Kaiarahi were all volunteers. They were sent away offsite for two days with the external coaching team who trained them on the fundamental coaching and facilitation skills required to fulfil their role and its cultural context. The training was a highly experiential process designed to be deeply meaningful for the participants. The external coaches became the Kaiarahi for the group and then the group became the Kaiarahi for the rest of the organization.

After the training, the Kaiarahi group then ran two separate conversations with groups within ATEED. These were loosely based around the appreciative enquiry process of *define, discover, dream, design, deliver* (Kessler, 2013) and AltusQ's own group coaching approach based on the four key phases of *awareness, reflection, choice and action*. Staff were invited to register to attend in groups of up to 40 people, which then broke out into smaller groups guided by up to 10 Kaiarahi in different roles.

In the first conversation, all staff were invited to envision what the city could be like as 'the world's most liveable city' and what ATEED's part in delivering this would be. The second conversation posed the question, "If we are going to deliver the most liveable city in the world, then how would we behave to get the best possible outcome for Auckland?"

These two conversations across the organization generated vast feedback from over 180 staff participants. By the end of the project over 80% of the organization took part in the conversations. The Kaiarahi were then faced with the daunting task of distilling all of this down into a set of values and behaviours for the organization.

At this point AltusQ coaches stepped back in. It was the role of the external coaches to create a safe and honest team coaching space until the Kaiarahi had distilled the captured meaning down into what resonated most strongly from the collection of conversations throughout the organization. This was a particularly challenging task for the Kaiarahi as they personally felt the pressure to deliver the best possible outcome to their colleagues. As one of the Kaiarahi said, "this has been the hardest thing I've ever done – and I've had three children!"

This phase of the cultural project culminated in February 2014 with the Kaiarahi holding a full organization gathering where they launched the values back to their colleagues. The event was held in a renovated shed on Auckland Wharf that symbolized the regeneration of Auckland; a fitting analogy for what the organization had set out to achieve.

The new values developed by the organization are summarized are follows:

Figure 11.1 ATEED values.

Great Company – *It's All About People*
- We respect and support each other and value our differences.
- We encourage each other to be the best we can be.
- We recognize and reward effort and achievement.

Great Communication – *Let's Be Clear*
- We are open and honest in what we say and do.
- We listen first and speak respectfully.
- We have straightforward conversations in a non-judgemental environment.

Great Relationships – *Connect and Collaborate*
- We seek to understand others and work together to make a difference.
- We celebrate our diversity and share our individual strengths.
- We are one team with a common goal, to grow our economy.

Great Thinking – *Bold Action, Smart Choices*
- We are courageous.
- We welcome fresh ideas, try new things and embrace change.
- We ask how we can do it differently, and do it better.

Great Results – *Get It Done and Make It Yours*
- We make things happen by taking personal ownership and responsibility.
- We believe time is precious and use it wisely.

Outcomes

Staff engagement was one measure used to determine the success of the project. In February 2013, employee engagement was 63% prior to the start of the Kaiarahi project. In February 2014, it had risen to 78%. The target for 2016 was to go to 85% (Source: IBM Kenexa employee engagement results).

When the final cultural charter was developed no one in the organization except the CEO, the leadership team and the Kaiarahi themselves knew of the external coaches' involvement. It was the objective of AltusQ to leave no fingerprints on the outcome and for the values to be fully owned by all the individuals that worked at ATEED.

At a strategic level, shifting the perspective of the organization to taking an internally integrated approach to 'new money and new jobs into Auckland' has required a multi-disciplinary approach and demanded a different mindset to approaching initiatives. This has been underpinned by the work of Kaiarahi through the conversations and culture work.

This mindset and behaviour have now become embedded in the organization with ATEED developing a reputation externally for being willing to take calculated risks and get things done. In addition, ATEED's owner, Auckland Council, is looking to ATEED to take a lead innovator role, both within council, and with key initiatives. ATEED today is seen as the 'agency of change'.

The future

Internally, a rich storytelling fabric lives on, with not just strong cultural values and behaviours aligned across the group, but a collective memory that staff were the collaborators in this project and shared the rich experiences of driving its own creative process.

The next phase of this team coaching project is currently in design. The aim is to evolve the Kaiarahi approach to give meaning to a shift to

Kotahitanga, meaning 'collective action' (Maori Dictionary Online). Kotahitanga is about going beyond working together internally with united values. It will involve leveraging collective action on initiatives that span teams from inside the organization and involve working across industry, Auckland Council and central Government with an approach of partnership and collaboration to deliver greater outcomes for Auckland.

As part of ATEED's move toward Kotahitanga the organization has chosen to hold its senior leaders' team retreats at Marae (local Maori tribe meeting houses) in Tāmaki Makaurau (Auckland). Shifting the mindset of the organization to Kotahitanga will require a refined approach that relies more on positive influence than direct control. Again, the influence of Maori culture is integral to the path forward that ATEED has chosen.

As CEO Brett O'Riley quoted in a recent conversation with ATEED leaders:

> If you were to ask us what is the most important thing in the world then I would have to answer…. *He aha te mea nui? He tangata. He tangata. He tangata* … it is people, it is people, it is people.

References

Kessler, E. H. (2013). *Encyclopedia of management theory*. Thousand Oaks, CA: Sage Publications.

Maori Dictionary Online. http://maoridictionary.co.nz. [accessed 20 January 2016].

12 Asia Pacific organizational coaching case study

Charlie Lang

PRINT3 is a leading manufacturer of 3D Printing Systems with global headquarters in the Middle East. Operating in a fast-evolving business environment, the company has been growing particularly rapidly in Asia with main offices in Hong Kong (regional headquarters), Singapore, Shanghai, Seoul and Tokyo.

PRINT3 works with both its own direct sales executives as well as distributors across the Asian region, often engaging both channels within the same country. PRINT3 maintains very close relationships with its distributors and therefore also invites the distributors' leaders and sales people to relevant development programmes PRINT3 organizes.

Progress-U has been supporting PRINT3 with individual executive coaching for various executives, Harrison Assessments and a 'Coaching for Sales Mentors' programme, the latter of which will be the focus of this case study.

The programme was based on Progress-U's framework developed in its first iteration in 2004 and continuously further developed since then:

This framework recognizes that the effective use of coaching in mentoring requires:

- a coaching mindset;
- key coaching competencies;
- a comprehensive and systematic process for each session, the A.S.S.A.P.P.P. model (the A.S.S.A.P.P.P model was developed by Progress-U in 2012 based on the GROW model by John Whitmore).

Challenges for the company

PRINT3 approached Progress-U because the management felt that their talent pipeline especially in the sales area was not commensurate with the rapid growth in the region. In fact, the slow development of new sales leaders among the teams of sales people both at PRINT3 and its distributors became increasingly a hindrance to further rapid growth.

Also, succession was a major challenge. PRINT3 often faced the situation that sales leaders both at PRINT3 as well as at their distributors' organizations

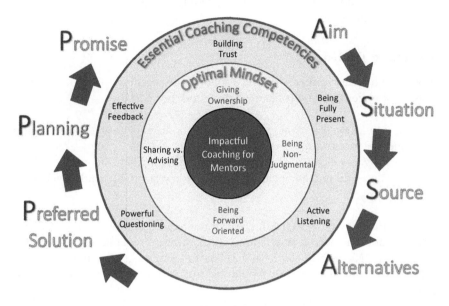

Figure 12.1 Coaching framework for leaders/mentors.

could not be replaced internally due to a too big gap between their sales people's current maturity level and the needs for these roles.

As well, the sales leaders had a tendency to micromanage their sales people because they felt they could not trust them to handle any significant deal by themselves. One of the reasons for this lack of trust was rooted in the fact that most of these sales leaders were frontline sales people themselves not too long ago – most of them had been promoted into the sales leader role within the past three years. As a result, the sales leaders themselves increasingly became a bottleneck hindering faster growth.

Progress-U together with PRINT3 analysed these challenges through a series of activities:

- a brief online survey among sales leaders and sales executives;
- interviews with a selection of 4–5 sales leaders in each of the five main locations;
- interview with the regional head of sales in Asia (who shadowed both sales leaders and sales executives during an extensive three-month tour across Asia).

Both parties concluded that the sales leaders would greatly benefit from a mindset change when dealing with their direct reports. The responsible PRINT3 executives realized that the challenges described above could be substantially reduced if the sales leaders would integrate coaching into their leadership repertoire.

Coaching for leaders

About two years earlier, PRINT3 piloted a coaching programme with another supplier that unfortunately didn't work out because

- the workshop was not practical enough, cases appeared remote, too much lecture and theory;
- the program did not include any embedding activities to ensure a high and successful implementation rate of action plans (Goldsmith & Morgan, 2004).

Because the previous programme was considered a failure, PRINT3 didn't want to label the agreed programme as 'Coaching Programme' but asked us to name it 'Mentoring for Sales Leaders Programme'. Nonetheless, it was agreed that this programme would have a strong focus on coaching as described below.

Expectations from this programme included:

- improvements in talent development and thus better succession through giving more ownership to sales people, leading to increased maturity and therefore reducing the talent gap between sales people and sales leaders;
- improvements in sales due to better mentoring/coaching of sales people, ultimately leading to higher sales and better margin;
- improvements in retention of the best talents – they tend to be most keen and open to being coached.

We learned during the initial investigation that one of the major issues were joint client meetings carried out by sales leaders together with their sales people. Whenever the sales leaders would meet customers together with their sales people, they would essentially take over and lead the conversation with the customer. As a result, the sales people – who were actually responsible for this account – mostly kept quiet during these meetings.

We found that this practice was deeply engrained and that any change would require a substantial mindset shift. Also, we were aware that the traditional business culture in Asia, especially in countries with a stronger Confucian cultural imprint (such as South Korea and Japan and to a lesser extent Greater China) would make the needed mindset shift even more difficult (Levi, 2013).

Thus, we realized that we would need to design the programme with a strong focus on experience and reflection so that participants would more likely buy into this paradigm shift from 'super salesperson' to 'effective sales leader and mentor'.

The programme contents were derived from Progress-U's 'Coaching for Leaders' programme that had been launched initially in 2004 and has since been continuously refined based on experience conducting this programme hundreds of times across the region as well as integrating the latest research in corporate coaching.

Tailoring of the programme towards this particular client was done in a number of ways:

- integration of Harrison Assessments Paradox Report (www.harriso-nassessments.com/paradox-technology.html) to fast-track self-awareness in related behavioural tendencies;
- restructuring the sequence of the different programme elements during the two-day workshop to create a meaningful flow for PRINT3;
- designing 'real-play' case studies that were as close as possible to what participants would typically experience in their daily work-life;
- establishing effective embedding of learning through group coaching with all participants and 1:1 executive coaching with selected sales leaders who struggled more with the adoption of the new 'Mentoring for Sales Leaders' approach.

The programme was piloted in Hong Kong with 12 sales leaders and then rolled out to groups of various sizes (10–18 participants per group) in Seoul, Tokyo, Shanghai and Singapore respectively. In Seoul and Tokyo, the workshop was conducted bilingually with English/Korean and English/Japanese interpreters. In Shanghai, the workshops were conducted in Mandarin Chinese, in the other locations in English only. A total of about 60 of PRINT3's sales leaders underwent this programme, piloted in mid-2015 and being completed with the last batch in the first quarter of 2016.

What the participants learnt

Already from the preparation questionnaire we gathered that a number of participants in each group were rather sceptical about this programme. We found that this scepticism was mostly rooted in the fear of giving ownership. They felt that they would lose power and recognition as a leader if they were not responsible for determining what is the right thing to do. Likewise, there was also the fear that some of the subordinates would not feel comfortable taking ownership.

These challenges were addressed by letting the participants reflect on their role as sales mentors and by having them discover the benefits and downsides of giving ownership. Once that was established by the participants, we helped them see how the impact of these potential downsides could be minimized.

The group coaching follow-up for the pilot intake was challenging as the 'show-up' rate was only 60–80% while we were aiming at 90–100%. Analysing the reasons why this happened, we found that a number of participants simply got side-tracked by their daily activities and essentially either forgot about the follow-up session or made other tasks/responsibilities a higher priority.

As a consequence, we highlighted right at the beginning but also a number of times during the workshops that the programme is not 'over' after the two-day workshop but that the most crucial part actually starts when they are back at work. We also kept highlighting how important the follow-up was in order to support them in the implementation of their action plans.

The 1:1 coaching sessions for selected participants proved to be particularly successful. They allowed them to deep-dive into the learning and address underlying patterns that might hinder these participants in becoming an optimal sales mentor.

What the coaches learnt

Conducting the workshop bi-lingually worked particularly well in Japan (due to a very strong and energetic interpreter) and a bit less well in Korea. It turned out that saying the same thing in the Korean language that our facilitator explained in English took significantly longer than in English which made the session a bit lengthy. If we were to re-run this programme in Korea, we would insist on getting the full programme delivered by a Korean native sales leadership coach.

Helping participants gain clarity in which situations it would be most beneficial to use the coaching approach and in which situations other approaches would tend to work better was another crucial success element for this programme. During the practice session at the workshop, we noticed that participants would quite naturally regress into other approaches that they were more familiar and comfortable with (e.g. giving advice). We found it to be more effective to interrupt during the real-play practice and ask them to rephrase what they just said. While this approach makes the flow less natural, we found that it enhanced awareness and essentially gave them the chance to immediately try out the coaching approach.

References

Goldsmith, M., & Morgan, H. (2004). Leadership is a contact sport: The follow-up factor in management development. *Strategy+business*, Fall, Issue 36.

Levi, N. (2013). The impact of Confucianism in South Korea and Japan. *Acta Asiatica Varsoviensia, 26,* 185–195.

13 Strength-based leadership and team coaching in Asia Pacific

Doug MacKie

CSA Consulting is a Business Psychology Consultancy that specialises in executive talent identification and development within organisations. Our practice is grounded in the field of Leadership Theory and Positive Organisational Psychology which emphasises that the identification and enhancement of individual strengths in relation to role seniority and challenges is a necessary precursor to effective organisational development.

Our strength lies in our ability to apply psychology in an insightful and commercially relevant manner.

Working with the operations leadership team

CSA Consulting was engaged by the Chief Operating Officer (COO) of one of the business units of a multinational resource company to undertake some individual and team development with the Operations Leadership Team (OLT). To add to the complexity, the team was based in a remote part of SE Asia and comprised expatriate Australians who were managing a largely indigenous workforce. The team, although relatively new, was acknowledged to be performing well against task delivery. However, there were some concerns about the sustainability of how the task delivery was being achieved and a perceived need for feedback from the key stakeholders on its performance to date.

This case involved a strength-based approach to both leadership and team development. All the participants were expatriates working overseas so the workshop and coaching were conducted in-country. The team had to deal with a high degree of complexity in that their project was a joint venture with the local government, the majority of the employees were non-English-speaking nationals, the remote location provided multiple infrastructure challenges and their key customers were also Asian nationals. In contrast, the OLT itself consisted entirely of Australian males which presented a challenge in terms of the lack of representative diversity. Consequently, although the programme was conducted in SE Asia, the culture of the team was typically Australian with a direct, hardworking and, at times, confronting style. Given this context, it was thought that a strength-based approach would be particularly helpful for a group that tended to focus on their deficits, comment critically on each other and showed a limited awareness of their own strengths.

The fact that they were an intact team in a complex environment and facing significant challenges required a bespoke solution. The team leader had had a successful individual coaching experience and was a keen sponsor. The project was moving from the start-up to the maintenance phase and this required a different, more sustainable type of leadership. A combination of both individual and team leadership development was designed to help the participants make the transition from individual leader development to applying that knowledge to the team level. The consistency of the strength-based approach gave them all a positive common language with which to discuss their individual development and how that applied to the development of the OLT as a team.

Individual and organisational readiness

During the initial individual interviews prior to the team coaching programme, an informal measure of individual readiness to change was derived from data collected around key questions (Franklin, 2005). This included assessing the capacity to experience some discomfort in the pursuit of enhancing leadership effectiveness, understanding the individual's implicit leadership theories and assessing their openness to developmental feedback. Together with some exploration of the individual's self-awareness of both their strengths and development areas, this narrative provided key data on some of the core constructs of developmental readiness (Avolio & Hannah, 2008; Franklin, 2005). Team members were thus primed in both the motivational and ability factors of developmental and change readiness that are necessary precursors of effective leadership development (MacKie, 2015).

The main team diagnostic used in this coaching process was the *Multifactor Leadership Questionnaire Team*. The MLQ Team (Bass & Avolio, 1997) is a 49-item questionnaire that measures nine elements of the full range leadership model (FRLM), namely idealized influence attributes (e.g. Display a sense of power and confidence), idealized influence behaviour (e.g. Talk about my most important values and beliefs), inspirational motivation (e.g. Articulate a compelling vision of the future), intellectual stimulation (e.g. Seek different perspectives when solving problems), individualized consideration (e.g. Help others to develop their strengths), contingent reward (e.g. Provide others with assistance in exchange for their efforts), management by exception active (e.g. Keep track of all mistakes), management by exception passive (e.g. Fail to interfere until things become serious) and laissez-faire (e.g. Avoid making decisions). The inventory also has three measures of leadership outcomes: extra effort (e.g. Heighten others' desire to succeed); effectiveness (e.g. Lead a group that is effective); and satisfaction (e.g. Work with others in a satisfactory way). It measures all items on a five-point Likert scale from '*not at all*' to '*frequently if not always*'. The survey also includes a research-validated benchmark which gives an ideal score for the various leadership ratings. The MLQ360 was also used for each individual participant to give them some specific feedback on their transformational leadership capabilities prior to completing the team version of the same scale.

Diagnostic results

The OLT scored an average of 2.5/4 for its transformational leadership as rated by all stakeholder groups. The benchmark for high performance is 3+. Given the relative youth of this team and the challenging operational context, this is a very encouraging score and represents a very solid foundation from which to develop. Amongst the five elements of transformational leadership, the OLT scored highest on Inspirational Motivation and lowest on Individualised Consideration (coaching and developing others) as rated by all others.

The OLT's scores for transactional and passive avoidant leadership were all within benchmark indicating those leadership behaviours are being performed at the right frequency. Amongst the different stakeholder groups, there was a consistent trend for the OT Executive to mark the OLT lower on ratings of transformational leadership. The OLT showed good alignment with its direct reports and advisor groups.

In terms of leadership outcomes, the OLT was rated as effective *sometimes* whilst its satisfaction rating was higher at *fairly often*. The OLT's strengths on individual items were largely related to inspiring others and setting high standards. The OLT's development areas on individual items were largely around spending time developing others, leveraging their strengths and constructively challenging each other around their problem-solving strategy.

The coaching process

The team coaching process constructed involved three discrete stages. First, individual team members were contacted prior to the team workshop to understand their context, assess their readiness for change and discuss their perceptions of how the team was functioning. Second, each team member received an individual debrief on their individual multi-rater leadership questionnaire (MLQ360) to help raise awareness of their individual strengths and development areas. These strengths were then utilised in the team coaching process with a particular emphasis on aligning strengths to roles. Finally, all participants attended the two-day team development and coaching workshop. The workshop took a strength-based approach to leader and team development (MacKie, 2016), provided input on high performing teams, assessed the team process and provided opportunities to generate insights and actions from the team diagnostic. This included a review of the necessary structures for high performing teams (Hackman & Wageman, 2005) and stage models that articulate the necessary processes for the formation of a high performing team (Hawkins, 2014). The output was a team development plan.

The workshop also utilised a team diagnostic (the MLQ Team) to gather data related to its leadership and performance from a wide range of stakeholders (Avolio, 2012). It is a major achievement of this process that so many stakeholder groups were included in the survey. The five groups were OLT, Executive and other senior leaders, Business Group Leaders, Direct reports of OLT and Business Advisors and consultants. This added significantly to the validity of the results.

Team strengths

OLT's key strength in relation to its role is its effectiveness in responding to a crisis. The team responds well to a clear and urgent issue and mobilises its significant resources to address this in a timely and efficient manner. It devotes significant and sustained amounts of energy in addressing these emergent issues. The OLT displays a strong values orientation in terms of facilitating the development of the national workforce in Mongolia. However, this strength was underutilised due to the time taken in crisis management.

The OLT also displayed a high task orientation and outcome focus. The members were seen to be collectively committed to delivering results no matter what challenges they encounter or what effort was required. In addition, the OLT displayed a highly directive style of leadership. Others were in no doubt of the short-term goals to be achieved and the urgency with which delivery was expected. The team members set high standards for performance. They both communicated these expectations with clarity and directness and modelled them internally in the OLT. Finally, they displayed a strong commercial mindset, monitoring a variety of metrics to ensure key milestones were met and business objectives achieved.

Team development issues

The OLT needed to prioritise and focus its efforts. Whilst it excelled at firefighting and performance under pressure, this came at a personal cost and the pace was agreed to be unsustainable in the longer term. Clarity within the team around the key objectives in the medium term promoted greater alignment within the team and partially addressed the existing issues around work-life imbalance. The team needed to focus more on the development of its members and direct reports. Initially the hectic pace and emergent challenges of the business provided little time for structured and focused development for its direct reports. This resulted in both excessive demands on OLT members and frustration at the direct report level in terms of a lack of development opportunities. The team was coached around how to make the development of direct reports a key priority and this norm was included in the team charter.

In addition, the OLT needed to manage its relationship with key stakeholders, especially the executive committee, more effectively. There was a perception that at times the OLT was not fully aligned with the executive committee and this gap needed to be closed. They also needed to ensure that there was sufficient diversity and challenge in its decision-making process. The current hectic pace and drive for results could at times mitigate against inclusive and robust decision-making and the team needed to ensure that contrary opinions were heard and respected in this process. Finally, the OLT's internal communication style was direct, confronting and at times vociferous. It needed to ensure it balances this advocacy with an equal focus on enquiry and ensure it created a climate where peers felt supported and empowered to engage, disclose and contribute.

The OLT prioritised its goals against three key criteria. First, where did the members personally want to make a change within the team? Second, what goals would have the greatest impact on the business? And third, what goals were achievable in a 6–12 month time frame? The OLT decided that given these criteria, it needed to address how it prioritised tasks, how, especially, it communicated this upwards and how it could internalise some of the gains made in the workshop through the development of a team charter. A critical aspect of the goal identification process was also the identification of strengths to leverage in the pursuit of these goals. A team development plan was constructed and success criteria and actions generated against each of the three development areas. The team elected a sponsor for each of the themes and built a plan review process into its team meeting structure.

Skill transfer and maintenance are recognised issues after any leadership development intervention (Baldwin & Ford, 1988). Given the significant logistical challenges of remaining engaged with such a remote team, considerable focus was given over to how to maintain and develop the insights and actions achieved during the programme. Building on the goals outlined above, the team decided to make team development a regular part of its weekly meeting so that development goals were reviewed and actions supported. It also focused on integrating the insights and actions from the programme with existing HR processes to assist the maintenance of these skills. The full report and development plan were sent by the OLT to all stakeholders which allowed them to be supported and held accountable by a much broader external group. The team was followed up periodically to coach the members around maintaining the gains and dealing with any obstacles to implementation.

Challenges observed and lessons learnt

This case study demonstrated the significant utility of transitioning from leader to team coaching. I had previously worked with the COO on an individual basis. Whilst there were many benefits to being familiar with the team leader, the challenge was how to manage that prior relationship with his team and not collude with the leader in the team coaching process. This topic was addressed in the individual coaching session prior to the team event and this allowed the formulation of a plan for the team leader to respond positively to some of the individual feedback he had received. It also integrated the concept of developmental readiness into the coaching process so that all participants were primed to tolerate some discomfort and challenge in pursuit of the team goals.

The case study also confirms the validity of a strength-based approach within an expatriate Asian context. This was particularly challenging for the Australian expatriates, ever wary of the tall poppy syndrome, but participants were convinced by the organisational benefit and were able to overcome their individual discomfort in pursuit of the broader goal. Finally, the utilisation of multi-rater psychometrics (MLQ Team) to diagnose both the strengths and development areas of the team confirmed the utility of other raters in both identifying and developing high performance teams.

References

Avolio, B. J. (Ed.). (2012). *Full range leadership development* (2nd edn). Thousand Oaks, CA: Sage.

Avolio, B. J., & Hannah, S. T. (2008). Developmental readiness: Accelerating leader development. *Consulting Psychology Journal: Practice and Research, 60*, 331–347.

Baldwin, T. T., & Ford, J. K. (1988). Transfer of training: A review and directions for future research. *Personnel Psychology, 41*(1), 63–105.

Bass, B. M., & Avolio, B. J. (1997). *Full range leadership development: Manual for the multifactor leadership questionnaire*. Palo Alto, CA: Mind Garden Inc.

Franklin, J. (2005). Change readiness in coaching: Potentiating client change. In M. J. Cavanagh, A. Grant & T. Kemp (Eds), *Evidence-based coaching* (pp. 193–200). Brisbane: Australian Academic Press.

Hackman, J. R., & Wageman, R. (2005). A theory of team coaching. *Academy of Management Review, 30*(2), 269–287.

Hawkins, P. (Ed.). (2014). *Leadership team coaching: Developing collective transformational leadership*. London: Kogan Page.

MacKie, D. (2015). The effects of coachee readiness and core self-evaluations on leadership coaching outcomes: A controlled trial. *Coaching: An International Journal of Theory, Research and Practice, 8*, 120–136.

MacKie, D. (2016). *Strength-based leadership coaching in organisations*. London: Kogan Page.

14 Empowering women leaders in STEM (Science, Technology, Engineering and Mathematics)

David Pierce, Kasia Gurgul, Sue Hubbard and Anna Blackman

Gender diversity and equality

Achieving gender diversity and equality is currently an important goal for many STEM organisations in Australia. The 2011–2012 Annual Report of the organisation in this case study showed that of the 199 staff, 69 are women, representing around 35% of the workforce. The roles primarily filled by women are:

- research scientists (18);
- research support staff (20);
- technical and corporate (31).

At the time, there were no women in the Executive Team and they were arguably under-represented at the executive and higher management levels of the organisation.

On 23 June 2010, the Australian Sex Discrimination Commissioner announced a Gender Equality Blueprint. The Blueprint describes the approaches to implementing the recommendations of the 2008 report *Gender Equality: What Matters to Australian Women and Men* (Cerise & Black and White Media Australia, 2008). The recommendations are:

- balancing paid work and family and caring responsibilities;
- ensuring women's lifetime economic security;
- promoting women in leadership;
- preventing violence against women and sexual harassment;
- strengthening national gender equality laws, agencies and monitoring.

The organisation identified that women are under-represented in leadership positions and needed specific consideration when planning their careers. Both these aspects are important for the organisation to support and retain women and to be an employer of choice for women. This is consistent with the Australian Human Rights Commission report findings. The organisation's leadership had decided to address this inequality. A step in that process was the subject of this proposal, which offered an opportunity for women to define their aspirations, explore their workplace options, identify their goals and define the actions required to meet those goals. Equality is about choice, choice is the essence of empowerment. Therefore, women were encouraged to decide what they wanted from their work at the organisation and then were supported by the organisation to attain these goals.

The organisation gave the participants a completely open coaching agenda for the coaching sessions despite the organisational aim being to develop women for C-Suite positions. Programme participants set their own goals for coaching in their first session with their coach. During the sessions, both work-related and personal barriers, and challenges that were preventing the participants from being fulfilled and empowered in their roles were addressed. Personal challenges such as communication, setting boundaries with self and others, and work/life balance were impacting the participants' state of mind and, therefore, the focus and confidence of participants. Removing these barriers to empowerment and success allowed the participants to remove distractions and be more confident and empowered both at work and at home.

The participants were asked to complete a pre-coaching and post-coaching survey about the coaching programme, to document their expectations and the impact of coaching, providing evidence of a progression from expectations to reality. The following factors were surveyed:

- expected achievements vs actual achievements;
- the best way to achieve the most important achievement;
- support of people around participants going through the coaching process;
- expected barriers vs actual barriers in the coaching process;
- important rating of the features of coaching and effectiveness;
- confidence levels about change and decisions;
- changes in behaviour in response to coaching;
- changes in beliefs in response to coaching;
- the most important feature of coaching;
- important characteristics that contribute to the effectiveness of a coach;
- factors that contribute to the participant's relationship with their coach.

Some of the results surprised the participants as the post-coaching survey results were, at times, different to pre-coaching expectations. Much of this can be credited to the raising of awareness of self and others through the coaching process.

Building the programme on an organising principle, in this case the Herrmann Brain Dominance Instrument, provided a common language and metaphor for the coaching. It also provided a framework around which the coach could communicate with the participant in their preferred English expression.

Programme format

The coaching programme consisted of three workshops with two to three coaching sessions between workshops 1 & 2 and 2 & 3. Participants were allocated six coaching sessions each. The workshops were conducted on-site and, as the organisation included participants in other locations, via video conferencing. The coaching was primarily face-to-face with the exception of five participants coached remotely. Phone coaching was used for these sessions.

The first workshop focused on awareness through the Herrmann Whole Brain Model (Herrmann, 1996) followed by an introduction to neuroscience and how habits and limiting beliefs could be changed if we understand brain plasticity. We also introduced the idea of coaching and the structure of the programme. This provided an opportunity for the participants to network with each other and the coaches.

The final workshop was a wrap-up of the programme and included lessons learned. The initial findings of the research were also tabled. Pre- and post-surveys were conducted prior to workshop 1 and before workshop 3.

Benefits

The programme describes a journey from goals developed to meet certain expectations and then these goals being adjusted to meet the changes the participants encountered along the way. The majority of participants found the process profound and something they would not have experienced without coaching. Most had been trained but never experienced the learning and capability development, self-actualisation, empowerment and possibilities of action that coaching provides.

The organisation benefited from the programme as disengaged women, who saw few opportunities and were cynical about the organisation's motivations, recognised the possibility of partnership and, consequently, changed their attitude and behaviour. Participants improved their leadership, communication and influencing skills, took responsibility for achieving their desired outcomes, all of which they reported improved their sense of worth at home and at work.

Main outcomes

The programme met a common goal, an empowered and engaged coaching cohort. This desire was both that of management and the women employees and contractors. Coaching empowered and unified, yet the pathway to achieving these outcomes for each woman was different. For the majority of participants, the coaching programme had a greater impact than they expected. In addition to personal, professional and career goals and development, the women also explored and made changes relating to achievement tools and work/life balance. Figure 14.1 demonstrates the hierarchy of achievement themes pre- and post-coaching.

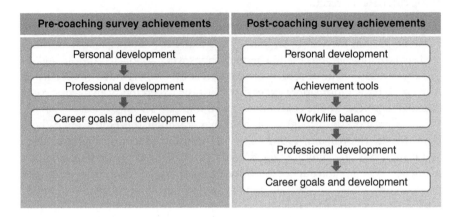

Figure 14.1 Hierarchy of achievement themes.

Personal development. The participants felt that personal development was the most important achievement gained from the coaching programme. Personal development was categorised into self-awareness, perspective and confidence. In the women's words, post-coaching achievements in personal development included "empowerment", "learning more about myself", "gaining perspective", "inspiration to deal with change", "personal satisfaction with work", "it's alright to take a risk".

Achievement tools. 'Achievement tools' were defined as leadership tools and skills that women can use to achieve their goals; tools such as communication, negotiation, defining values and priorities, strategic review and planning, seeking alternative strategies and identifying information sources. These tools had not been identified pre-coaching; therefore, leadership capability development was not an outcome the participants had expected for themselves.

Work/life balance. This was identified as an achievement, yet was not an achievement expected from coaching by participants. Post-coaching, the women indicated that "better strategies for work/life balance", "making time for family and friends", "making time when time doesn't seem to be available" and "what makes me happy at work and at home" were important achievements in this category.

Professional development. Participants noted that the most important professional development achievements post-coaching were "improved networks", "better networking skills" and "workforce planning". Survey results showed that the most important post-coaching achievements in the Career Goals & Direction category were "gaining clarity between work and personal goals" and "analysing and setting career goals".

Decision-making and managing change. The coaching impact on decision-making was mixed with some participants feeling more confident about making decisions after the coaching programme and some less confident.

Survey results also showed that overall participants were less confident in making change after the coaching programme finished. The length of the programme could be an important consideration in this.

Barriers that may affect successful outcomes from coaching. The women were surveyed on potential and actual barriers that may affect successful outcomes from coaching. Preoccupation with other work matters and lack of time were identified as the highest barriers to both pre- and post-coaching (41–45%). Preoccupation with other personal matters was 14.3% before coaching and 12.6% after coaching, and family commitments dropped from 6.7% to 0%.

Most important characteristics in a coach. Pre-coaching and post-coaching showed a shift between expectations and experience. From a coaching perspective, the expectation that the coach was experienced and knowledgeable became less relevant as the coaching programme progressed. As the participants experienced coaching, they became more aware that the coach's role was to guide them through a development process, assisting them to discover their own solutions and be neutral regarding the content of the session. Nevertheless these two aspects were important at the start of the programme when the participants were asked to select a coach. Discipline experience and knowledge provided the participant with the sense of comfort that the coach would appreciate their circumstances better.

The top five pre- and post-coaching characteristics are shown in Figure 14.2 below. Coaches would be encouraged by the post-coaching characteristics as they represent core meta skills. The ability to become non-judgemental, open-minded and an active listener were identified as important characteristics post-coaching.

Factors that contributed to the participant's relationship with their coach:

- *Age:* A similar age match was found to be more important post-coaching (42%), compared to pre-coaching (18%).

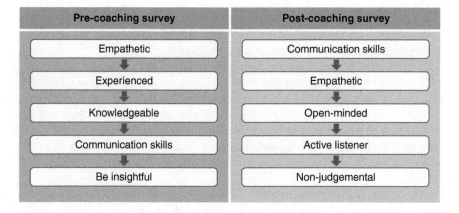

Figure 14.2 Most important coach characteristics.

- *Gender:* Gender match was considered to be more important post-coaching (47.1%), versus pre-coaching (27.3%).
- *Personality:* A personality match between coach and participants became less important post-coaching, compared to pre-coaching. Before coaching, personality was considered important by 91% of participants, after coaching 33% said it was unimportant, and 42% said it was neither important or unimportant.
- *Values:* Values were deemed to be about equally important pre- and post-coaching.

The lessons learnt

The organisational intention of enabling women to prepare for advancement to the C-suite shifted throughout the assignment. For many women in this programme, their sense of engagement was not defined by advancement, but by the ability to choose their own career path and professional development. Some of the women did not aspire to advance through to the C-suite. The stage of life was the biggest motivator with many happy to trade promotion and remuneration for a better balance in their lives between self, work and family.

Giving women an open coaching agenda to focus on the most pressing needs for them supported them to develop the skills they needed at that time to have more influence and confidence in their work and life situations. Resolving personal and work-related challenges supported women to bring more skills, energy and focus to their work. Giving participants the option to discuss personal matters in coaching sessions, such as relationship and communication challenges outside of the workplace, allowed them to remove or reduce these personal barriers to successful outcomes from coaching.

Coaching around an organising principle was effective for the group and the individuals. The programme used the Whole Brain Model (Herrmann, 1996) as a foundation for self-awareness. Our sense of control influences our mindset, and our mindset influences our behaviour and attitudes to work. This helped with understanding what motivated the women in their work, giving them a better sense of control and influence.

Insights arrive unexpectedly during the coaching process and occur not only during the coaching sessions but also during moments of personal reflection between sessions. One moment was an epiphany during a group check-in session where the group of participants in the programme watched one of the women work her way to insight during discussion. With the support and encouragement of her fellow participants she broke through a barrier and was able to reconcile an internal conflict that made an aspect of her work less stressful.

The ability for the coach to be non-judgemental, open-minded and an active listener were considered to be important coach characteristics post-coaching but not pre-coaching. This is an important factor for consideration for coaching engagements between internal coaches and employees, as it is likely to affect coaching outcomes if the coach does not have this coaching mindset and skillset. Post-coaching, an age and gender match between coach and participant were more important factors than personality or values. Thus, it may be of benefit to match coaches based on gender and age.

Coaching via technology for five participants was effective and made coaching more accessible for some participants. The participants preferred the privacy that audio-only coaching via phone offered them when dealing with challenging emotions, allowing them to freely discuss matters that they considered difficult and confidential, especially with regards to challenging relationships at home and in the workplace. Several participants preferred to do their coaching sessions on a day off or a day when they were working from home to be able to better focus on the coaching session.

The length of the coaching programme is an important consideration, demonstrating the case for ongoing or future on-demand coaching support, as each decision and change is a new and unique situation.

References

Cerise, S., & Black and White Media Australia. (2008). Gender equality: What matters to Australian women and men. In C. Goldie & K. O'Connell (Eds), *The listening tour community report* (pp. 1–24). Sydney: Human Rights and Equal Opportunity Commission.

Herrmann, N. (1996). *The whole brain business book*. New York: McGraw-Hill.

15 Leadership coaching

An Australian context

Julia Milner and Mike Armour

Building leadership

People leaders in this organisation are technical experts in their field whether it is Medical, Legal, Claims, Actuarial or other disciplines and increasingly represent diverse backgrounds in terms of age, gender and ethnicity. Despite their expertise, most have had little in-depth or formal training in areas of leadership and interpersonal skills, which are core to the role of today's people leader.

Combining coaching and mentoring along with 360° feedback[1] on leadership interpersonal behaviour has provided a structured, evidence-based approach to leadership development, which is beginning to pay rich dividends in changing the conversations that people leaders are having with their employees and shifting the leadership culture from the role of technical manager to the professional leader.

The combined approach, which is part of a long-term process, is what has been driving lasting change. While the coaching approach used in the leadership development programme has been well received by participants, there is a growing awareness of issues of diversity and the need to incorporate what Rosinski (2003) describes as alternative ways to communicate and understand values. Passmore (2013) also refers to Rosinski (2003), commenting that "by integrating the cultural dimension, coaching will unleash more human potential to achieve meaningful objectives" (Rosinski, 2003, p. 7 cited in Passmore, 2013, p. 2).

Coaching is a core leadership skill for people managers and team leaders. Training is only one part of the learning process; it is important to transfer theory into practice, providing managers with ample room for application, feedback and exchange with peers. The training sessions were over several stages, giving the manager room to implement their learning into the workplace.

Over the past few years, individuals have gained significant value through individual coaching assignments focused on career goals or improving the way they interact with and manage their team. The use of coaching as part of the leadership development programme has been deliberately designed to help embed these changes and reinforce the right behaviours and culture. Coaching has also been a key element in developing our leaders and, within the leadership essentials programme, two separate training sessions have been provided to increase the effectiveness of managerial coaching. What is very clear is that ongoing, constructive feedback and coaching has been essential to bringing about change. Many leaders within the organisation have commented that only through feedback have they grown and had the courage to try new things. We have intentionally created a framework where coaching, mentoring and feedback are the bedrock of building leadership capability and continue to use this in a variety of ways to support individuals and groups.

Leadership and coaching programme

Over the past three to four years, the organisation has placed an increased emphasis on leadership development with a specific focus on coaching and mentoring skills to support the regular task-based management activities. Coaching has been a key element of the emerging leaders programme, and two separate training sessions were provided to all people leaders to increase the focus on managerial coaching as a mechanism to help individuals focus on specific goals. The coaching programme as a whole has been an integral part of the capability development programme, and a long-term investment in moving away from more traditional managerial styles to a more flexible and responsive leadership approach.

One of the best outcomes of the leadership and coaching programme is that we have been able to bring in other experiences such as providing leaders with time to reflect using ideas from adult learning principles. *Time to Think* (Kline, 1999) and *Appreciative Inquiry* (Cooperrider & Whitney, 2000) have also been used to address issues of engagement and communication between various groups and teams. For the participants, the key outcomes have been learning new coaching models and being able to use these skills in their daily interactions with their team members, colleagues and higher managers. The organisational impact is difficult to measure at this stage. However, during the follow-up coaching sessions many of the managers comment that the one-to-one discussions with their people are more focused and that this has led to an improvement in overall performance. Time will tell if this can be sustained.

Participants came with a different skill level and understanding of coaching and represent an increasingly diverse background in terms of age, gender and ethnicity. It was important to create a base line and common definition of coaching first, as well as incorporating the experience from leaders in the room. With previous experience of coaching leaders from a diverse range of backgrounds, there was a recognition that one approach would not work in every situation and that the greatest asset a coach can employ is the ability to ask the right questions and listen for what was important for each individual. Allowing enough, but not too much, time between face-to-face workshops was important to optimise learning and application.

On reflection, if any changes were to be made to this approach, they would include an increased emphasis on follow-up and peer coaching to expand the impact and effectiveness of each process.

Embedding a coaching and mentoring culture

Developing capability and a future leadership pipeline have been core elements of our coaching and leadership development programme, with a primary goal to embed a coaching and mentoring culture. While the organisation provides specialist Indemnity Insurance and ancillary products and services, the key challenges it faces are similar to many other organisations – a continuously changing business landscape, competition on price and product differentiation, increased expectations from our customers, having the right people with the right skills and capabilities, and balancing commercial disciplines with excellence in customer service.

The organisation is somewhat traditional in its outlook but recognises that it needs to keep changing to meet the demands of an increasingly competitive business environment. In terms of the culture and diversity of the organisation, the majority are women; in terms of executive managers the ratio is 60:40 men to women while in the senior management level the ratio is 28:20 men to women. Overall, however, taking total people leader numbers of just over 100, the ratio is well balanced at 52:50 for men and women respectively.

Backgrounds are also varied, with the majority from a European background. However, an increasing number of leaders (9%[2]) come from the Asia Pacific region, in particular the Philippines, Thailand and China, and there is a growing shift that senior managers and people leaders are often younger than many of their team members.

Reshaping the culture

Lasting change takes time, with the leadership development programme and coaching training working in tandem to reshape leadership culture from strongly technical expertise, to deep skills as people leaders. What the organisation has done through coaching and mentoring has in no small measure enabled it to embrace these new experiences and build engagement and communication across the organisation. More importantly, leadership has improved as a result.

While the primary focus to date has been the establishment of generic coaching skills, the increased focus on gender/equity issues and growing number of leaders from non-European backgrounds will challenge our ability to develop relevant and culturally appropriate programmes in the future. We are not there yet by any means, although the tools and insights offered by Rosinksi and Abbott (2006) in terms of communication styles and the need to understand the requirements of "collectivist versus individualistic beliefs" (Passmore, 2013, p. 66) provide a number of signposts for further development.

Developing professional leadership

The challenge this organisation has sought to address is to develop the professional leadership capability of its leaders to meet its future strategic challenges. The organisation's strength lies in its deep technical expertise, with promotional opportunities being given to those who have excelled in their specialised field. This is not uncommon in many professionally based organisations. However, like many organisations worldwide, there is a recognition that people leadership demands the same level of training and professional development as any other field and that technical expertise, while critical to competitive advantage, is not enough to ensure success. The experience of a number of high-profile organisations over the past 10 years of leadership failure suggests that we need to do much more to develop leadership skills and qualities that create a culture that is open, transparent and where the leaders' role is to empower and support their people to achieve excellence. Given this 'high dream', coaching is a key enabler to support the essential transition process.

The programme

The programme was designed in collaboration with key stakeholders. Several meetings were planned, allowing a dialogue to truly understand the context and environment in which the organisation operates as well as current (leadership) challenges and review previous development programmes. The current programme was designed in several iterations, getting feedback from the organisation during the process. We then started a pilot workshop with a smaller group, allowing room for adjustments.

Apart from participants involved in dedicated leadership development programmes, the target group for the coaching and mentoring training was all people leaders in the organisation. Some have had coaching in the past; however, there was little awareness of coaching tools and techniques, the distinction between coaching and mentoring and how or where coaching skills could be applied as distinct from other managerial roles. In training the participants, it was important to understand the different skill levels of each person and incorporating this into the workshop.

The programme was conceived in two stages. In the first session, the focus was on the development of core skills in listening and a simple coaching model such as Whitmore's GROW model, which proved a useful general model for many common managerial coaching situations. Stage two of the programme took place almost 12 months later and built on the initial training with LEADER, a new coaching model developed by Milner and Couley (2014). The LEADER model offers two important elements for organisational coaching. First is the notion of alignment, which provides the link between what an employer expects and the employees' personal goals and objectives. The second process highlights the importance of action and

reflection, which support and enhance the training process. This model is significantly more nuanced and designed specifically for organisational settings.
Furthermore, we focused more on group coaching settings in the second
workshop whereas the first workshop looked more at one-on-one coaching
situations.

While the programme started with external training sessions, ongoing
support and guidance on coaching are now provided from within the organisation. Since the training sessions, there has been an increased uptake in
leaders wanting to discuss the best way to approach a particular interaction,
either with their manager (influencing upwards) or a different approach to
undertaking a performance or goal-setting discussion with one of their team.

Along with the other leadership initiatives, practice and feedback are
important steps in supporting the change process. Coaching circles or peer
coaching groups are the next step in this process. These coaching circles
would ensure that leaders have the opportunity to regularly exchange their
thoughts and issues on coaching in a group coaching manner, hence not only
sharing ideas with peers but also continually practising coaching.

Calculating change

A number of different methods were used to measure the impact and effectiveness of the training. Starting with assessments of the presenter and content,
the evaluation also included an assessment of individuals' knowledge before
and after the training intervention. This equates to Level One and Two of
the Kirkpatrick Evaluation model,[3] which measures Reaction and Learning
outcomes. Level 1 – reaction data – demonstrated very high levels of satisfaction with ratings of 92% overall for the course and the content of each session
and 96% for the facilitator (Dr Julia Milner). In the Level 2 evaluation of the
48 participants in the sessions, the average level of knowledge before the
training was 55% and after the training this had jumped to 81%, a 25%
increase overall.

While these data provide helpful signposts to indicate that the training was
working, the more important indicators relate to behaviour change and what
outcomes the individuals are achieving in the conversations they are having.
Practice and application of these skills is ongoing and combined with feedback has become a powerful learning tool for many of the participants. Key
learning areas include the application and use of specific coaching models and
tools and avoiding jumping in to solve the issue as significant areas for further
development.

The 'proof of the pudding is in the eating' so to speak, and the best measures to indicate that this training has been working so far have been the follow-up discussions with the participants on how they are applying these skills.
This is where training and experience in coaching can offer significant value
as the skills are role-modelled and played back in a context of continuous
learning.

Of all the feedback received from this training, the anecdotal comments from participants describes what they have found most effective. A selection of the recurring comments include:

- "Don't jump in to solve the issue – ask questions and push back or allow them to do it – this helps people make their own decisions."
- "Using the Scaling tool is a great way to help me and my team set and achieve goals."
- "Engaging my team in problem solving helps them take accountability for the outcomes."
- "Coaching is a very useful management tool – it means I don't have to come up with all the answers, but it is still hard not to offer solutions."
- "Focusing on individual strengths rather than weaknesses provides a more constructive approach." (This session also used the online 'Strengths Finder tool'.[4])

Key challenges

Key challenges were, first, to shed light on the importance of coaching – explaining the 'why' of the workshops in order to get buy-in from the participants as well as the unique role of the leadership coach compared to other types of coaching (Milner & Couley, 2016). Only if managers understand how a leadership coaching approach might help will they be open to truly engage in the learning journey. Second, it was important to make people understand that coaching is not the right tool for every situation – explaining the 'when' of coaching (Milner & Couley, 2014) and the challenges that a leader as coach might encounter (McCarthy & Milner, 2013). As with many training workshops, a third issue was balancing content input and application with limited time constraints. We only had a limited number of training days available and, even during the workshop, some managers had to leave the workshop for a couple of hours due to emergencies. Ensuring that this did not interrupt the workshop for the rest of the participants and incorporating the managers when they came back into training was another key challenge.

Participants came with a different skill level and understanding of coaching, so it was important to create a base line and common definition of coaching first as well as incorporating the experience from leaders in the room. Allowing enough, but not too much, time between face-to-face workshops was important to optimise learning and application.

For the future

If the budget and time constraints allow, it would be very beneficial to create peer coaching supporting groups between sessions, ideally initially facilitated by an experienced coach. This way, participants can debrief their application, challenges and insights in a group setting and share their learning with others.

Peer group coaching sessions (either face-to-face or via video conference technology) with a smaller number of participants are envisaged to ensure that the learning is embedded. This could be added with smaller skill input in the form of new coaching tools. It is also clear that, with an increasingly diverse mix of leaders and employees, coaching will need to take more account of differences in communication style and perhaps provide a model which offers the best of individual coaching while acknowledging the value of the collective, an approach which aligns strongly to the 'team of teams' approach (McChrystal, Collins, Silverman & Fussell, 2015).

Coaching in this new cultural milieu is not about new coaching models and theories as such. Rather, it is a shift in emphasis, focusing on the role of coaching in empowering individuals to achieve their goals, a willingness to explore a diversity of views and listen as each person's reality emerges. Listening in this context takes a considerable amount of time with perhaps the biggest challenge being moving from an individual to a more collective approach.

Notes

1 The 360° feedback used the Circumplex Leadership Scan 360° (CLS360) to provide feedback on eight dimensions of leadership interpersonal behaviour correlated with leadership effectiveness (see www.cls360.com).
2 This figure mirrors the Australian Bureau of Statistics (ABS) data. The 2015 ABS report estimated that 9.1% or 2.15 million of Australia's resident population come from the Asia Pacific region.
3 See: www.kirkpatrickpartners.com.
4 www.kirkpartickpartners.com.

References

ABS. (2015). *Australian population by country of birth.* Retrieved 10 April 2016, from www.abs.gov.au/ausstats/abs@.nsf/Latestproducts/3412.0Main%20Features32014-15?opendocument&tabname=Summary&prodno=3412.0&issue=2014-15&num=&view=.

Cooperrider, D. L., & Whitney, D. (2000). A positive revolution in change: Appreciative inquiry. In D. L. Cooperrider, P. F. Sorensen, D. Whitney & T. F. Yeager (Eds), *Appreciative enquiry: Rethinking human organisation toward a positive theory of change* (pp. 3–28). Champaign, IL: Stipes Publishing L.L.C.

Kline, N. (1999). *Time to think: Listening to ignite the human mind.* London: Cassell Illustrated.

McCarthy, G., & Milner, J. (2013). Managerial coaching: Challenges, opportunities & training. *Journal of Management Development, 32*(7), 768–779.

McChrystal, S. A., Collins, T., Silverman, D. & Fussell, C. (2015). *Team of teams: New rules of engagement for a complex world.* New York: Portfolio/Penguin.

Milner, J., & Couley, A. (2014). *Coaching how to lead: How managers can use coaching skills effectively in the workplace.* Calwell, ACT: Inspiring Publishers.

Milner, J., & Couley, A. (2016). Manager as coach: The challenge. In C. van Nieuwerburgh (Ed.), *Coaching in professional contexts* (pp. 29–40). Croydon, UK: Sage.

Passmore, J. (2013). *Diversity in coaching: Working with gender, culture, race and age.* (2nd edn). London: Kogan Page.

Rosinski, P. (2003). *Coaching across cultures: New tools for leveraging national, corporate and professional differences.* London: Nicholas Brealey.

Rosinski, P., & Abbott, G. N. (2006). Coaching from a cultural perspective. In D. R. Stober & A. M. Grant (Eds), *Evidence based coaching handbook* (pp. 255–275). Hoboken, NJ: John Wiley & Sons, Inc.

16 "The different me-s"

Using the multi-selves model for peak performance and alignment

Marion Neubronner

I am one of the Asian faculty at Behavioral Coaching Institute (BCI) in Singapore founded by Perry Zeus and Dr Susanne Skiffington in 1994. Most of our participants are Human Resources Directors, CEOs, founders and coaches who want to deepen the psychological understanding of their work and practice.

While many other courses run in Asia and in Singapore, our intensive four-day coaching programme is popular with executives and leaders who are already using coaching in their professional context. They want to dive deeply into many coaching methodologies and the psychological principles behind them.

The participants

It is important to know participants' coaching experience when they first attend the course. On the first day of the programme, we ask the participants to rate themselves on a scale of 1–10 for coaching knowledge and skills. Most will say their knowledge is at a 5 or 6 on a full score of 10. They often say they are already coaching, mostly from a sense of what they think coaching is or from some course they have undertaken during a leadership or human resource management class. Most cite a lack of expert knowledge of coaching psychology for their self-reported low score. Many feel that they have learnt to coach on the job and definitely lack a holistic sense of what is going on in the actual process.

On the skills rating, most, especially those from a Human Resource background, rate themselves at 7 or 8 out of 10. However, they say they predominantly coach on issues like job loss, adjusting to new job roles and 360 feedback. They coach less often on issues like anger management, remediation, leadership development and mentoring.

Why do they come?

Participants mostly come for an easy coaching tool-box. They want to know which coaching technique to use for which purpose and situation. They have seen the basic GROW models and they have seen the humanistic models of rapport and paraphrasing and probing questions. Yet they want to see more. Many have taken certifications in Neural Linguistic Programming (NLP), DISC personality tests and Myer-Briggs profiling tools and they use these to inform their coaching choices with a presenting coachee. This is why they feel they want to have an intensive psychology-driven course to put all these tools into a larger and meaningful context.

The challenges

In my years as faculty, the three most common challenges that the participants say they face in change management and executive coaching in most corporations are: resistance to change, moving from advising to coaching and getting to a psychological safe place in a corporate setting.

The challenge of resistance to change. In Asia, change management is a buzz word as there is a constant need for the old and hierarchal ways of leading to be reviewed. Participants are always concerned about how they can be able to coach their colleagues and leaders despite the resistance to changing outdated workplace behaviour. There are many reasons why coaching can be seen as an asset during this period of change. There is a high millennial population in India, Thailand and Vietnam and this evokes generational tensions in leadership and communications. At the same time, numerous multinational companies and leaders enter Asia on a regular basis to set up their own company and culture, causing transition and culture changes. Finally, many traditional industries are closing or re-vamping their former ways of production. Change is the norm rather than the exception. Many professional managers, executives and technicians have had to re-make themselves and their careers. Most of the participants have seen and felt a great resistance in their leadership teams and employees as they ride the waves of such changes.

The challenge of the move from advising to coaching, from telling to envisioning. The change has to be the decision of the coachee, never the coach. The buy-in has to be from the employee, especially since many millennials prefer to be coached than told what to do. The push from the millennials for a different leadership style, is a great driver for leaders to review the way they lead and their desire to learn to coach or use coaching skills in their management style.

Many of the participants who attend have had years of listening and advising. Most are good listeners and great advisors. But, they are not always good at coaching because of their tendency to be too much of a listener. They may lack a confrontational and caring question stance or become instead too directive in their advice, by-passing their employee's or team member's input and own inner meaning-making of the situation. Many would cite the lack of time for their choice to advise rather than coach. The feedback such leaders get, is that their team has not bought in to the mission and many times they feel disempowered. Poor employee engagement surveys are a testament to that feeling.

The challenge of holding a safe space. Creating the psychological safe space for effective coaching sessions is a huge difficulty when we are coaching in the office. Everything around the coachee reminds them to play a corporate game or stay in a certain way of thinking. Rather than an environment of support for coaching discussions on a coachee's full potential, it is very likely the coaching will be done in the very same meeting room where they were recently told off by their superior. This makes the coaching far from effective. I have suggested and taught my clients to use mindfulness practices to get themselves and their coachees into a state of relaxation and openness before they begin. This is crucial for any coaching conversation, especially in an office setting or when they are seeing the coach in between busy work sessions. The five minutes of slowing down one's breathing and focusing on one's breath rather than on one's problem solving or work-related thoughts is the key to setting up a coaching session.

Ideally, the coaching session can happen outside the workspace. However, as many of my participants are part of the internal coaching teams, they want to make coaching a seamless technique for managing people at work. Many coffee meetings or mentoring off site are acceptable; however, to be realistic, coaching is never a time simply set aside, it is part and parcel of managing daily. While a special time is set aside for external executive coaches for their coaching sessions with the senior leaders (as part of their leadership development), the participants in my coaching programmes are using coaching as a daily technique to grow high talent or diffuse conflicts between team members.

The framework: deep, psychological, fast, professional, self-reflexive and safe

Even as I write that sub-heading, I am judging myself and wanting to put up disclaimers. We know change takes time and we know that 'deep' is subjective and I cannot prove that this method I am about to share is the definitive answer to that proposition. I can, however, safely say it is a method that opens the door for the coachee to continue exploring these questions for themselves on a daily basis and also offers a place for them to negotiate with aspects of themselves that they dialogue less frequently with.

To get to deep psychology, fast and safe, I use a theoretical understanding of the Peak Performing You Model based on the Multi-Selves Model in the Certified Master Coach certification by the International Coaching Council. I use this as an education for coaches and coachees to understand their different social selves and how that affects their behaviours and choices at work and also home.

We begin by drawing an iceberg and then labelling the parts as shown below. The coaches then explain each aspect to the coachee as follows:

On top above the water, the light tips of the model represent the aspects of personality that can be observed; that is, a person's outward behaviour.

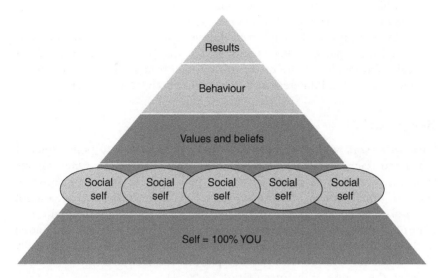

Figure 16.1 Peak Performing You Model.

Source: Marion Neubronner, adapted from *Journal Psyche* (2017).

This *result* and *behaviour* are influenced by unseen factors such as the values and beliefs that the person holds, the person's perceived social self and, finally, the person's true self.

The darker sections are subconscious or unconscious and usually play a large role in influencing how we act. They are under the water and are unseen and unconscious. The *social selves* are influenced by a person's culture and perception of societal expectations. It is an aspect of a human that results from taking on social roles and is the perspective that we assume to view and analyse our own behaviours. For example, social roles in the workplace could include the friend, the supervisor, the achiever, the millennial, the old guard, the slacker, the community builder, member of this particular clique, etc.

The self, on the other hand, is 100% adaptable. It explains why we unconsciously act in a particular way. We highlight to the coachee that from this space and essence they can and do many things. In fact, most of their amazing behaviours arise from this space where anything is possible. Their only limit is when they choose one role over another. So, by being the 'old guard' they talk and think like that and do not use other roles or see other perspectives. This social role gets them in conflict, perhaps, with the newer members of the organization or with people who are acting from opposing social roles.

An example of social selves in conflict is provided below:

A man is a father and husband and then undergoes a divorce. He goes into a depression because he no longer knows who he is. His past routine and lifestyle are disrupted as he cannot be around the same routine as he was before as a father to his children. And he is no longer a husband.

He does not understand that while his social self 'husband' and 'full-time father' may have been removed, his 'self' (100% YOU) is not about a social role. He is more than a role. He can re-marry, he can be a father but in a new and different way of being in his children's life, etc.

Being 'me'

I regularly work with the military, air force, healthcare and police force. I coach and train their trainers on aspects of mental resilience. One example that often comes up is the social role of 'police officer' in the organization and their other personal pursuits and values. Many times, the coachee cannot find a place to be 'me' in the very hierarchical and conformist nature of such high performing and high security organizations. While they are committed to their social roles as employees, leaders and culture creators, many actually bemoan the loss of their own personal pursuits and identities in that effort to maintain the culture of the organization.

Most recently, a 32-year-old police officer who has given 10 years of his life to the force mentioned that he originally joined the police force mainly because of financial reasons. Then, he began to love and respect his work. However, his passion was in racing motorcycles and he had garnered quite a bit of attention for his talents. He was even being courted for the Johor Bahru circuit by the Sultan of Johor's son. In his mind, he could not reconcile ever following that dream, given his stable financial and social identity as a police officer and father and devoted son to an ageing father.

When we began the coaching, I got him to first acknowledge his multiple social selves, which gave him the relief he so sought and the language for each of his desires. They used to be binary – this or that. The dominant discourse of police officer and 'responsible' won and his passion was pushed aside as a hobby and a dream.

When we started working and allowing both roles to speak to each other to find a way to be both police officer and champion racer, the creative juices and insights came up fast and furiously. He sought a way to show his talents at work rather than hide them and to ask the police force to support his hobby as a means to show the police force in a favourable light. The process involved a huge shift from 'a this or that' mentality to the possibility of being a police officer 'and' a father 'and' a champion rider 'and' a devoted son. There was a renewed sense of hope and excitement and achievement milestones to pursue. This was in contrast to a 'let's beat myself up' for having desires which are in opposition to my company or the dominant values. He mentioned swimmer Teo Zhen Ren, a National Serviceman in the Singapore Police Force (www.redsports.sg/2013/12/06/swimmer-teo-zhen-ren-red-sports-interview/) who competed in the South-East Asian Games while still being a police officer as an example of what the police force could do to bend their customary rules when they realized what he could do.

Choose behaviours

We remind coachees that they can choose the results and behaviours by realizing they are coming from versions of themselves: am I speaking to my team as *a friend, a boss, someone who needs their recognition* or *an authority figure* (like I learnt from my former boss). If you see your new behaviour being stuck, then it's almost because your social selves are in conflict.

This model helps with building self-awareness around the social roles we play. Many people are not aware that the unconscious or subconscious aspects of themselves affect their lives so powerfully. Also, putting examples and labels for the different behaviours coachees exhibit, as if they were multiple actors on the same stage of one's life, makes the unconscious or subconscious something we can dialogue about with a bit of distance, even though it can be an emotional topic. We find often that we only need to provide examples of another's tensions between their multiple selves and the coachee immediately self-corrects as they start seeing this same psychological dynamic in themselves.

When we try to fix ourselves or a person, too many times we use tools and techniques that are ineffective and for short-term gains when we should look at underlying principles and addressing our Self, the 100% You. This keeps us open to being and doing anything and allows us to be more flexible and adaptable with our behaviours.

We need to understand how flow, clarity and new ideas actually come about and how they are blocked when we believe we have to be only one or a few social roles or selves or identities. As an extension to coaching, we do role-plays and give voice to each social role that is in conflict so the coachee gets the opportunity to develop that distinct and powerful identification and awareness with these often-repressed or under-acknowledged aspects of themselves. To be helpful, the coach can offer some options of common archetypes of social and mental roles played in the world.

Lessons learnt

As a model and a conversational framework, this has been an effective tool to speak deeply and quickly in a coaching session within 45 minutes of beginning. After the coachee is comfortable with the terminology, they seem to be able to review their actions a little faster and with a little less resistance.

Peak Ideology Questions that prompt deep reflection include:

"What selves are in conflict here?"
"What triggered that reaction, what self or role were you protecting or promoting?"

"What if you played another role here?"

"Where can you find more alignment for your different selves and the 100% You?"

Often a role-play between two different identities in conversation reveals more in terms of the psychological conflict than most questions uncover. Allowing the coachee to claim their repressed or vulnerable roles, gives voice to a tension that if not addressed comes up in other unhealthy workplace actions instead.

This external, reinforcing self-reflection structure, that both parties use to guide the discussion, has given many people comfort as it is not merely a simple trust exercise in following the coach wherever he/she may lead each session.

Using this model helps with the challenges of resisting change and finding and holding a safe place. It is a model for everyone. It allows for some distance and that addresses the challenge of resistance. It also allows for psychological discussions about the challenge of holding a safe place as well as time for introspection without having the coach pry too much in a professional setting. We do not need to problem-solve the coachee's emotions; we merely need to allow each of their social roles and emotions to express themselves.

Reference

Journal Psyche. (2017). Freud's model of the human mind. Retrieved 17 August 2017, from http://journalpsyche.org/understanding-the-human-mind.

17 High performance team coaching

Morné Maritz

Situation/challenge

A dilemma that has troubled many employers and leaders for years is how to make groups and teams more effective. One tool that has emerged as a powerful intervention for the development of individual and team performance is business coaching or executive coaching. Translating these into team coaching, however, has proved a bit more challenging since the dynamic and approach are quite different. The traditional approaches to teams have been predominantly from a 'business theory' point of view. Since business coaching has some of its roots in sport coaching, one way to understand team coaching is from a team sports perspective.

Like individuals, teams can benefit from focused team coaching aimed at improving their functioning and performance. It helps teams review performance, improve results, communication and build rapport. In this sense team coaching is a significant part of the remedy for team performance shortfalls. Coaching therefore can also provide a vehicle for inspiring individuals and their teams to challenge their current constraints and to explore new possibilities.

The case presented here gives understanding and insight into how effective team coaching assisted the national rugby team of South Africa, the famous Springboks, and how they rose from a very underperforming and humiliated team to end up winning the World Cup in 2007.

Coaching was not a new concept to the team or the management staff. However, the approach of the head coach at the time, Jake White, was significantly different from his predecessor. A fresh approach was required as the morale of the team was at its lowest point and they were failing to achieve any newsworthy achievements at the time, despite the credentials and experience of the players.

I wanted to explore and validate, first, what behaviour helped the head coach to function in an optimal manner and helped to facilitate team coaching that caused the team to excel and perform in an extraordinary way. Second, I wanted to map such behaviour into a high performance coaching framework that can be used together with other coaching frameworks or as a stand-alone approach.

Solution

I chose a positive deviance model (Figure 17.1 below) as a functional framework and roadmap as a valid framework for high performance team coaching. White's story as a high performance team coach is interpreted through the positive deviance framework.

What will be shown is how White's virtues and strengths impacted on him as well the Springbok rugby team. However, this does not mean that the successes of the team should be attributed solely to the core qualities, facilities and outcomes embedded in White's positive deviance, since there may be other mediating factors inherent to individual team members, such as the team dynamics and other external factors. The process almost happened chronologically as explained in the framework, and the more elements present in the foundation, the more compounding effect they had on the next layer which in turn enforced and supported the desired outcomes, making the behaviour more sustainable with less effort. It does not mean that all the *qualities* need to be in place in order to work on the *facilitators*, but working on *facilitators* without any qualities firmly in place will have little or no results. As you will see when implementing the framework, qualities will naturally give birth to the facilitators and start supporting them, which in turn will produce the designed outcomes.

Amplifiers

Positive emotions. Virtuous behaviours create positive emotions such as optimism, joy, pride, zest and enthusiasm which in turn may reproduce virtuousness and an elevation in well-being. When White took over the coaching position, the Springbok rugby team was extremely demoralised and at 'their lowest ebb'. The Springboks suffered a series of defeats, including a disastrous 2003 World Cup tournament. The international media also exposed the scandal referred to as 'Kamp Staaldraad'; a demeaning boot-camp where players were forced to participate in humiliating actions. The coverage, losses and shame of the scandal left the team broken, without direction and purpose and with a very low morale. The intentions of this 'retreat' may have been pure as the previous coach wanted to address aspects such as courage, determination, tenacity and a winning mentality but, without any foundation of qualities present, it almost had the exact opposite effect. As a result, at the time, the image and the esteem of the squad were not held in high regard, neither by the players nor the local and international rugby communities. White's first action, besides choosing his captain and his team players, was to 'restore the Bok pride', fostering those emotions that lead to excellent and virtuous behaviour both on and off the field and, in doing so, eliciting positive emotions.

To accomplish this task, he employed the services of a company specialising in team-building techniques to address current issues both inside and outside that affected the morale, virtue and well-being of the team and to

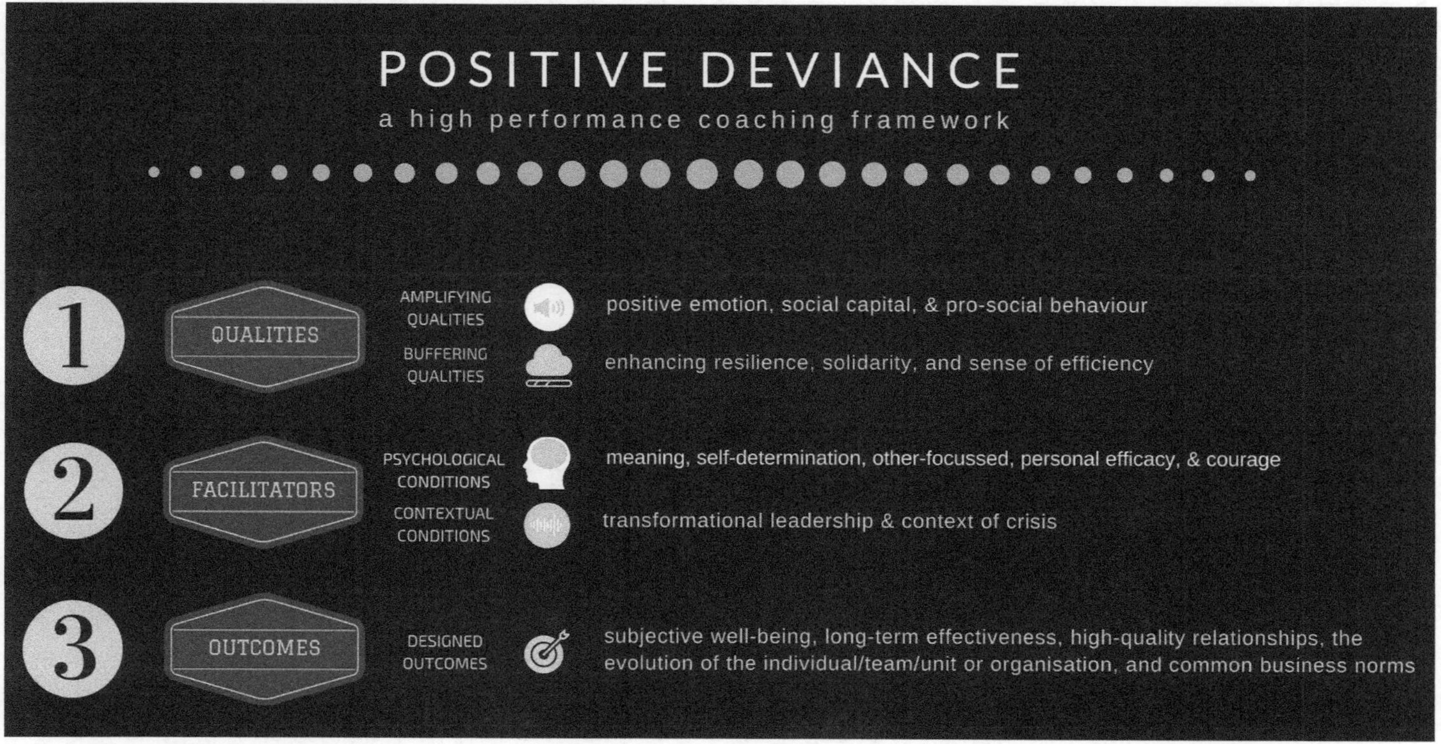

Figure 17.1 A model of positive deviance: qualities, facilitators and outcomes.
Source: compiled from Cameron, Dutton and Quinn (2003) and Spreitzer and Sonenshein (2003).

give the players a safe platform to voice their concerns and frustrations. To add to the positive momentum that was happening off the field, White made the players play in the traditional Bok jersey. They emphasised the culture and heritage by getting previous Springbok and Rugby legends to come and share their stories of the past. This was in many ways a symbolic way to celebrate the return of pride, honour and virtue that was once associated with being a Springbok. The culture became alive again and once the pride and honour were reintroduced there was a different mood in the camp. The negativity was gone.

Social capital. Social capital is the existence of positive interpersonal relationships among individuals, which facilitate virtues such as care giving, empathy and trust that in turn tend to build high quality relationships among team members (cf. Cameron et al., 2003). White invested social capital through facilitating open communication in allowing players, for the first time, to voice their bottled-up feelings and express themselves verbally without being punished. White also made himself and any member of his management team as approachable as possible. By inspiring and motivating the players he was able to move them to higher levels of commitment which benefited the overall team performance and he strengthened relationships by getting players from different backgrounds and cultures to transcend their differences and perform in unison. A common theme related to social capital here is trust and loyalty. From the start, White wanted to build a foundation of trust and mutual respect between the players and more specifically towards him and the decisions he made as coach. White didn't just chop and change team players for the sake of having the best team for the present; rather, he focused on the bigger picture by building a more experienced team able to function better together. As a result, by expressing his loyalty he was able to foster social capital in the form of better relationships, commitment, trust, participation and sharing of knowledge of team players that in turn led to optimal performance on the field.

Pro-social behaviour. This occurs when individuals behave in ways that benefit other people. It seems that White wanted to engage in pro-social behaviour with each individual team member, which in turn motivated the member to reciprocate such behaviour. In order to make sure that he would be able to behave in a pro-social manner that would benefit his team players, White had a particular way of selecting them; he didn't just look at talent but also considered each player's character. This is quite different from the norm as most coaches select on merit and talent first as do many organisations and other teams or units. What White managed to do well is choose on character first and foremost, because when you do that players will start to complement each other and act in a way that is to the benefit of the whole team rather than in their own interest. It is also easy to see how this further enhances a strong culture with a high moral fibre and in any team.

Buffers

Resilience. Resilience enhances the team's ability to absorb threat or trauma and to bounce back from adversity. Right from the beginning, White reassured his team, in a personal letter to each individual, that he had faith in their abilities and that he would protect them from the media and any negativity that might come their way. As a coach or a leader of a high performing team, you must be able to turn the negatives/challenges into positives and turn adversity into advantage. In South Africa, especially during the 2006 season, White and the team faced public and media scrutiny as they were underperforming. There were calls for White's resignation and for some players to be dropped from the team. Resilience is born out of the experience the team gains of playing or working together; it builds more trust and confidence in their own ability as players, in the ability of the team and in the ability of the team to 'have your back' so you can take risks and gain more skills. Very often it is during this process that players or coaches are dropped or the manager/leader sacked. Not only will you lose the experience but you will also lose the ability to weather the storm.

As a result of building continued resilience, despite the setbacks in 2006, they managed to overcome these threats, winning the World Cup only one year later with White being awarded Coach of the Year by the International Rugby Board (IRB). Seeing it through and allowing mistakes to build experience and resilience, they were able to turn an underperforming team into a unified and victorious one in just four years.

Solidarity. This refers to unity or agreement of feeling or action among individuals with a common interest and fosters mutual support within a group. White had the ability of getting the team dynamics right and when you work with a team this is easier said than done, as most teams are put together by skill or 'best in class' rather than considering how they complement each other. White continuously stated that the single most important concept was relationship, because "sport and business is mainly built on relationships". The single common denominator in business or in sport is people, and the ultimate ability of an effective leader and a high performance coach is how to deal with people and to understand how to manage people.

A simple example of how White got the team to function better as a unit and to get them to know, trust and feel positively toward one another was when he got the team to meet the other players' families, girlfriends and children and contrived a big family experience so that team members got to know their fellow players. It was a very simple gesture but it worked and was very effective in accelerating a sense of solidarity among the team. In fact, it went beyond the team and fostered a level of support among their respective families as well.

Once this gained momentum, White and his management staff ensured that there was a high level of transparency, openness and communication to help individuals deal with issues and experience a sense of belonging. As a result, the players all started to talk the same language and the unity among the players was incredible. Another example of how the team started to show signs of solidarity was when they, as a collective, protested against the South African Rugby Union (SARU) on behalf of those players who had not yet had contracts. This was a significant shift for players to focus on seeking the best for the team as a whole rather than each individual player just worrying about himself.

Sense of purpose (shared vision and goals). One cannot elicit positive responses without a shared vision and a sense of purpose. This serves as a fixed point during an ever-changing environment. It is essential for a coach to have a vision for the team and the ability to share that vision in such a way that it is both inspiring and motivating. The overall vision or goal to win the World Cup might be an obvious choice, but before that goal can be reached there have to be other visions and goals in place that pave the way to the overarching vision for the team. The first rule of motivation is that it should be challenging but not unreachable. For high performing teams, it is all about that focus, definiteness of purpose, really buying into the vision. To help achieve this and to break the overall goal into smaller measurable victories along the way, each player received a diary for daily planning and every page had the slogan 'see it, believe it, achieve it' with a picture of the World Cup trophy linking the daily task with that of the main vision. Everything they did tied into the larger vision and sense of purpose. This assisted the team to gain a clearer understanding of the larger vision that needed to be attained and then to go about putting in place a set of specific goals without focusing only on the end goal and, so, to instil in them that they owned and held the belief that they can win, a significant paradigm shift. Once that change in thinking had been set in motion, the vision became more realistic and attainable, getting individuals to play to win instead of playing not to lose. Finally, having vision is also about an understanding of where the team is in the journey towards the end goal: if they move too fast, they will lose faith; but move too slowly and they will become disillusioned.

As the qualities are cultivated they start to overlap and connect. This is essential to sustain the associated positive behaviours and to drive long-term outcomes. This is similar to building a tower with a deck of cards; focusing on only one thing and moving to the outcomes too soon will cause the deck to fall down. Whereas the stronger the base, the more secure the next layer and the higher you can build the tower and, therefore, the likelihood of continued high performance.

Facilitators

Besides the amplifiers and buffers identified above there are key facilitators or conditions contributing to positive deviance. While each condition is not absolutely required for positive deviant behaviour to occur, each contributes to an individual's willingness and ability to engage in positive deviant behaviour that will ultimately drive and lead to high performance of a team.

Meaning. Personal meaning is reflected in the degree or extent to which individuals are prepared to take action or to stand up for a cause. It involves deep caring that what people are doing matter to them in important ways. As a high performance coach, White was proactive in his approach to coaching and his desire to make a difference in rugby, because that was what made him tick and drove his sense of purpose. This sense of personal meaning discovered by White through his engagement in rugby was authentic and as such was instilled in the rugby team members. There is also a sense of transfer that occurs here as passion ignites passion and that energy drives meaning. As mentioned earlier, the first thing on the agenda was to restore pride and honour and cultivate a winning culture. This drove meaning as it gave the group a sense of belonging to something bigger them themselves. Similarly, having a shared vision and goals also drives meaning if you can attach them to personal goals. This answers the core fundamental question, "What's in it for me?" As can be seen, each of the previous qualities start to merge and promote meaning as a core facilitator, which in turn is a key ingredient for resilience.

Other-focus. Being other-focused is consistent with servant leadership, implying that an individual will grow as a result of serving others. A core attribute of a high performance coach is the ability to develop each player and empower them to be able to think for themselves, instead of coaching players to do what the coach wants them to do; it's essential to develop people to become even better. This is what high performance coaching is all about. This implies that a coach must allow other people to make mistakes and not be scared of failure. If executed successfully, being other-focused will empower the members of the team to such a point that the coach is not needed. In the beginning, it was Jake White and his captain, but that wasn't good enough to win the World Cup. By the time they arrived for the tournament any one of a number of players could have fulfilled that role which shows the extent White had developed the team and its capacity for leadership. During his tenure, White was willing to go out of his way to make himself available to his staff and to people in general; nothing was too much trouble if it benefited the team and that willingness had a great bearing on how the team gelled, not only the players but also the coaching and management staff.

Self-determination. When people have a sense of self-determination they have an internal locus of control and their reason for taking action is internalised rather than coerced by external forces. Self-determination is very often confused with confidence which is a quality gained from experience and practice and through failures. Self-confidence is what individuals and teams rely on when confidence is low and where they draw energy from in order to follow through on their vision. For most high performance sports there are very slim margins in which to operate and interference of any kind can be very destabilising. From time to time White faced strong opposition during 2004 to 2007 from various sources such as SARU, the media, the public and initially even team members, which could have severely limited positive deviant behaviour. White, however, was able to transcend these challenges because of his strong sense of internal locus of control expressed as a determined World Cup winning mindset, which facilitated an environment which made it possible for the team players to experience a greater sense of self-control and the ability to take initiative. White had a clear vision and methodology on how and what he wanted to accomplish. Some of it may not have been successful, but he wanted to be responsible for his own decisions and not for someone else's. As he put it, "if I'm going to take the heat, then I want to do it the way I want to do it, because too many times you get fired for listening to all the other people".

Personal efficacy. Personal efficacy refers to an individual's ability to perform a specific task. When individuals feel effective they believe that their chances of success are greatly increased, leading to higher goals to be set and dedication to reach those goals. These beliefs in turn affect motivation levels and the length of time individuals will persevere in the face of obstacles. While White had a stellar track record as a coach, from early in his coaching career, he was able to embrace losing as an opportunity to learn as it helped him to see where improvement was needed. The failures made him realise who he needed to recruit to assist him in executing his role as a high performance coach. White also realised that coaching doesn't need to follow a traditional one-to-one or one-to-many approach; in order to be successful in high performance sport you must be able to identify those individuals who can assist you with the job.

Confidence is an important factor to consider for personal efficacy as it increases commitment, cultivates interest and defies the norms of conventional practice. Personal efficacy can only be bred though experience, failures and successes. Very often, success is used as the only feedback mechanism for efficacy, but this is too narrow an idea as it doesn't encompass resilience and tenacity. For personal efficacy, all three aspects need to be present.

White expressed his confidence on the very first day when he addressed a team that was still discouraged because of their unhappy past, envisioning that they would have extraordinary results. He did not focus on their current state, but rather on what they could become by the next World Cup. White's efficacy came to fruition four years later when they won the World Cup trophy and they made a clean sweep of the major categories 24 hours later at the IRB awards. White was chosen as Coach of the Year for the second time and the Springboks won the Team of the Year prize.

Courage. Courage provides individuals with the backbone to engage in positive deviant behaviour, to stand up for what they believe in and do what is thought to be the right course of action. It seems plausible that White's love, passion and enthusiasm for rugby provided him with the courage to overcome the many challenges he had to face such as a declining relationship with SARU's executives, being sometimes unpopular with the media, the expectations of an unforgiving rugby-mad nation and challenges with his personal relationships. Without a sense of risk there is no need for courage. An example of him displaying courage was to send over a less experienced side to Australia during the 2006 Tri Nations series in order to rest his core players, despite a lot of opposition from the media and the public. South Africa did not win the Tri Nations Tournament that year, but his decision played a vital part in that not one of his core players was injured during the World Cup tournament the following year, which was not the case for most of the other teams. Playing with a less experienced side also served as a platform to see how younger players perform under pressure and White and the management team learned a lot about the younger group. It also takes courage to say no and not allow short-term successes to blind you from the bigger prize.

Leadership. White himself attributes his leadership to the fact that he was fortunate enough to "learn from the successes and mistakes of a variety of good coaches". As mentioned earlier, he also realised that a coach does not have to possess all of the skills himself, so he surrounded himself with people who complete the required set of skills needed. Appointing a captain was key in White's ability to facilitate transformational leadership. This was a particular challenge as there was a politically driven, higher transformation agenda in South Africa at the time. The bottom line is that part of the aim for leadership is that team members should be so empowered that responsibility is owned instead of assigned, in which case you have a captain in any player at any given point during the game. But this result is first and foremost started by a solid relationship between the coach and the team captain.

Context of crisis. Few things go according to plan and when people are faced with crises and challenges, the necessity to follow rules and procedures becomes mitigated. White faced a crisis when he took over the head coaching position in 2004. The team's morale was extremely low following the humiliation of 'Kamp Staaldraad' and subsequent coverage of the incident in the media. Furthermore, the underperformance of the team had been reflected in a series of defeats. What amplified the severity of the situation was a lack of unity and trust amongst the team members. White also had had some skirmishes with SARU and its management. On a few occasions White was not sure of his position as head coach, which greatly increased his levels of stress, but also created a sense of uncertainty amongst his staff and team members. On numerous occasions he was discredited by the media and the public for some of his selection decisions and his coaching style. Despite all these numerous challenges and crises, White managed to transcend these contingencies by overriding them by breaking the accepted norms of traditional South African coaching practice. White protected the team fiercely from the media and the politics. Moreover, White implemented innovative coaching methods by bringing in experts in their respective fields to assist with optimal on-field performance and obtained the services of expert behavioural consultants to assist with building their morale and comradeship. For White and his team, therefore, the crisis they faced when he took over the head coaching position for the Springboks may be regarded as a positive trigger event.

Innovation. A common condition present with individuals that perform extraordinarily is their innovative ability. White borrowed innovative ideas from other disciplines, which allowed traditional thinking to be challenged. White therefore could stimulate and challenge his team with new ideas and practices. For example, he acquired the assistance of a vision expert, something rather unique and unheard of at the time. Players' minds were trained off the field with use of personal laptops and customised programmes specific to each player's function and skills. White also went with a selected team over to America to learn from their basketball and football coaches, something not done before. This allowed for the game to be less predictable and added some adaptations that greatly improved their chances of success.

Planning. One of the key conditions of deviant behaviour is that it is intentional, in other words, planned for. For White and his management team and the challenge they faced, the plan was to close the door on previous failures, bad publicity, negative stigmas, low morale and make sure there was a plan for four years on how they, as a team, were going to become world champions. Planning was about breaking down goals into the smallest detail in order for it to be measured. This directed the journey towards the end vision and made it practical and focused. This allowed the players to focus on either training or the match at hand and their particular role. Good planning limits unforeseen surprises or events and, when they do occur, provides for what the countermeasures should be. White made sure "the planning that was done was done so with the team in mind and with their input, keeping in mind the vision". This ensured that the team took accountability for its execution on and off the field. Thus, the whole team collaborates on a game plan and strategy, they stick to it and afterwards re-assess why it worked or why it didn't work.

High stake environments cannot just rely on talent. The problem with relying on talent is that attention to detail gets overlooked and raw talent almost never compensates for a lack of proper planning. Only relying on talent leaves a gap in the foundation of the team and is only helpful in the short term. Thus, planning can't be done with only talent in mind. Rather, planning should be done with the team in mind and how each team member's skill complements that of other team members.

Recognise opportunities. White referred to the facilitating component of recognising opportunities as 'luck'. In the sports and business world there are constant circumstantial events that could be considered lucky or unlucky, but a positive deviant coach is able to recognise those opportunities and capitalise on them. For example, just because an event is considered to be lucky you must also be in a position to recognise it as such and act upon it. For the executive coach, the more they are surrounded with individuals that complement the required skillset and experiences required, the easier it will be to recognise opportunities and act upon them.

Outcomes

Possible outcomes for positive deviance and how it could make a difference to the individual, the organisation and other stakeholders are numerous and they depend on the design of the engagement and the ultimate goals. In this case winning the World Cup, the team's recognition for best team and the coach's award for best coach are all part of the outcomes desired but there are four outcomes that transcend results and don't rely on success.

Subjective well-being. Subjective well-being is the way in which people evaluate their overall quality of life, their pleasures and pains. In the case of the Springboks, the team's and the public's subjective well-being increased as the team's performance grew over the four years. Furthermore, as the team's performance increased under White's coaching, their levels of hope, optimism, resiliency and confidence (self-efficacy) led to overall increased levels of objective well-being.

High quality relationships. The relationships between the positive deviant, in this case White, and the recipients of the deviant behaviour, in this case the Springbok team members, were strengthened as a result of the positive deviant behaviour of White. The team members appreciated White's loyalty, courage, sense of responsibility, openness, fresh approach to coaching and fairness. This kind of positive coaching behaviour did not only restore their pride in playing rugby but also facilitated a winning mindset. White created a sense of comradeship amongst the team members and strengthened relation-ships among them when he encouraged them to share in each other's hopes, dreams, fears and to take an interest in each other's immediate families.

Long-term effectiveness. Positive deviance should have implications for the long-term effectiveness of individuals and organisations. White and the team developed significantly from his appointment as head coach up until the World Cup final. From an inexperienced team with only 175 test caps between them, they had managed to obtain 659 test caps four years later. White's success as an extraordinary coach can be attributed to his emphasis on experience as a key contributor for effectiveness and, as pointed out before, the leadership develop-ment went far beyond just the development of one player as captain. The process has developed the team and its capacity for leadership in such a way that a number of players could fulfil the captain's role.

The evolution of common norms. Positive deviant actions help change common norms and gear them more towards excellence. Positive deviant behaviour, therefore, should promote and set new standards to aspire towards. From the story above, it is apparent that White's actions and coaching set new norms for excellence in team coaching.

The lessons learnt

Some of the key learnings in applying a positive deviant coaching model are that, first, it moved beyond the traditional, individual focus of coaching towards that of team coaching. Second, a theoretical model for positive deviant behaviour has been created to interpret high performance team coaching. Third, this model was validated as an appropriate framework for high performance team coaching. The framework may serve as a basis for providing the core qualities, facilitators and outcomes of high performance team coaching, even in the business environment as a stand-alone roadmap or in conjunction with other frameworks.

References

Cameron, K. S., Dutton, J. E. & Quinn, R. E. (2003). Foundations of positive organisational scholarship. In K. S. Cameron, J. E. Dutton & R. E. Quinn (Eds), *Positive organisational scholarship: Foundations of a new discipline* (pp. 3–14). San Francisco: Berrett-Koehler.

Spreitzer, G. M., & Sonenshein, S. (2003). Positive deviance and extraordinary organizing. In K. S. Cameron, J. E. Dutton & R. E. Quinn (Eds), *Positive organizational scholarship* (pp. 209–224). San Francisco: Berrett-Koehler.

18 Coaching in Asia Pacific from the perspective of the coachee

Siqiwen Li, Anna Blackman and Alison Carter

Testing the claims

While there have been many articles written about what coaching is advocating for, its adoption and descriptions of how to coach, little critical, systematic, empirical research has been published about the effectiveness of coaching for either the individual or the organisations they work for (Joo, 2005; Leedham, 2005). Few coaching programmes have been formally evaluated within organisations (McDermott, Levenson & Newton, 2007) and, until recently, little academic research has examined coaching (Kilburg, 2001; Passmore & Gibbes, 2007). Coaching has, however, become a topic of academic interest and there has been a growing number of empirical studies published since 2005 (Ely et al., 2010; Jarvis, Lane & Fillery-Travis, 2006). This emerging empirical literature offers an opportunity to begin to assess the many claims made for and about coaching.

The Coaching for Effectiveness survey was developed to test the extensive number of claims made in the literature about coaching effectiveness. This case presents a slice of the data collected, coachees' opinions and their observations of coaching in the Asia Pacific area. The primary data were gathered from a questionnaire designed by the researchers with both quantitative and qualitative aspects included. Consistent with this approach, a questionnaire asking questions relating to the coach, the coachee, the organisation and the coaching process/experience was designed containing both structured and unstructured questions. The survey included scale items developed from the literature on best practice in the coaching process. By asking these questions, the researchers were able to determine what factors respondents felt were effective and what factors need to be included in the coaching process in order for it to be successful.

The questionnaire was divided into six sections. The first section, *Section 1 – Your Coaching Programme*, was used to determine whether respondents were currently going through the coaching process or not. Sections 2 to 5 were divided into each of the following components, namely, *Features of the Coaching Programme, Features of the Coach, the Coaching Process/Experience, the Organisation*, and questions about *the Coachee*. The last section of the questionnaire was titled *Section 6 – About You*. This final section of the survey aimed at extracting a general profile of the participants in terms of gender, age, marital status and whether or not they had children.

The survey was distributed online to national and international professional coaching organisations, associations and networks worldwide and was online from March 2013 until May 2014. The responses used in this case are, as indicated earlier, a slice of that data from coachees with an Asian-Pacific background with the majority being Australian. Respondents represented 13 different industries (Table 18.1 below).

Analysis

Analysed below are the responses from the coachees regarding their coaching experiences. Included are coaching models and/or frameworks, highlighting the implementation of coaching and the main outcomes from the participation.

The perspectives of the coachee emerge from three aspects: the description of the coaching programme they were involved in and the perceived effectiveness of it; their experiences with the coaching practices evaluated by six criteria (*confidence, work-related performance, creativity, time management, self-awareness* and *action plan*); and the coaching context. An exploratory factor analysis (Courtney, 2013; Kaiser, 1960) was conducted to explore further the factors that explain each aspect in greater detail. A list of all factors in relation to each aspect is presented in Figure 18.1.

Based on the 13 industries covered in this study, coaching in Asia Pacific as a whole can be grouped into 15 factors (Figure 18.1). The design of the coaching programme, such as the length and frequency of sessions, is closely linked to the

Table 18.1 Industries and professions of respondents

Industry	Profession of the coachee
1 Education	Academic
2 Training, Development and Coaching	Human Resources (HR)
3 Utilities, Public Sector and Government	Administration
4 General Business and Business Support Services	Senior Management
5 Property Development	General Manager
6 IT	Librarian
7 Consulting and Legal	Medical Practitioners
8 Mining, Energy and Manufacturing	Business Partners and/or Owners
9 Hospitality and Leisure	Legal Practitioners
10 Health	Government Officers
11 Telecommunication	Consultant/Trainer
12 Finance	Non-Profit Practitioners
13 Others	Accountant

Note
The listed items in column 2 and 3 don't necessarily match horizontally.

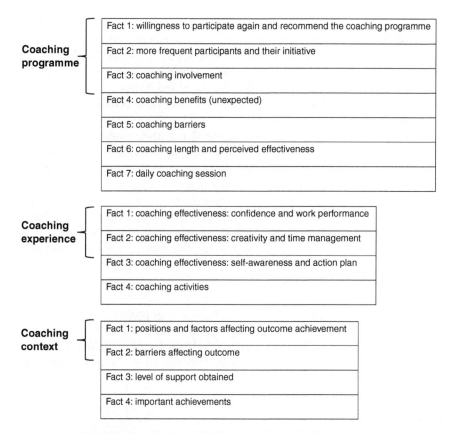

Figure 18.1 Coachees' perspectives of coaching in the Asia Pacific region.

perceived effectiveness of the programme as reported by the coachee. The willingness to continue the coaching programme and to recommend it to peers also emerges as a criteria to evaluate the programme with 97% willing to participate again and above 98% of coachees saying they would recommend the coaching programme. This demonstrates a certain degree of success within the existing coaching programmes in the Asia Pacific region. Almost 71% of the coachees reported unexpected benefits from their coaching programmes. Benefits of coaching included networking and new career possibilities.

The researchers also looked at who initiated the coaching: 75% were self-initiated and 8.6% were initiated by the coach while there was no record of organisation-related initiative (Carter, Blackman, Hicks, Williams, Hay, 2017). Barriers were also identified with the highest ranked barrier being *the lack of agreement with the coach on the goals and/or unclear development goals (13%), the coaching programme not being challenging enough (12%),* and third, *emotional barriers (9%).*

The results found that, to enhance the experience of coaching for coachees, the coaching should focus on six main areas for the coachee: confidence, work performance, creativity, time management, self-awareness and developing an action plan. Most useful were found to be: *the development of action plans, identifying and questioning assumptions and evaluations* and *goal-setting*. Respondents found that respectively 57%, 66% and 55% of coachees think they are very useful while 12%, 11% and 21% think these activities are somewhat useful.

Coachees in the Asia Pacific region found that their position and background are most likely to affect their coaching outcomes and expected achievement. The level of support provided was seen as the most important achievement in order for the coachee to reach their targets. Barriers such as preoccupation with other work and personal matters were regarded as the most important issues with 44% and 31% of coachees agreeing to these barriers and 12% and 10% strongly agreeing while lack of time (25% agree and 12% strongly agree) was ranked as the third highest barrier to coaching outcomes.

The coachees' position title and self-employment status also attributed to coaching outcomes and affected the expected achievements. The majority of support obtained for the coachee during the coaching programme came from family members with 18% of respondents confirming this had been the case. The greatest support at the organisation level was from senior management such as the boss or the line manager with 15% reporting strong support and also support from colleagues and peers.

Lessons learnt

Overall this study helped to confirm the importance of the three main parts of coaching: the coach, the coachee and what the coach does (the coaching process). Also of importance to coachees is the relationship between the coach and coachee and the barriers that may be encountered when embarking on a coaching experience. The study also provided empirical evidence to suggest that coaching can be effective and that respondents felt that coaching was effective in helping them achieve their goals.

For coachees within the Asia Pacific region the benchmarks set by coachees can be influenced when certain factors are repeatedly raised during the coaching experience. These include the level of confidence the coachee has, the professional and personal development they receive and the increase in productivity-related work performance.

References

Carter, A., Blackman, A., Hicks, B., Williams, M., & Hay, R. (2017). Perspectives on effective coaching by those who have been coached. *International Journal of Training & Development*, Wiley, *21*(2), 73–91.

Courtney, M. G. R. (2013). Determining the number of factors to retain in EFA: Using the SPSS R-Menu v2.0 to make more judicious estimations. *Practical Assessment, Research and Evaluation, 18*(8), 1–14.

Ely, K., Boyce, L., Nelson, J., Zaccaro, S., Hernez-Broome, G. & Whyman, W. (2010). Evaluating leadership coaching: A review and integrated framework. *The Leadership Quarterly, 21*, 585–599.

Jarvis, J., Lane, D. & Fillery-Travis, A. (2006). *Does coaching work?* London: CIPD.

Joo, B. (2005). Executive coaching: A conceptual framework from an integrative review of practice and research. *Human Resource Development Review, 4*(4), 462–488.

Kaiser, H. F. (1960). The application of electronic computers to factor analysis. *Educational and Psychological Measurement, 20*, 141–151.

Kilburg, R. (2001). Facilitating intervention adherence in executive coaching: A model and methods. *Consulting Psychology Journal: Practice and Research, 53*(4), 251–267.

Leedham, M. (2005). The coaching scorecard: A holistic approach to evaluating the benefits of business coaching. *International Journal of Evidence Based Coaching and Mentoring, 3*(2), 30–44.

McDermott, M., Levenson, A. & Newton, S. (2007). What coaching can and cannot do for your organization. *Human Resource Planning, 30*, 30–37.

Passmore, J., & Gibbes, C. (2007). The state of executive coaching research: What does the current literature tell us and what's next for coaching research? *International Coaching Psychology Review, 2*(2), 116–127.

Part III

Mentoring cases

19 Can a 'white-fella' be mentored using traditional 'black-fella' wisdom?[1]

Akram Sabbagh

Modern, western modalities of coaching and mentoring tend to focus on an intellectual 'thinking' baseline of applying frameworks, models and tools to specific issues or agendas. The focus is on 'doing'. Ancient wisdom and teaching-based cultures are more focused on ontological and experiential development and learning. The focus is on 'being'.

In the 21st-century business world, where leaders are seeking (intellectual) skills in the areas of mindfulness, purpose, engagement, storytelling, etc., this case study shows that these and other 'skills' do not need to be 'learned' as much as 'remembered' by exploring a mindset grounded on 'being' rather than 'doing'.

This chapter explores the use of traditional wisdom and ontological experience in the Australian Aboriginal context. Experiences drawn from field work in the Australian desert will be used to draw parallels to modern, western-based coaching modalities and it will be argued that the 'full circle is coming closer to being drawn' on providing holistic and sustainable change in the lives of those seeking it by using both western and locally based coaching and mentoring methodologies to create and manage change. In essence, combining the wisdom and process of ancient cultures with modern coaching methodologies, coaching and mentoring can provide the bridge to reconnect the ancient to the modern, the commercial and the cultural.

Akram Sabbagh is a Partner at AltusQ Australia. He has been a coach for more than 14 years and has over two decades of experience with national and international corporations. Nick 'Bodhi' Aldridge runs Bodhi Aldridge Coaching and is also a Partner in Spirit Adventure Tours Australia. Bodhi works with a wide range of individuals and organisations. He has a particular interest in working with young men looking for more in their career, starting their own business and interested in a holistic approach to life and work.

A process of discovery

Our contact to the inner world of ancient Aboriginal sacred rites, rituals and traditions is Nick 'Bodhi' Aldridge. Bodhi has been coaching business professionals for well over 16 years and in his previous work he was a successful commercial lawyer on the north coast of New South Wales.

AltusQ Australia Pty Ltd has known and worked with Bodhi for most of that time. He's partnered with us over the years to work with many of our clients across the country on the 'softer' and 'deeper' aspects of personal and professional development. In fact, we've often used Bodhi as a coach, guide and point of reference for how we are 'being' as a business.

Together with his business partner Andrew Leitch, Bodhi runs Spirit Adventure Tours, a company that takes people into the Australian desert to experience a depth of Aboriginal learning that cannot be found on the typical tourist track where the 'throwing of a boomerang' or the 'eating of a Witjuti[2] grub' shallowly defines a modern understanding of what is an ancient and noble culture.

For some years, Andrew and Bodhi have been taking people from all walks of life – lawyers, doctors, HR professionals and others in the professional and corporate world, to meet and work with Aboriginal elders like Uncle Mike.[3] On these 3–5 day excursions, the participants go through a process of discovery, awakening and healing and come away empowered to make (or not make) the choices needed for sustainable change (commercial and/or personal).

With the intention to empower and enrich the lives of people seeking change at work or at a personal level, Bodhi is using the power of one of the oldest living, unbroken cultures on the planet. It is a resilient culture with ancient lineage and tradition. It is a culture founded in the wisdom of centring one's self in a place of 'being'.

"Taking the typical executive who lives in a world of 'doing' and agendas, into a place of real 'being' can be a challenging thing. Especially in a world where most of us still intellectualise – rather than experience 'being'," Bodhi says.

With countless books being published on mindfulness and states of being, the modern world still lives within the construct of intellectualising the process. We rarely give ourselves the time, space or permission to really explore the depths of being or to experience the profound shifts that can occur once we reach those depths.

Using the tradition of dreamtime storytelling, rituals and experiences, ancient Aboriginal culture is helping to create sustainable change. This, it can be argued, is essentially one of the oldest ontological models in existence – one that encourages a state of *being* before acting from a state of *doing*.

In essence, the programme provides a 'Peak Experience' that serves as a contextual circuit breaker. Once the circuit is broken, the re-wiring that occurs is specific to the individual. The programme and process allows the participants to enter deep points of reflection as to what is flowing or not flowing in their world. With the clarity that only comes from deep reflection, participants are offered the opportunity to make choices that are often profound and life changing.

The time in the desert, and the participant's personal experiences there, provide an anchor point which can be used to bridge the ancient learnings with the modern expectation of 'action'.

But can a white-fella see the world through a black-fella's eyes? Yes. But first the white-fella must suspend their model of the world. Drop the various agendas running in their head, and drop the suppositions that they have to 'do' anything.

Meet Uncle Mike

Uncle Mike is a descendant of the Arremte people – originally one of the largest Aboriginal tribes of central Australia. He could best be described as an 'urban Aboriginal', growing up in the space between the world of the white man and the aboriginal. Dressed in jeans and an Akubra hat, Uncle Mike made a living as a jackaroo.[4] He was a hard worker, heavy smoker and an alcoholic.

His life changed the day that his grandfather pulled him aside and, encouraging him to change his ways, began sharing with him the teachings, rituals, customs and stories of his origins. Today Uncle Mike shares his wisdom and learning with those who are ready to open up to the opportunity of slowing down time and listening to the magic which occurs somewhere in the space between the dark of night and the light of day.

In the heart of our country, Uluru is one of Australia's most treasured and well-known landmarks. Close to 350 metres high and over nine kilometres in diameter, Uluru is more than a big rock in the desert. For the local Pitjantjatjara people, it is a sacred site. It is an ancient meeting place, watering hole and hunting ground. It is a place of deep spiritual significance and if you just stand there and 'be' with it, Uluru captivates you in ways that cannot be described.

At sunset and at dawn, Uluru is known for changing colour. But when observed during those times it is hard to discern the changes. You know it is happening but just cannot 'see' it. The best way of capturing these subtle changes is by taking photos. Then, on reviewing those photos, you can see how the rock changes colour – moment by moment.

It is in these shifts of colour – the spaces occurring *between the moments* that best describe the way Uncle Mike works with Aboriginal dreamtime stories and rituals to help people come to awareness and make the choices to change. Anthropologically, these spaces are called liminal spaces and were first defined in the West by Arnold van Gennep in 1909,[5] and re-discovered by Victor Turner in 1967 who broadened its application to apply to non-tribal societies.[6]

Liminality is the space 'between worlds' in ritual where participants are no longer in a pre-ritual state (a state of darkness) but have yet not begun the transition to full enlightenment when the ritual is complete. In a modern coaching context, we would often call this the 'point of awareness' or the moment between confusion and clarity – the 'ah-ha' moment.

Uncle Mike is a master of the liminal moment, creating these spaces for participants by taking them on a journey using the rituals, rites, stories and wisdom of his ancient heritage. It is a journey that helps people find their awakening between the dark and the light.

The experience and the story

Participants generally arrive in Alice Springs in the afternoon or evening, staying overnight in a local hotel. Before dinner they are met by Andrew and Bodhi and the group begin to get to know one another. Uncle Mike turns up towards the end of the evening.

The next morning, after breakfast, the group jump into four-wheel drives and head 'out bush'. It is an 80 km drive, but takes four hours to reach the destination. The group stops multiple times along the way, around every 20–30 minutes, to visit sacred places and hear stories of the local area. In essence this is a 'welcome to country' by Uncle Mike to the group.

With each stop along the way, and with every story told, the group get a deeper understanding of what it means to be in the desert, of the experiences living around them in the wildlife, trees, rocks and other structures. Gradually, through this process, the group is gently welcomed into Uncle Mike's country, the place he – and his spirit – were born into.

Ointments made from natural ingredients are placed upon members of the group as Uncle Mike describes the spiritual energies that go into each ointment and shows how the healing oils work to allow the body to absorb the creative spirit locked into the country. Along the way, there are stories about specific trees, hills or birds. The group experiences other rituals, all designed to invite them into and share in the opportunity that will unfold in the coming days.

Arriving at the Ross River camp site, the group sets up camp and settles in. The coming days will be filled with exploring the outer world of the bush, the desert, canyons and river beds as a context for journeying into the inner world of self-discovery and awareness. During this time Uncle Mike shares his stories and invites the participants to wander around to 'find your place in this place'. As one participant shares:

> I felt I was being drawn into what feels like the source of life itself … my modern self was stripped away to the core of who I am, allowing me to fully explore who I really am. It was a continual process of being immersed and being given amazing insights into the working of nature, the vibration of nature. We were then invited to explore how that vibration is working in us at that moment and stage in our lives, careers, etc.

After these points of personal reflection, the group re-forms to tell their stories, sing and share insights. This process provides the perfect balance between the individual and group conversations.

The energy within

In the context of discovering spirit and identity, the world around the group is used to create metaphor and meaning. Uncle Mike takes them to specific sacred places that are specific to gender. Sacred sites for men and women, and in some case, for both.

As an example, at one place, Uncle Mike introduces them to 'big daddy' and 'big mamma', two trees with baby trees around them. Big daddy tree has a girlfriend tree 'to the side' as well! The group is asked to be open to the *energetic* reality of these contexts and stories, to hold the perfection of masculinity and femininity, of the maternal, flirting energy of the female themes, as well as the lessons around loyalty versus playful masculine themes. Individuals are then asked to contemplate those energies within themselves, and how they manifest in life, home, work, etc.

Throughout the programme, each participant works on their own agenda and outcomes. For many, the results are profound shifts of insight, changes in perspective or personal agreements to make significant and life-altering changes. For others, the programme is an entry point for starting a journey of self-discovery and personal awareness. As one participant states,

> The best way to consider this programme is in the context of building 'spiritual fitness'. The US Army talks about three capacities of spiritual fitness: The first is the capacity to have a clear sense of self and purpose; the second, being able to access your own personal resources to enable you to fulfil that purpose; and the third, to take the first two and form meaningful connections with a diversity of people and situations in the outside world.

Another participant's perspective is that

> the programme enables me to build an inner confidence for when I go back into the modern world … the programme has opened my heart, mind and soul to how I relate to the world in general. I go back to the 'real world' fully re-charged. My personal meditation practice has also been enhanced greatly and will be something I put into daily practice.

Profound effects

The time, stories and experiences shared with Uncle Mike have a profound and long-lasting effect on those taking the journey. Building (or re-building) the inner sense of self, purpose and confidence are all outcomes shared by many participants of this programme. The outcomes manifest in various ways. Some use the experience to change their leadership and management styles and perspectives, other use the experience to achieve more personal goals like changing life choices around health, fitness, relationships, etc.

Combining the desire for professional or personal self-development with the wisdom and process that is manifest in ancient cultures can provide a powerful milieu for change. The use of stories and experiences are a powerful bridge between the ancient and the modern and despite the antiquity of some modalities, there is strong evidence to show that meaning can be found in context, regardless of the age of the modality.

"We are all visitors to this time, this place. We are just passing through. Our purpose here is to observe, to learn, to grow, to love ... and then we return home" – Aboriginal Proverb.

Notes

1 'White-fella' is an Aboriginal Australian term used to describe non-Aboriginals of European descent. It is not a term considered to have any racial or other prejudice associations. 'Black-fella' is similarly used to describe someone of Aboriginal descent.
2 Witjuti (or witchetty) grubs are the larvae of moths found in central Australia. The larvae feed on the roots of trees and have for millennia been a food source for traditional Aboriginal Australians.
3 Uncle Mike is not his real name. We have changed his name in respect of some Aboriginal tribal beliefs and rules regarding the publication of real names and/or photographic images.
4 A jackaroo is someone who works on sheep or cattle stations. They are generally involved with working on the land, mustering herds and other activities associated with work on rural properties.
5 Van Gennep, A. (2004). *The rites of passage*. London: Routledge Library Editions.
6 Turner, V. (1967). *The forest of symbols: Aspects of Ndembu ritual*. Ithaca, NY: Cornell University Press.

20 Mentoring within the Pacific Islands

Christopher Nunn

As a professional sports coach working at the Australian Institute of Sport for 13 years, the results of the athletes I coached reflected the 'value' I was to the organisation. If an athlete won a medal at an international competition, then I was a 'valuable asset'. However, after many years of achieving excellent results, it was not the technical aspects of coaching which gave me the greatest level of satisfaction, but rather the development of the athletes and other coaches I had the chance to work with.

I realised very early in my career that the greater the level of belief I could show in an individual, the greater self-belief they developed. Through an increase in confidence came a higher sense of self-worth and a greater level of commitment, which ultimately led to a better performance result. Interestingly, there is no Key Performance Indicator within elite sport which measured the role I played in the development of others. As a result I have stepped completely away from 'sports coaching' to 'personal coaching' and mentoring.

Whilst Australia presents many opportunities to work with a mentor or coach, my involvement with individuals from the Pacific Islands has highlighted the lack of access to personnel who can provide ongoing personal and workplace improvement.

Working with athletes with disabilities

I have been fortunate to be given the opportunity to work in the Pacific Islands through the Oceania Paralympic Committee which received funding to enhance the identification and pathways for athletes with disabilities and their coaches. The first country I worked with was Papua New Guinea (PNG) through its Paralympic Committee in 2008 at the National Sports Institute in Goroka. The Institute is extremely remote and a far cry from those you would find in Australia or throughout any European or North American city. I conducted the workshop with two other colleagues from Australia and at the time we felt we had met our objectives. However, despite two additional visits and the identification of several athletes with potential, we were unable to identify and develop the key staff to a level where the development of the athletes could be maintained.

In 2009, the Australian Prime Minister announced at the 40th Pacific Islands Forum the release of additional funds to establish and support sport partnerships between the Australian Government, Australian National Sports Organisations and Pacific Island counterparts. The Pacific Sports Partnerships (PSP) programme was established.

Table Tennis Australia and the Oceania Table Tennis Federation were successful in receiving a grant to implement a three-year programme with the objectives of building capacity of the local partners, promoting sustained increases in sports-related participation and contributing to positive social development outcomes. The islands of Fiji, Kiribati, Papua New Guinea and Vanuatu were the targeted countries in the first iteration of the Smash Down Barriers programme. Currently, the programme is operating in Fiji, Kiribati, Solomon Islands, Tonga and Vanuatu with a total team of 12 development officers.

The Smash Down Barriers programme

Heading up this programme was Mr Christian Holtz. At the time of his appointment Christian had no experience working in Pacific Island Countries nor was he a table tennis person. He was 'thrown in the deep end' with only three weeks to prepare before his first assignment, a six-week visit to Vanuatu. Due to the unique nature of the project, it was crucial that Christian visited each country for six weeks to assess the networks of disability organisations, gain the support of local ministries and initiate and sustain a table tennis disability programme. Pacific Islanders value personal relationships and therefore gaining the trust and friendships of local coaches and development officers was an essential part of the programme in order to maximise the sustainability of the programme and encourage a sense of ownership.

The approach taken by Christian has made a significant impact within the Pacific region. He had to form relationships with the development officers and understand the unique challenges involved in delivering a disability programme in each country. This task couldn't be completed remotely and thus Christian was required to visit each country for a period of six weeks to establish relationships and map the disability landscape. Christian identified development officers (DO) with capacity to undertake the roles he needed filling at a local level. He contacted every national coach and players registered with the Oceania Table Tennis Federation and worked alongside them during the six-week period, ultimately offering the successful candidates a role as a development officer of the Smash Down Barriers programme. During this period, Christian developed excellent rapport with the local organisations and the DOs, thus establishing an environment of open and honest communication. This was critical to the implementation of the mentoring programme.

Christian is based on the Gold Coast in Australia and is therefore geographically limited in the number of times he can visit the islands and work with the DOs face-to-face. Internet access is also limited at times which restricts the effectiveness of Skype and similar virtual modalities to enable effective immediate feedback. Therefore, Facebook was chosen as the mentoring modality between Christian and the DOs. Pacific Island countries are often a few years behind the rest of the world when it comes to adopting new technologies and Facebook is no exception. Facebook's popularity was increasing as each programme was firmly established and DOs and coaches were becoming increasingly more comfortable using social media. Facebook offers a number of communication channels that are perfect for virtual teams, including instant messaging, uploading photos and videos of activities, Facebook pages to centralise announcements and the use of hashtags to track activities.

The critical difference between the PSP programme overseen by Christian and that which was undertaken in PNG was the mentoring he implemented for each DO on a regular basis. Christian communicates with the team DOs daily using Facebook for updates and speaks with each individual to assess progress and identify areas of support. However, a more formal exchange occurs via email, especially when reporting or sending confidential, programme-wide announcements.

Christian adopted a pay-for-performance approach where communication is the top priority rather than actual performance. Therefore, all DOs must send a monthly progress report with participation data and brief summaries in order to receive their salaries. The actual performance doesn't affect their salaries but the lack of communication does. If a DO conducts 20 activities per week but doesn't report on any of them they add no value to the programme. Conversely, if a DO underperforms it is important to understand why this is occurring. Furthermore, because Christian established personal relationships with the disability organisations, they are invited to offer feedback on the programme and assess the performance of the DOs. This enabled Christian to collect a comprehensive picture of the programme and understand the needs of the disability organisations and the work done by the DOs. Finally, Christian visits each country in the programme on a quarterly basis; this allows him to assess progress and maintain the personal relationship with the DOs and participants of the programmes.

The significant element contributing to the establishment of the mentoring process was the amount of funding available to each programme. In PNG, funding was provided to conduct workshops only. The PSP programme provided significantly more funding which enabled Christian to be employed full time and, therefore, it was considered a component of his role to undertake the development of the DOs. He was able to build into his work schedule time to undertake a mentoring role.

This highlights the need for funding agencies to appropriately resource remote and regional programmes to ensure mentors have the time to work with the mentees. Without being able to develop relationships and provide regular feedback, progress through mentoring is limited. Unfortunately, none of the countries in the Pacific Islands have funds allocated for mentoring. The small amount of funding goes into sending personnel to other countries to undertake development opportunities and there is no evidence that the learning which takes place is effectively transferred to other locals on return, or if, in fact, there is any effort made to share the new knowledge with others. Without the Australian Government funds, the PSP programme would not exist and the mentoring within the islands would not be possible.

Working within cultures

The main challenge in establishing a mentoring programme in the Pacific region was gaining an understanding of the cultural and personal differences between Christian and each of the DOs. Pacific Islanders value and respond better to a leadership approach that is nurturing and values personal relationships over a transactional approach. One of the first observations noted by Christian was that the DOs started each day by greeting and catching up with work colleagues. Often the first 30 minutes of work would be spent doing this, even though they may have seen each other the previous day. So rather than 'diving into work' each morning, Christian would ask as to the well-being of the family, their upcoming plans, their ambitions and he would also ask questions about the culture and traditions of their communities. Spending six weeks working alongside each DO allowed Christian to form strong relationships and gain a better understanding of the intricacies of each culture. Christian stated "I learnt more about cross-cultural management in the first six weeks of the programme than I ever could at university. Three years later and I'm still learning about them and about myself."

In addition to the PSP programme the Australian Department of Foreign Affairs and Trade also provides funding for the Australian Awards Fellowships. During 2015, I was working with a colleague from the University of Canberra and with the support of the Australian Paralympic Committee we successfully applied for funding to conduct a three-week tour of Australia titled 'Enhancing Sport: A Targeted Program for Sport Leaders and Senior Sport Officers'. This programme included series of workshops covering topics such as disadvantaged schools, inclusive practices, integrated sports practices, understanding behaviour and engagement with the 2018 Commonwealth Games Organising Committee.

Normally the process of identifying Islanders who warrant access to this intensive learning opportunity is a little 'hit and miss'. People often nominate for the programme knowing that if successful they will be given the opportunity to travel to Australia, experience various locations and enjoy a quality of accommodation and food which is not possible within their islands. For example, participants from Kiribati live on an island which has an elevation of three metres and no building has more than two storeys. As part of the tour they were accommodated in a 26-storey building with views over the entire Gold Coast in Australia; this was a 'life experience'.

With the effective implementation of the PSP programme we were able to attract excellent calibre Fellows. Christian played a key role in nominating individuals he had established mentoring relationships with and who he knew would have the capacity to benefit from the Australian Awards Fellowship programme. He was able to brief each person prior to their engagement about their particular focus during the Fellowship programme which would assist them on their return to the islands.

The quality of the relationship Christian had with the Fellows nominated from the PSP programme allowed for open conversations with all involved. The Fellows who had the benefit of Christian's mentoring were more engaged from the start of the Fellowship programme. They had a higher level of self-confidence than many others who were not in a mentoring relationship and were better equipped to engage in meaningful discussion with the various workshops. It was evident that their engagement was a direct reflection of the quality of mentoring they had received and their willingness to be mentored.

As recently as November 2016, I conducted two workshops in Kiribati through funding provided by the Agitos Foundation, which is the development arm of the International Paralympic Committee and since 2012 has become "the leading global organisation for developing Para sport as a tool for changing lives and contributing to an inclusive society for all". The key focus is to distribute resources and expertise to parts of the world where they are most needed and the Agitos Foundation recognises that para-sport is all too often expensive, unavailable or not well-promoted, especially in developing nations.

Each of the above programmes have been mentioned for good reasons. Given my awareness and roles with each of the funding programmes, PSP (through Christian), the Australian Awards Fellowships and the Agitos Foundation, I have been able to maintain a 'global view' of development for various individuals within the Pacific region. Individually, funding for each programme is limited and thus ongoing development of personnel is restricted. Collectively, they provide a greater number of contact opportunities for Pacific personnel, who can then engage in opportunities to further develop their skills and receive mentoring and feedback.

Case study

An example of how this collective approach works can be seen through a PSP development officer in Kiribati, Mr Tokannata Ioatene (Toka). Toka was appointed as one of the table tennis development officers within Kiribati. Christian visited the island and identified the work which needed to be done and, together with Toka, travelled to various schools and organisations, explaining the mentoring programme and contract requirements.

After several months working within the PSP programme and maintaining regular contact, Christian then successfully nominated Toka for an Australian

Awards Fellowship. As part of the Fellowship programme, Christian was invited to speak with the group about two specific objectives. First, to provide an overview to all the participants of the work he was undertaking within the Pacific and, second, to enable the opportunity for Christian to meet with the PSP participants face-to-face whilst on the Gold Coast.

During November 2016, I conducted two workshops in Kiribati for the Oceania Paralympic Committee through the Agitos Foundation. In order to organise the logistics for my visit we called on Toka to act as the Kiribati liaison for me. Toka was briefed by Christian as to the objectives of the visit and provided direction as to who was required to attend and the processes involved in having everything in place for the visit.

Without question the Kiribati para-sport workshops have been the most successful to date within the Pacific islands. On each day of the workshops, more than 50 delegates attended, almost double the number from other islands with bigger populations. The dissemination of information, arrangements for meetings, venue bookings, meal arrangements and transport for locals to attend the workshops were all undertaken by Toka. (Side note: this involved hiring a truck to load and transfer the wheelchair users as the mini-buses do not cater for wheelchairs in the islands!)

I need to point out here that the skills exhibited by Toka in preparing for these workshops would be expected of a university graduate. However, within the Pacific region my experience has been that these skills are rarely exhibited by people working at a community level equivalent to the role Toka performs. Toka was able to implement many of the things he had learnt through his relationship with Christian and engage a wide range of people from athletes, coaches, teachers, and people with disabilities through to the High Commissioners from Australia and New Zealand and the President of the Kiribati Paralympic Committee. He was methodical, organised and not fazed by hierarchy or protocol.

There is no doubt the skills developed by Toka are evidence that the quality of mentoring provided by Christian and the processes he implemented have been incredibly effective. Christian has a greater level of mentoring engagement through the better funded PSP programme than either the Australian Awards Fellowship Program or the Agitos funded workshops. However, collectively the programmes provide a wonderful opportunity for individuals within the Pacific region.

Mentoring is integral to successful outcomes

I have cited just one example here, but there are several others within the Pacific islands. Mentoring as part of the PSP programme has been integral to the successful outcomes. Since the inception of the Smash Down Barriers programme in February 2014, the programme has expanded in terms of funding, scope and, more importantly, participants. As at November 2016, there are currently 762 people with disability participating in ongoing table tennis activities across five countries in the Pacific. Of those participants, 44% are female and on average each person is engaged for 3.5 hours per week. The data indicate a significant increase in the levels of physical activity by people with disability. Furthermore, the programme aims to promote the social inclusion of people with disability in Pacific communities. For this reason, Christian collects 'stories of change' to capture individual experiences focusing on a person's sense of belonging before and after their involvement with table tennis.

In summary, the experience from within remote islands of the Pacific region highlights the importance of mentoring in the development of human potential. Organisations and funding agencies supporting programmes for development must therefore consider the following:

1　Mentoring is the most effective method to build capacity within the Pacific islands.
2　Time must be given to enable the mentor to develop a meaningful relationship based on cultural awareness with the mentee.
3　Financial allocations must be adequate enough to enable effective mentoring programmes to be implemented.
4　Funding agencies should consider long-term programmes as a priority to increase the likelihood of enabling sustainable change.
5　Workshops are an effective method of introducing the roles of the mentor and the mentee but must be followed up with regular mentoring.
6　Once the relationship is established, mentoring is most effective via email in remote regions.

21 The Mentoring for Effective Teaching (MET) programme

Peter Hudson and Suzanne Hudson

The MET programme

This is a case study about an Australian award-winning mentoring programme, the Mentoring for Effective Teaching (MET) programme. MET aims to facilitate understandings and skills for advancing mentoring and teaching practices for mentees (e.g. preservice teachers and beginning teachers). The MET programme is based on a five-factor model originating from Peter Hudson's PhD thesis in 2004. More than 10 years on, the MET programme, which has undergone continuous development, has had an impact nationally and internationally.

The MET programme is evidence-based. There have been more than 40 research papers in journals and refereed conferences around the MET programme over the last six years that assist to provide evidence of what works, why it works and what requires further development (see http://eprints.qut. edu.au/view/person/Hudson,_Peter.html). The research embedded within the MET programme aims to advance the various components of the programme. To illustrate, the first session in MET outlines the importance of the mentor-mentee relationship where the mentor willingly accepts the role. Analysis from eight MET programmes (approximately 25–30 participants in each programme) indicated distinct mentor actions for forming and sustaining the mentor-mentee relationship. Responses were collated into themes (Creswell, 2014). Participants claimed that a two-way sharing of experiences for learning about each other would initially help to form the relationship. Respect and trust were shown at the centre of this two-way interaction (see Figure 21.1, see also Hudson, 2013a). Ongoing mentor support, sharing of teaching practices and resources with collaborative problem solving were actions claimed to further form and sustain the relationship. The model and related information were then incorporated into future MET sessions.

As another example, specific to mentoring teaching practices, 24 mentors observed a final-year preservice teacher through a professionally video-recorded lesson in the MET programme and provided written notes for feedback. Findings showed that the mentors' written feedback varied considerably when open-ended observations occurred and could be categorised within

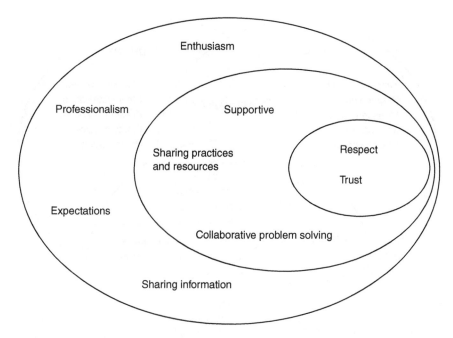

Figure 21.1 Model for forming and sustaining the mentor-mentee relationship.

three domains (i.e. visual, auditory and conceptual). For instance, Figure 21.2 outlines the positive feedback provided by these mentors within the three domains (see also Hudson, 2013b). Figure 21.2 was then incorporated into future MET sessions on feedback to highlight the domains of mentor observation.

Researching into mentoring promoted the development of instruments to measure participant views and to gather first-hand data. To explain, each MET session had graphic organisers to facilitate participant engagement. Session three is about understanding the mentor's personal attributes that help to engage with a mentee. A graphic organiser provides a structure with six key attributes (e.g. attentive listening, comfortable with talking, instilling confidence and positive attitudes) where participants record their thoughts about how to develop these attributes. Data from participants who had signed research consent forms were used to put forward strategies for developing personal attributes in future participants. Similarly, a number of Likert scale instruments (strongly agree to strongly disagree) were developed to gauge participant viewpoints on specific components of the mentoring programme, which were also used as evaluative tools. Many of these instruments have been published.

Australia has produced many education reform recommendations over the last decade (e.g. Commonwealth of Australia, 2007; Masters, 2009), emphasising

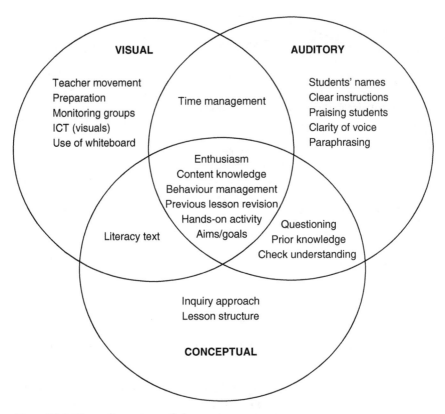

Figure 21.2 Three dimensions of observation.

that teaching and teacher education must change to improve educational opportunities for all. Research (Hudson, 2010) shows that mentoring pre-service teachers is varied in both quality and quantity, thus part of education reform involves embedding mentoring for enhancing preservice teacher education. In 2009, Peter Hudson and Suzanne Hudson received a significant structural reform and diversity grant while at Queensland University of Technology (QUT) from which they took the opportunity to advance the two-day Mentoring for Effective Teaching (MET) programme. During the grant period (2009–2011), various QUT staff, school principals and school executives refined the MET programme as a train-the-trainer model over an 18-month period.

As statements of impact, the MET programme has been delivered to more than 25 Australian institutes with over 1,200 facilitators trained and involvement from more than 1,000 school representatives. In addition, MET has been delivered internationally, including Manila's University of the East and Hong Kong University. The programme received an Australian citation award in 2012 and a coveted national programme award in 2013.

Mentoring beginning teachers

The vision for the MET programme is to empower classroom teachers, in their roles as mentors and co-educators, to provide mentees (preservice teachers and beginning teachers) with insightful learning experiences when they enter schools.

MET is based around a theoretical and empirically tested five-factor model that emanated from the generic literature on mentoring in education, which can be summarised as follows:

1   analysing the mentor's personal attributes, which surround the mentoring process;
2   mentoring system requirements, particularly with the inclusion of a national or state curriculum;
3   articulating pedagogical knowledge practices for differentiated learning;
4   modelling teaching practices; and
5   providing quality feedback to the preservice teachers.

Other key components in the MET programme (conducted as 10 one-hour sessions) include: developing and sustaining the mentor-mentee relationship (i.e. the professional relationship between the classroom teacher and the preservice teacher); inducting mentees into the school culture and infrastructure; analysing feedback tools for mentors and mentees to employ within the school setting; instilling the notion that a mentoring role is a leadership role; and providing ways for mentors to advance their own practices through action research.

As education reform emphasises mentoring as a way forward for the teaching profession, enlisting participants was initially organised through the principals and school executives who were proponents in the programme development. As a train-the-trainer programme, MET continues to have considerable influence and impact. For instance, a deputy principal from an Education Queensland state school, who was trained as a MET facilitator, took 18 dedicated teaching staff through the two-day MET programme over a weekend. The deputy principal later wrote in an email,

> I truly believe this program has had an impact on the way teachers will mentor students [preservice teachers] in the future. It also had the added benefit of encouraging them to reflect on their own practices and hopefully build mentoring relationships within our staff in the future.

Prominently, endorsement from the New South Wales Institute of Teachers (now Board of Studies, Teaching and Educational Studies NSW) for a five-year period has helped participant uptake of the MET programme. In addition to participants seeking out MET training, the programme is offered free of charge to school and university staff associated with QUT and Southern

Cross University as part of giving back to the wider community; however, there are fees for others to ensure programme sustainability.

Positive responses to the MET programme

Across Australia, participants have commented on how the MET programme provides insights. As a testament, a teacher from Bertram Primary School in Western Australia (WA) emailed, "I was privileged to go through the MET course last year at Murdoch University. I am soon facilitating the course in regional WA to some teachers and supervisors." Similarly, a senior lecturer from Charles Darwin University in her role as a MET co-facilitator wrote,

> Well, we did it! We facilitated a day for both mentor teachers mentoring preservice teachers and Assistant Teachers/tutors who are mentoring non-indigenous teachers new to the school community. The feedback was very good with clear mention made of the clarity, focus and organisation of the first 5 units that we delivered. Many thanks again for a splendid program, both for participants and facilitators.

MET has been cited in seminal reports such as Renshaw's (2012) report outlining that the programme is well recognised and the Caldwell and Sutton (2010) report, which further demonstrates the systemic nature of its reach and impact.

Internationally, participants from Asian universities involved in the programme have responded positively. For example, Dr Cheri Chan from Hong Kong University (HKU) wrote,

> The MET workshop was very inspiring for all the participants. It made me reflect a lot on the current practices of mentoring in the HK socio-cultural context. So the MET workshop has empowered me to move forward to think about what I can do about this.

Associate Professor Tammy Kwan from HKU also noted,

> How nice to have gone through your two-day wonderful, wonderful MET workshop! I felt I have been refreshed by learning from you. I also felt confirmed of what we have been doing here in our Faculty that we share our passion, mission and vision in a very, very similar way. I am thrilled to see the participants being so involved, so willing to take part and to share in this powerful learning journey.

Various staff from Philippine universities became MET facilitators in a programme conducted at the University of the East in January 2015. Evaluative responses indicated that many of the participants will implement the MET programme in their own educational contexts.

What we've learnt

Involvement in mentoring for over a decade has led towards considerable learning about this valued field for building teaching capacity. Reading through the literature and conducting research around mentoring have provided professional insights into getting the most from our mentors and, consequently, the most from our mentees. We have learnt that mentors require real-world examples of effective mentoring practices with significant opportunities for sharing knowledge and experiences. We have learnt that developing models and associated strategies can be used as a way for continued advancement of the mentoring programme. In addition, we have learnt that mentoring is not inherent but rather requires strong theoretical frameworks based on evidence to guide the mentor's practices.

To date, MET has been delivered to representatives from seven schools in Alice Springs and various rural areas in South Australia. The plans for the future include offering the programme to those in more remote areas across Australia. The Australian Government supports and advocates mentoring as a way to build capacity. MET will continue to grow by embedding further research into the programme components and by embedding educational reform measures such as mentoring with stronger links to the Australian Curriculum.

References

Caldwell, B., & Sutton, D. (2010). *Review of teacher education and induction: First report, full report*. Brisbane: Queensland Government.

Commonwealth of Australia. (2007). *Top of the class: Report on the inquiry into teacher education*. Retrieved 17 August 2017, from www.curriculum.edu.au/leader/top_of_the_class,18080.html?issueID=10733.

Creswell, J. W. (2014). *Educational research: Planning, conducting, and evaluating quantitative and qualitative research* (4th edn). Upper Saddle River, NJ: Pearson Education Inc.

Hudson, P. (2010). Mentors report on their own mentoring practices. *Australian Journal of Teacher Education, 35*(7), 30–42.

Hudson, P. (2013a). Developing and sustaining successful mentoring relationships. *Journal of Relationships Research, 4*. doi: http://dx.doi.org/10.1017/jrr.2013.1.

Hudson, P. (2013b). Feedback consistencies and inconsistencies: Eight mentors' observations on one preservice teacher's lesson. *European Journal of Teacher Education*. doi: 10.1080/02619768.2013.801075.

Masters, G. N. (2009). *A shared challenge: Improving literacy, numeracy and science learning in Queensland primary school*. Camberwell, Victoria: Australian Council for Educational Research.

Renshaw, P. (2012). *Literature review and environmental scan supervising professional experience students*. Education Services Australia. Retrieved 10 December 2012, from www.aitsl.edu.au/verve/_resources/Supervising_Professional_Experience_Students_LiteratureReview_June2012.pdf.

22 To mentor or not to mentor

A mentor speaks

Ya-Hui Kuo

As the mentor in this study, I report on my first experience on mentoring a new graduate (Maggie, whom I had taught as a senior in college). Being a mentor of a college student was like being a mother taking care of a new-born baby who demanded a great deal of attention and guidance as he/she grew up. Mentoring is a unique interpersonal relationship between two individuals (Janasz, Behson, Jonsen & Lankau, 2013). In fact, it is a life-long relationship that does not end or go away even after the baby turns into an adult or, as in Maggie's case, graduates from college. Thus, being asked to serve as a mentor was a great honour for me. It was also a great motivation for me to help Maggie, a student from the Department of Foreign Language Instruction, become a more effective student/researcher.

Mentoring undergraduates or mentoring undergraduate research has never been the focus or practice in Taiwan. This may be one reason why Maggie had been turned down by six teachers prior to meeting me. This research focuses on one mentor and mentee relationship and the challenging and rewarding experience of being a mentor.

The current study was based on my own experience as a mentor, so reflexivity was adopted throughout the research process. Reflexivity helps with understanding how researchers construct meaning (Gilbert & Sliep, 2009). Additionally, reflexivity is a significant part of the data because researchers reflected on their participation in the study (Atkins & Williams, 1995). It facilitates the understanding of the research process (Watt, 2007). Furthermore, Dowling (2006) indicated that applying reflexivity in research, researchers should be aware of their relationship to the research topic and people involved in the research.

I knew that researchers do have influence on data generation and interpretation and insights of the phenomenon researched (Buckner, 2005). Thus, applying reflexivity in this study can be viewed as a means of adding credibility to the research (Dowling, 2006) and can provide the evidence for sound qualitative research (Johnson & Waterfield, 2004). Furthermore, to assure that I presented the results accurately, I contacted Maggie and presented the study to her personally and invited her to make any comments.

I also invited Maggie's feedback and comments on the study as a further way of ensuring the credibility and trustworthiness of the present study.

Beginning a mentoring relationship

Prior to reading the mentoring articles I provided, Maggie knew nothing about mentoring or the role of a mentor. Yet, prior to meeting and working with me, Maggie clearly explained what assistance she would like from a mentor. She expressed a wish that she wanted to do research with a faculty member and she was looking for someone who could read what she read and grow with her. Planning to study for a Masters in the United States was probably the most important reason Maggie sought a mentor to help her gain research experience in preparation for thesis writing. After all, mentors are good resources for gaining research experience (Hughes & Fahy, 2009). The added benefit of having a positive and meaningful research experience at the undergraduate level would inspire confidence and motivation in an undergraduate such as Maggie to pursue advanced degrees and a career in research (Abdel-Qader, 2004; Abudayyeh, 2003). Most importantly, mentoring provides "rich one-on-one mentoring experiences, guidance/preparation for graduate school, and career and hands-on-research experience" as stated by Horowitz and Christopher (2013).

I told Maggie that I was honoured and glad that I was able to help her. I learned from Maggie that I was not the first faculty member she had asked to mentor her in doing research. Maggie said that she had wanted to get involved in research as a sophomore, but had been turned down by six teachers for various reasons. One teacher, for example, told Maggie her focus should be on learning English, not doing research. In contrast, I had always been approachable and generous with time. Thus, when Maggie responded to my invitation to come to her for anything, this mentoring relationship evolved.

Challenges and dilemmas

The foremost challenge I encountered was to think back to my own experience as a mentee at graduate school and as a faculty member. Casto, Caldwell and Salazar (2005) wrote a research paper about their own experiences of a mentoring relationship to provide guidelines for mentoring relationships. They reported that a mentor who did not have his or her own mentor as a new faculty member or as a graduate student might feel ill-prepared or reluctant to become a mentor herself/himself. On the other hand, mentors' own experiences as students and faculty influence how they mentor their mentees. I, from time to time, would tell Maggie that I admired her and wished I could have had a mentor at school. After all, I had no mentor like those in the Rippe (2001) study who had regular meetings with their mentees when I was a graduate or undergraduate student.

Nor had I had the same experiences as those in the Katz and Coleman (2001) study in which the mentee presented several papers at conferences with her mentor. In addition, I wondered why she herself didn't contact her supervisor for advice, resources, support, or didn't simply just email her supervisor regarding what she has been up to after graduation. I think her situation was like participants said in the Rippe (2001) study: a change in location, the feeling that the supervisor and supervisee relationship was meant to be short term, and not feeling a connection with the mentor all resulted in not anticipating further contact.

Mentors themselves find publishing hard to do even though publication of research is one of the standards of academic excellence. I did want to put pressure on Maggie to publish, to collect data or to write for publication. After all, mentors play an important role in helping mentees preparing manuscripts (Straus, Chatur & Taylor, 2009). Furthermore, supervisors' involvement in undergraduate researchers' research is the key to success (Mah, 2013). Yet, in reality, both I and Maggie at times were overwhelmed by our respective responsibilities at school as faculty members and as a senior college graduate. Consequently, publishing became impossible since it needed time and patience.

Additionally, Maggie had many extra-curricular activities such as tutoring a young boy with Asperger syndrome, being a teaching assistant, auditing a graduate class and working as a part-time assistant to a retired professor. Those activities took away from her time to publish or get a research paper done. Therefore, at times when Maggie seemed not to be doing her work, I was encouraging rather than being judgemental.

At the same time, the mentor acknowledges the importance of regular meetings with Maggie and also believes time is a valuable commodity a mentor can offer to his or her mentee (Pita, Ramirez, Joacin, Prentice & Clarke, 2013). Simply, regular meetings allow mentors to check progress, answer questions and minimize potential miscommunication concerning with mentees' research (Mah, 2013). Yet, the next challenge I and other mentors might encounter is to find the suitable or best time for regular weekly meetings with mentees. After all, many mentors might be married and their duties at school and in the family can be overwhelming sometimes. In addition, many mentees might have a full-time or part-time job. As a result of busy and different class or working schedules, both parties have personal and professional responsibilities which make demands on their time.

(Not) setting boundaries

I met with Maggie on a weekly basis during the school year. However, that year, I had a heavy teaching load and meeting weekly with Maggie meant that I had no time for a short break or something to eat. In addition, depending on the length and number of the articles I and Maggie were reading, the discussion could be as short as one hour or as long as three hours. This reduced the time I could spend before my evening class. She was especially stressed at the times she had a fully booked schedule and was afraid that she did not spend enough time for class preparation.

Furthermore, I was surprised to learn that Maggie did not want a break when school was not in session. When a mentee expresses her/his desire to continue working with the mentor during the break, a mentor who wants to be a good mentor has no reason to turn her down. In addition, I did not want to or give Maggie the feeling that she occupied my time even when she did. For many mentors, that could be an issue. After all, school break is an important time for faculty to recharge themselves after the pressure of teaching, doing research and outreach work.

Additionally, at first, there were times when Maggie was late for the meeting. Excuses such as she overslept were truly unacceptable or irresponsible. I was disappointed. Instead of blaming her, I gave Maggie a few mentoring articles in which mentors in the study indicated their disappointment at having unpunctual and undedicated mentees. I discussed those mentors' concerns with Maggie at the next meeting. Subsequently, Maggie would call if she could not make it or would be late for the meeting. I can only say that Maggie would have been a more disciplined mentee if I had initially corrected Maggie's behaviour as it happened. I should have discussed with Maggie how often and in what manner she established contact.

The mentor's role

Many mentors would agree with Abdel-Qader (2004) that mentoring students to do research is not an easy task. It is especially challenging with undergraduates who are not used to searching for information. Instead, they demand quick answers from mentors.

According to Scott (n.d.), a mentor is a person who makes a mentee feel more confident about the steps he/she takes. Furthermore, mentors are experienced people or role models who are sources of guidance and wisdom. Mentees in the Milner and Bossers (2004) study of mentor group relationships in an occupational therapy university curriculum reported their desired qualities of a mentor as someone who is wise, insightful, honest, approachable, inspiring, enlightening, professional, friendly, personable, encouraging, a good communicator, trustworthy, respectful, a role model/leader, dedicated, enthusiastic, willing to share ideas and perspectives and learn from mentees.

Similarly, Hudson (2005) examined 331 preservice science teachers' perceptions of their mentors' personal attributes and found that having a mentor who is supportive, attentive and comfortable in talking about teaching does help mentees' teaching practice. Indeed, supportiveness is a vital component of a successful mentor's character (Cramer & Prentice-Dunn, 2007). Furthermore, a mentee in the Kamvounias, McGrath-Champ and Yip (2008) study described a mentor as someone a mentee can look up to and someone who is interested in mentees' interests. Mentors are also people who sometimes might put mentees ahead of their own interests. Katz and Coleman (2001) indicated that mentors are those who are willing and enjoying committing time and energy to help mentees. Additionally, mentors should be people who believe their mentee is worth helping. Therefore, mentors should never penalize or criticize mentees (Brown, 2004). According to Hughes and Fahy (2009), the nature of the mentor-student relationship is voluntary and primarily very informal. However, it needs to be noted that not everyone is a competent mentor and arranged mentor-mentee matching are not always ideal (Darwin & Palmer, 2009).

Mentoring undergraduate research is a very time-consuming process. While some mentors find editing writing style and correcting formatting time-intensive (Jensen, Martin, Mann & Fogarty, 2004), many mentors find scheduling time to meet with mentees is the major challenge for them. However, I was surprised to find that mentees and mentors met so frequently in the Rippe (2001) study of the benefits of a mentoring programme at the University of Nebraska Omaha. Mentees in the Rippe (2001) study met with their mentors anywhere from daily to every two weeks. All mentees in the study said they met with their mentors on a regular basis even when they were still in their coursework in the university. I was surprised to learn that Mentee F, a high school teacher in Rippe's (2001) study, stated that his mentor, with whom he worked to develop a website for the building, updated him at least twice daily and that they spent a minimum of 15 minutes daily together. Generally, it is rare to have a mentor who could devote time to mentees every day.

Having experts as mentors to inexperienced mentees can be a challenging task for both mentors and mentees. For example, Shim and Roth (2007) studied how expert teaching professors transfer their knowledge to mentees. They reported that very often experts may not able to explain how they do their jobs or exactly what they know. A mentee in their study also commented on shadowing her mentor and observing how she interacted with students. The mentee said she could learn, view, feel and see how her mentor did that, but her mentor really could not put it into words.

Unlike a teacher, whose responsibility mainly focuses on class teaching, a mentor does more than teach. A mentor usually has a mission to help mentees succeed in their professions and fulfil their needs. Furthermore, having a mentee is like raising a child. Parents are excited to have children, but they feel their hands are tied when it comes to educating their children and have limited time to spend with them. Similarly, mentors want to share the success of mentees, but they do not have time or do not want to devote too much time to mentees. No doubt, not all mentees can succeed without help from mentors. In the following, I discuss my challenging and rewarding experiences being a mentor to my mentee, Maggie.

Challenges and rewards

Reading and discussing articles with a mentee does not sound like a lot of work for a mentor. Maggie, at first, would send articles to me which she had read or was planning to read. I was indeed glad to read all of them and to discuss them with Maggie. However, there were times when I was over-loaded with my own work and reading those could disturb my schedule or delay the original proposed working schedule. Furthermore, at first, it took me some time to digest the Asperger syndrome articles that Maggie was interested in.

Additionally, the way I read Maggie's articles were different to the way I would read my research articles. Instead, I read as if preparing a lesson plan. After all, I was not sure if Maggie could comprehend all the articles despite the fact that those articles were chosen and sent by her. However, later in the meetings, articles tended to be chosen by me, so I was fully prepared for dis-cussion. Thus, this was not a problem. Yet, it did raise another question: when the readings originate mainly from me, does that mean Maggie is relying on the mentor and she is not making any progress in searching the literature? Perhaps I should have used literature as a reference to teach Maggie how to research, like Rivera did with his mentees (2014).

The Atkins and Williams (1995) study registered nurses' experiences of mentoring undergraduate nursing students. I experienced a similar satisfaction from working with Maggie as those mentors in their study. Mentors in their study said that it was quite a nice feeling to see that mentees had taken their advice and had done something positive and creative. Throughout the men-toring, I taught Maggie how to organize the literature review and the import-ance of organizing knowledge especially when doing research. I showed Maggie her own filing system and how to retrieve articles easily. I was pleased to learn when I visited her that Maggie had adopted the practical advice and examples of organizational strategies she had been offered. Mentors can point mentees in the correct direction or even open doors for them, but mentors cannot do the work for them (Advice to mentees, 1997).

A mentee in the Lee (2008) study expressed that he/she wanted to call his/her supervisor the moment she/he solved the tough math problem. Sim-ilarly, the mentee, Maggie, in this study shared all the good things that hap-pened in her life including passing the first screening of the school's outstanding student competition, earning it afterward and being reported in the newspaper with the mentor who had spent all day with her to get her recommendation letter out. Interestingly, Maggie told me that, if students were selected as outstanding students, teachers who wrote recommendation letters would join the celebration luncheon with school officials. I felt greatly honoured by that. In the event, I was not invited to the luncheon with those selected outstanding students, but Maggie's homeroom teacher was. Despite that, I was surprised and touched when later Maggie came to my office and asked to have a photo taken with me the day she received the recognition plate from school. Maggie has been very grateful to me. Having a mentee who remembers and appreciates what a mentor has done for her/him and to her/him means a great deal to a mentor.

Reciprocal learning

I have learnt greatly from mentoring Maggie, especially from her personal development. I agree with Lee et al. (2006) that mentees should not underestimate their professional knowledge. On the other hand, mentees might offer a lot of information, knowledge and enthusiasm to their mentors in return for their support. Mentoring Maggie helped me learn what the new generation is thinking, doing, surfing, eating, expecting and hoping.

While I attempted to teach Maggie, Maggie taught me in return. For example, by passing articles to me for discussion, Maggie introduced me to sources that I would not normally have come across. Additionally, Maggie had been the tutor of a boy with Asperger syndrome for two years. I got to know and compare the Asperger syndrome learners to what I read and heard. This helped me to reflect on my own teaching style and method in class in which there might have been Asperger syndrome learners.

Furthermore, during the mentoring process, the mentor also learns how to be a good role model – role modelling is another good method for mentees to learn from mentors. On the other hand, mentees learn through observing their mentors (Jones, 2013). However, I also believe that not all mentors are comfortable with having mentees job shadowing what they are doing. Nonetheless, Atkins and Williams (1995), looking at registered nurses' experiences of mentoring undergraduate nursing students, found that a mentor believed her mentee's presence as an observer had facilitated learning even though she knew observing how nurses interact closely with patients was not easy. As another mentor said in the Atkins and Williams (1995) study, role modelling will push mentors' desire to do things properly. Similarly, I wanted Maggie to learn research skills from me and, more importantly, that I could be a role model for her. Thus, I hope my own desire for learning and reading could make me a good role model for Maggie.

The feeling of being a mentor is quite interesting because the researcher becomes very protective and takes her mentee under her wing. The mentor wants her mentee to do well and she feels like she needs to help her succeed. Maggie was well nurtured; she should have no regrets about her college life as I had contributed to her success.

I believe being a mentor will help teachers develop a bond with students. It is only when the mentor and mentee both have the same or a similar research interest that the mentor is able to provide sound advice. I and a mentor in the Lee (2008) study both believe that a mentor's job is to get mentees to the stage of knowing more than the mentor. It is my hope that colleges and universities will develop a mentoring programme for undergraduates.

References

Abdel-Qader, I. (2004). An undergraduate research mentoring model in digital signal and image processing. *International Journal of Electrical Engineering Education, 41*(2), 146–302.

Abudayyeh, O. (2003). Undergraduate research mentoring model in construction engineering and management. *Journal of Construction Engineering & Management, 129*(1), 65–69.

Advice to mentees: How to get the most from the relationship. (1997). *Getting results … for the hands-on manager: Office edition, 42*(4), 2. Retrieved from Business Source Premier database.

Atkins, S., & Williams, A. (1995). Registered nurses' experiences of mentoring undergraduate nursing students. *Journal of Advanced Nursing, 21*(5), 1006–1015.

Brown, W. K. (2004). Resiliency and the mentoring factor. *Reclaiming Children & Youth, 13*(2), 75–79.

Buckner, S. (2005). Taking the debate on reflexivity further: Psychodynamic team analysis of a BNIM interview. *Journal of Social Work Practice, 19*(1), 59–72.

Casto, C., Caldwell, C. & Salazar, C. F. (2005). Creating mentoring relationships between female faculty and students in counselor education: Guidelines for potential mentees and mentors. *Journal of Counseling & Development, 83*(3), 331–336.

Cramer, R. J., & Prentice-Dunn, S. (2007). Caring for the whole person: Guidelines for advancing undergraduate mentorship. *College Student Journal, 41*(4), 771–778.

Darwin, A., & Palmer, E. (2009). Mentoring circles in higher education. *Higher Education Research & Development, 28*(2), 125–136.

Dowling, M. (2006). Approaches to reflexivity in qualitative research. *Nurse Researcher, 13*(3), 7–21.

Gilbert, A., & Sliep, Y. (2009). Reflexivity in the practice of social action: From self- to inter-relational reflexivity. *South African Journal of Psychology, 39*(4), 468–479.

Horowitz, J., & Christopher, K. B. (2013). The research mentoring program: Serving the needs of graduate and undergraduate researchers. *Innovative Higher Education, 38*, 105–116.

Hudson, P. (2005). Mentors' personal attributes for enhancing their mentees' primary science teaching. *Teaching Science: The Journal of the Australian Science Teachers Association, 51*(2), 31–34.

Hughes, A., & Fahy, B. (2009). Implementing an undergraduate psychology mentoring program. *North American Journal of Psychology, 11*(3), 463–469.

Janasz, S. D., Behson, S. J., Jonsen, K. & Lankau, M. L. (2013). Dual sources of support for dual roles: How mentoring and work-family culture influence work-family conflict and job attitudes. *The International Journal of Human Resource Management, 24*(7), 1435–1453.

Jensen, B. E., Martin, K. A., Mann, B. L. & Fogarty, T. (2004). Easing your pain: A method for evaluating research writing from students. *Measurement in Physical Education & Exercise Science, 8*(1), 43–52.

Johnson, R., & Waterfield, J. (2004). Making words count: The value of qualitative research. *Physiotherapy Research International, 9*(3), 121–131.

Jones, J. (2013). Factors influencing mentees' and mentors' learning throughout formal mentoring relationships. *Human Resource Development International, 16*(4), 390–408.

Kamvounias, P., McGrath-Champ, S. & Yip, J. (2008). 'Gifts' in mentoring: Mentees' reflections on an academic development program. *International Journal for Academic Development, 13*(1), 17–25.

Katz, E., & Coleman, M. (2001). Induction and mentoring of beginning researchers at academic colleges of education in Israel. *Mentoring & Tutoring: Partnership in Learning, 9*(3), 223–239.

Lee, A. (2008). How are doctoral students supervised? Concepts of doctoral research supervision. *Studies in Higher Education, 33*(3), 267–281.

Lee, S.-H., Theoharis, R., Fitzpatrick, M., Kim, K.-H., Liss, J. M., Nix-Williams, T., Griswold, D. E. & Walther-Thomas, C. (2006). Create effective mentoring relationships: Strategies for mentor and mentee success. *Intervention in School & Clinic, 41*(4), 233–240.

Mah, J. (2013). Dear mentors/professors: Tips to maximize research value from your undergraduate research assistants. *Council on Undergraduate Research Quarterly, 33*(3), 18.

Milner, T., & Bossers, A. (2004). Evaluation of the mentor-mentee relationship in an occupational therapy mentorship programme. *Occupational Therapy International, 11*(2), 96–111.

Pita, M., Ramirez, C., Joacin, N., Prentice, S. & Clarke, C. (2013). Five effective strategies for mentoring undergraduates: Students' perspectives. *Council on Undergraduate Research Quarterly, 33*(3), 11–15.

Rippe, K. (2001). *Anecdotal responses collected through interviews with selected mentees in the educational administration program.* (ERIC Document Reproduction Service No. ED 453168.)

Rivera, F. O. (2014). Enhancing the mentor-mentee relationship. *Healthcare Executive, 29*(2), 66–69.

Scott, R. A. (n.d.). Commentary: Mentoring matters. *Long Island Business News* (Ronkonkoma, NY). Retrieved from Regional Business News database.

Shim, H. S., & Roth, G. L. (2007). Sharing tacit knowledge among expert teaching professors and mentees: Considerations for career and technical education teacher educators. *Journal of Industrial Teacher Education, 44*(4), 5–28.

Straus, S. E., Chatur, F. & Taylor, M. (2009). Issues in the mentor-mentee relationship in academic medicine: A qualitative study. *Academic Medicine, 84*(1), 135–139.

Watt, D. (2007). On becoming a qualitative researcher: The value of reflexivity. *Qualitative Report, 12*(1), 82–101.

23 Young women in leadership, Massey University

Vasudha Bhide and Beth Tootell

The Young Women in Leadership programme (YOUWiL) is the brainchild of Dr Sarah Leberman, Deputy Pro Vice-Chancellor, Massey University, New Zealand. Designed and organised by the Massey School of Business, it was first rolled out in 2014. The objectives of the programme are to both inspire and educate young women about leadership. The programme is targeted at young women with leadership potential and explores how leadership styles and characteristics relate to them. We have been involved in different capacities with various parts of the YOUWiL programme, alongside other faculty and support staff.

YOUWiL supports and actively reinforces the leadership programmes organised by primary and intermediate schools in New Zealand and expects that over time this would lead to building and enhancing confidence in young women, a step towards change. YOUWiL promotes the School of Management, Massey Business School and Massey University to secondary school girls in the regions. It is conducted in the Albany and Palmerston North campuses of Massey University annually. In 2016, YOUWiL had 85 Year 12 female students from 13 schools in Albany, and 81 Year 12 female students from eight schools in Manawatu, both cities on the north island of New Zealand.

Young women in leadership roles

The continued challenge behind the low number of women in leadership roles (Catalyst, 2014; Grant Thornton, 2014, 2015) was the reason behind the inception of this programme. A number of reasons have been identified for this issue, one of them being the lack of confidence among women (Ibarra, Ely & Kolb, 2013). Dr Leberman observes that "women feel they need 80 to 100 per cent of the required skills before they apply for a job, while men are comfortable applying with only 50 to 60 per cent of the skillset" and YOUWiL aims to address confidence issues at an individual level.

YOUWiL supports the perception that leadership can be exerted in a way that is unique to individuals and encourages young women to identify their strengths and utilise them. It is unique in that it specifically targets young women who may not have had the opportunity to undertake traditional leadership roles in their current school environment and encourages a pluralistic view of leadership that includes both more traditional charismatic forms of leadership but also more quiet forms of leadership (Dinh et al., 2014).

Dr Leberman hopes that YOUWiL "sows a seed for them [participants] to grow to be the best they can be" and the young women who participate in the programme are expected to gain the confidence to "put up their hand and get noticed". This is achieved by experiencing leadership and teamwork first hand through a combination of various interactive sessions on leadership skills, confidence building, public speaking, connecting with people, teamwork and decision-making; working in teams on projects that are chosen, planned and executed by them with the support of mentors; interacting with mentors and sharing and presenting their project work.

The programme

The participants for the programme are selected from secondary schools in Manawatu through a rigorous selection process monitored by senior academicians from the school. Since the programme also aims to expose young women to the idea that leadership comes in a variety of forms, including quiet leadership, the participants might not be those who would typically raise their hand and are often the introverts in their classrooms. The goal is to identify students with 'leadership potential', and young women who desire to make a difference or identify the need to develop and practise leadership skills are chosen over those who are already engaged in leadership activities in other ways in their school environment. This supports the goal of increasing the number of women engaged in leadership as well as broadening the scope and understanding of diverse leadership styles. Mentors are identified from all walks of life across the region. These are women who have exhibited leadership skills, successfully met their career goals, are eager to share their leadership and career experiences, and are keen to mentor young women. They are matched with similar interest groups for the projects.

YOUWiL is conducted in two stages spaced 13 weeks apart. In the first stage the participants are exposed to leadership lectures, guest speaker sessions and interactive workshops designed around central topics such as leadership, personal values, ethics, decision-making, interpersonal skills, the influence of values and ethics on leadership and understanding how experiential learning and reflection enhance the practice of leadership. The focus of the various sessions in the first stage of the programme is on personal development as well as development of leadership skills. Guest speakers provide personal leadership stories that are motivational and enable an understanding of the diverse leadership styles and characteristics. The goal is to challenge common assumptions about leadership and encourage individual leadership skills and capabilities.

In this stage, the participants are also introduced to the projects component of the programme, grouped on the basis of similar interest areas and assigned into project teams. Projects give participants an opportunity to demonstrate and work on their own leadership capabilities by working in teams on projects chosen by them. They present the results of these projects in the second stage of YOUWiL. It is at this stage that each team is assigned a mentor to guide and support them in their project work. Mentoring can most simply be thought as "a more experienced person guiding a less experienced person" (Eby, Rhodes & Allen, 2007; Levinson & Darrow, 1978) and in the context of YOUWiL, mentoring provides support to the teams during the project work phase. Mentors are expected to be approachable, reachable and available throughout the project phase to guide, support, advise and provide feedback (Dougherty & Dreher, 2008; Kram, 1985) to the teams on:

- project ideas
- project planning
- overcoming issues, challenges
- presentations.

The mentor's role

The role of a mentor is to participate in and sometimes initiate exploration of possible projects; and support the team with project planning, implementation and presentation. The mentors also provide a layer of general guidance and leadership advice besides specific project guidance. Mentors are encouraged to be available for the teams as well as individuals for advice and feedback as required and not to 'hand hold' the participants, following the developmental mentoring model (Clutterbuck, 2009). This encourages and enables the development of confidence and leadership skills in individuals. At the same time, mentors also ensure that each person in the team is heard and gets the opportunity to exercise their skills.

Some students may not have had the opportunity to interact with such a group of mentors and may be hesitant or shy. Therefore, the mentors are encouraged to communicate with the students through the Facebook page, text, email or phone. They are encouraged to send inspirational stories, quotes or other interesting news/articles that they think the students would appreciate. The idea is not to put the young women on the spot but rather to establish a level of comfort and familiarity that would make it easier for them to reach out without hesitation. Contact details of the mentors are given to all the participants and they are encouraged to contact the mentors when required. Team as well as individual contact with mentors is encouraged so there may be participants who reach out for advice outside of just the projects (e.g. similar interests, career or future study). The Massey team also provides support by constantly being in touch with the students and mentors and being available for any kind of support if required.

In the second stage of the programme, the students present their project work to the other teams, mentors and the team from Massey. They are asked to reflect upon their project journey, leadership moments, learning experiences and how their assumptions and anticipations were challenged while working on projects. Therefore, the focus is not just on the project outcomes but also on the learning during the projects. The project presentations also contribute towards public speaking experience for the students. A guest speaker once again reinforces the diversity in exercising leadership by sharing their life story. The programme concludes with YOUWiL certifications.

Benefits

Benefits of the YOUWiL programme extend to the participants, mentors and Massey University. YOUWiL provides participants with the opportunity to be part of a leadership development programme designed specifically for young women from secondary schools, to interact with other students from across the region, to work on projects and the opportunity to exercise and develop leadership skills. The selection process ensures that young leaders who have leadership potential and drive but do not display traditional leadership traits are able to avail the opportunity as well. Participants have reported that they are inspired both by the stories and experiences of their mentors and course leaders but, perhaps more importantly, also by the stories of other programme participants. Responses to key learning outcomes for students include:

- "knowing what qualities leadership takes, being confident and the tips about public speaking";
- "... a lot of tips on public speaking";
- "that everyone shines as a leader in different ways and that we all show our talent/inspiration in certain areas";
- "to believe in yourself & have confidence";
- "that it's okay to be brave and bold and express yourself in a unique way that suits me – be myself";
- "to step up and out of my comfort zone";
- "how important having a reliable team of people is and having support from others can influence how well you do as a leader";
- "a leader can be a small or a silent role, which involves a range of qualities".

Students are also encouraged to undertake self-reflection activities and think about what they would do differently in the future having taken part in the workshops. Some of the comments here include being more confident, putting themselves forward for new opportunities, speaking up and asking for help when needed and taking more risks. Participating students have also expressed their desire to recommend the programme to other students.

YOUWiL mentors have reported learning and development themselves from the mentoring process. Mentors appreciate the opportunity to 'pay forward' their own mentoring experiences and report being motivated and inspired by the passion displayed by many of the young women. The mentors' feedback suggests that the programme provides a unique mentoring opportunity to mentor young women from secondary schools, engaging with young leaders and guiding and advising them during the project phase. Inspirational guest speakers demonstrate various leadership styles and provide role modelling and encouragement. By being asked to reflect on their own leadership pathways speakers report an increased engagement with their own career stories.

YOUWiL is an enabler for leadership and this is the larger benefit of the programme for Massey University. Some of the projects have expanded benefits to the community through fundraising, raising awareness about issues, etc. Other benefits for Massey include relationship building with schools in the regions and an audience that is captured for the future, showcasing strengths (staff, research and teaching) as well as exposure in the media, and building connections with enterprise and enhancing social reputation.

Refining the programme

Since the time YOUWiL was first rolled out, the Massey team continues to reflect upon the programme, learn from experience and continuously improve. The mentors, too, have reflected upon learning to manage the mentoring relationship with a strong age/power imbalance. A lot of the mentors had assumed, based on their prior mentoring experience, that the students would be more self-motivating in terms of contacting the mentors. However, they learnt that they needed to be more proactive in letting the young women know that it was acceptable to contact the mentors and ask for help and what kind of support to expect or what the mentors could help them with.

Some of the issues that were observed by the Massey team and are under consideration for improvement include the timing of the programme (time of year), scheduling and logistics, expanding more sessions across the year, utilising the Massey online environment and social media and expanding the reach and scope of the programme. One particular challenge is that the difference in the nature of the cohort of students each year also means that there is a need to continuously adapt and change the programme to be beneficial to the participants. Future plans include rolling the programme out to more schools and increasing the number of participating students.

References

Catalyst. (2014). *Women on boards*. Retrieved 17 August 2017, from www.catalyst.org/knowledge/women-boards.
Clutterbuck, D. (2009). Coaching and mentoring in support of management development. In S. J. Armstrong & C. V. Fukami (Eds), *The Sage handbook of management: Learning, education and development* (pp. 477–497). Thousand Oaks, CA: Sage Publications, Inc.

Dinh, J. E., Lord, R. G., Gardner, W. L., Meuser, J. D., Liden, R. C. & Hu, J. (2014). Leadership theory and research in the new millennium: Current theoretical trends and changing perspectives. *The Leadership Quarterly, 25*, 36–62.

Dougherty, T. W. & Dreher, G. F. (2008). Mentoring and career outcomes: Conceptual and methodological issues in an emerging literature. In B. R. Ragins & K. E. Kram (Eds), *The handbook of mentoring at work: Theory, research and practice.* Thousand Oaks, CA: Sage Publications, Inc.

Eby, L. T., Rhodes, J. E. & Allen, T. D. (2007). Definition and evolution of mentoring. In T. D. Allen & L. T. Eby (Eds), *The Blackwell handbook of mentoring.* Malden, MA: Blackwell.

Grant Thornton. (2014). *Women in business: From classroom to boardroom.* Retrieved 17 August 2017, from www.grantthornton.global/en/insights/articles/Women-in-business-classroom-to-boardroom/.

Grant Thornton. (2015). *Women in business: The path to leadership.* Retrieved 17 August 2017, from www.grantthornton.global/en/insights/articles/women-in-business-2015/.

Ibarra, H., Ely, R. & Kolb, D. (2013). Women rising: The unseen barriers. *Harvard Business Review, 91*(9), 60–67.

Kram, K. E. (1985). *Mentoring at work: Developmental relationships in organizational life.* Glenview, IL: Scott, Foresman & Company.

Levinson, D. J. & Darrow, C. N. (1978). *The seasons of a man's life.* New York: Ballantine Books.

24 Familial mentoring in Hawaii

Understanding the influence of culture on mentors and protégés

Donnel Nunes

Familial mentoring

Since early 2000, my practice and research has focused on the intersection of learning and human relationships. My goal has been to find ways I can assist families and organizations to build and nurture a culture of shared learning that promotes the healthy exchange of knowledge between members. In 2013, I began examining this exchange through the lens of *familial mentoring* (Sanchez, Esparza & Colón, 2008) which is mentoring that takes place between family members. Though familial mentoring exists across multiple contexts, I have found family owned business settings to be particularly rich for exemplary cases. Professionals in the field of family business advising have recognized the value of these types of mentoring relationships for decades. In fact, these relationships have been identified as a key factor for successful business succession amongst some of the most lasting international family owned businesses (Jaffe, 2016).

When compared to non-family mentoring relationships, familial mentors and protégés differ primarily because of the additional interpersonal complexity that comes from the overlap with family. What is important to note is that family members do not become mentors by virtue of being a parent or caregiver for a member of the younger generation (Bearman, Blake-Beard, Hunt & Crosby, 2010). What makes them distinct from other familial members is their sustained effort to advance the participation of younger generations within culturally congruent communities of practice (Nunes, 2013; Nunes & Dashew, 2017). Further, these efforts must be done in a manner that includes skill sets and knowledge that would otherwise make them viable mentors to non-family members. Lastly, it is also important that the child be a willing participant and the interactions of the relationship remain protégé centric.

The following case presents highlights from a naturally occurring mentoring relationship between a father and son in Hawaii. The purpose of this case is to present a familial mentoring relationship and to demonstrate how cultural expectations influenced the focus of their interactions. My relationship to this case was that of a researcher.

Family destiny

Travelling thousands of miles, the giant winter waves of the northern Pacific are summoned by storms that race across the mid-northern latitudes. From their humble beginnings off the coast of Japan, the storms track eastward, stall, and intensify just south of a slender claw of volcanic islands known as the Aleutian Arc. It is here where they find themselves among some of the most massive and powerful storms on the planet. Waves born from these winter cyclones can reach colossal heights as they travel south and eastward across the open ocean at speeds in excess of 50 mph.

When these waves finally arrive at the outer edge of Waimea Bay on the North Shore of Oahu, they are greeted by a group of elite athletes waiting to test themselves against one of the greatest forces in nature. And for more than 40 years, one of those athletes included native Hawaiian and world champion big wave surfer, Clyde Aikau. Starting in early in 2013, Clyde's son, Ha'a, could be spotted on his surfboard alongside his father as giant waves rolled through. Since Ha'a was a young child, his father has been interacting with him in ways that transcended traditional parenting and into the realm of mentoring.

As a familial mentor, Clyde intuitively sought opportunities for his son to both observe and participate in the activities and communities associated with his roles as a professional surfer and public figure. According to both father and son, these kinds of interactions remained common throughout their relationship. As Ha'a got older, these activities started to include conversations and coaching that were focused on his desire to become a professional surfer like his father. In spite of what appeared to be a clear purpose for their mentoring relationship, review of supplemental data sources revealed that 'becoming a professional surfer' was actually only a small part of a much larger and profound mission. The greater mission was a broader family succession plan that was deeply connected to the very foundation of who they were as members of the Aikau family and as Hawaiians.

For native Hawaiians, connection to family ancestry is paramount to their cultural sense of identity. For the Aikau family, one of the most significant moments in their history took place during the late 18th and early 19th century when the Hawaiian Islands were under the rule of King Kamehameha I. As was the custom of that time, King Kamehameha entrusted the care and oversight of his land and resources to his closest advisors. One of these appointments was given to the great, great grandfather of Clyde Aikau, Kahuna Nui Hewahewa. Hewahewa was delegated to the care of Waimea Bay and Valley. When Hewahewa died in 1837, the family connection to Waimea seemed lost.

Over a century later and at a time when Clyde and other Hawaiians were experiencing an ever-increasing sense that they were being marginalized in their own land, the Aikau family connection to Waimea was given a second chance. In 1967, Clyde's brother Eddie, became the first official lifeguard of

Waimea Bay. In Hawaii, this was a prestigious appointment and, given the political and social climate of the time, was seen by many Hawaiians as a validation of their place in society. Clyde described his reaction to his brother's selection as an overwhelming feeling of homecoming for their family. In the ESPN documentary, *Hawaiian: The Legend of Eddie Aikau*, Clyde passionately refers to his brother's selection as the fulfillment of 'destiny'.

When Eddie's life came to an early and tragic end in 1978, his status as a waterman and ambassador to the Hawaiian community quickly elevated his eminence to mythical proportions. In 1984, with the establishment of the Eddie Aikau Big Wave Invitational, the cultural legacy of the Aikau family and its connection to Waimea Bay was solidified. The event, which carries the Aikau name, has become the most prestigious big wave surfing event in the world. For over three decades, Clyde perpetuated his brother's legacy as both a world champion surfer and a public figure. By the time Ha'a was ready to paddle out in Waimea Bay, Clyde and his son seemed confident he was on track to take his father's place as the ambassador of Hawaiian big wave surfing.

A father/son mentoring relationship

From surfing to finding his place as a contributing family member, Ha'a was constantly at his father's side. His mother, Elani Aikau, can remember him being drawn to the activities of his father. "He was just this little guy and he would follow Clyde everywhere, even down to the water. He would wrap his arms around Clyde's neck as he paddled out." Consistent with some of the earliest forms of mentor-like behaviour, social learning theorists have observed this kind of adult/child interaction in traditional societies dating back for millennia (Lave & Wenger, 1991; Rogoff, Paradise, Arauz, Correa-Chávez & Angelillo, 2003). During interviews with other parent/child mentoring dyads I found it was common for parents to describe similar scenarios when parents talked about how they had *mentored* young children. While it is important to note that the mentoring relationship between Clyde and Ha'a formed naturally, it is also important to pay attention to how it evolved into a more formal relationship as Ha'a became a young adult.

In addition to instrumental support related to the physical act of surfing, Clyde tried to help his son see a bigger picture associated with becoming a professional athlete. Clyde stressed. "I don't care how great a surfer you are, the attitude that you give out is what will actually carry you a lot further in life." He added, "I'm trying to teach him to basically be a good person, be a kind person, be a caring person."

Fundamental to any emerging professional surfer is having the ability to financially sustain themselves in ways that allow for them to be on the water when the conditions are just right. Based on his own experience, Clyde encouraged Ha'a to develop working skills in multiple professional domains. Since Ha'a was a boy, he and his father have partnered on jobs ranging from animal care and food service to surfing instruction and guided ocean excursions.

As a role model, Clyde sought out opportunities to model behaviours for his son. When he was called to lead cultural ceremonies or to speak in front of large audiences he always brought Ha'a. Clyde also used these events as opportunities to build and expand Ha'a's professional networks. Often, members of the audience would include potential sponsors and Clyde capitalized on these events as opportunities to introduce his son. After being involved in the "professional surfing world for over 40 years", Clyde knew many of the owners of big companies and tried to leverage his relationships for the benefit of his son.

As Ha'a got older, the mentoring and coaching between him and his father became more formal. They expressed their focus on helping Ha'a to become a professional surfer. They began having discussions about how to approach sponsors and Clyde started to seek out members of his network who could help his son. Clyde also starting 'sitting out' on surf sessions so that he could critique his son's performance from the beach.

Unfortunately, in 2015 Ha'a was dealt a major setback after being violently thrown onto the reef during a surfing accident. The impact caused a severe injury to his shoulder that required surgery and resulted in him missing the entire 2016 winter season. On 25 February 2016, at 66 years old, Clyde Aikau rode his final waves in the Eddie Aikau Big Wave Invitational and announced his retirement. Where father and son had hoped to fill his departure with the rising of a son, there remained uncertainty. Perhaps bigger than just the uncertainty of Ha'a's professional surfing career there was a second, unspoken, goal of their mentoring relationship that also seemed in peril; they had relied on Ha'a's success as a professional surfer to be the vehicle for him to carry the Aikau name forward as stewards of Waimea Bay.

Mentoring values and goals

Without considering the cultural values of the Aikau family, the relationship between Clyde and his son might otherwise have appeared as a typical familial mentoring relationship. From this perspective, mentoring goals focused on formulating a vision and strategy to support Ha'a's efforts to join the tightly knit community of professional surfers. However, once we factor in the role of family legacy for Hawaiians, the limitations of this assessment become clear. Ultimately, this was not just a case about a son trying to gain entry to the world of professional sport, it was a case about a father and son trying to perpetuate a cultural legacy. For practitioners working with Polynesian clients, this case serves as a reminder to look beyond the presenting features of mentoring relationships when assessing recommendations for clients.

From other cases that participated in my pilot, I found emerging evidence to suggest that Hawaiians have historically relied on fathers to take part in mentor-like relationships with their sons. Where other cultures may follow a dyadic model, Hawaiians appeared to have emphasized a network model of mentoring. Under this model, the primary role of a mentor-father was to help the son to identify and connect to a community of mentors. As the primary mentor, the father was also responsible for teaching the son how to cultivate those relationships. In addition, I also found several cases in Hawaii where mentoring relationships were exchanged between families who possessed differing areas of expertise. In one case, a father approached another father in the community and offered to mentor his son in woodworking, if he would mentor his son in Hawaiian cultural practices.

As familial mentoring relationships become more accepted in the greater body of coaching and mentoring research, I anticipate the emergence of a new field of familial mentoring practitioners. These practitioners will work alongside parents and children, in the contexts of business, education, cultural practices, and other domains in ways that will empower them to negotiate the complexities of learning relationships between family members. They will also help to reframe values, visions and goals in ways that represent the actualization of the younger family member's greatest self and unique contributions. I suspect the most skilled practitioners will be those who not only help family members to see their own priorities with greater clarity, but also help them to see how the perpetuation of values and legacy can be expressed through multiple forms.

Since my initial interviews with Clyde and Ha'a, they have celebrated moments of accomplishment while also confronting setbacks. They could gain much from inevitable advances in the fields of mentoring and coaching that should include the development of further research and specific strategies for family mentoring relationships.

References

Bearman, S., Blake-Beard, S., Hunt, L. & Crosby, F. J. (2010). New directions in mentoring. In T. D. Allen & L. T. Eby (Eds), *The Blackwell handbook of mentoring: A multiple perspectives approach* (pp. 375–395). Oxford: Wiley-Blackwell.

Jaffe, D. (2016). *Releasing the potential of the rising generation: How long-lasting family enterprises prepare their successors.* Milton, MA: Wise Counsel Research.

Lave, J., & Wenger, E. (1991). *Situated learning: Legitimate peripheral participation.* Cambridge: Cambridge University Press.

Nunes, J. D. (2013). *Father/son mentor/mentee: The parent as the mentor.* Paper presented at the 2013 Mentoring Institute Conference. Albuquerque, NM.

Nunes, J. D., & Dashew, L. (forthcoming 2017). Mentoring between generations: A family affair. In D. Clutterbuck, N. Dominguez, F. Kochan, L. Lunsford, B. Smith & J. Haddock-Millar (Eds), *Sage handbook of mentoring.* London: Sage Publications.

Rogoff, B., Paradise, R., Arauz, R. M., Correa-Chávez, M. & Angelillo, C. (2003). Firsthand learning through intent participation. *Annual Review of Psychology, 54*(1), 175–203.

Sanchez, B., Esparza, P. & Colón, Y. (2008). Natural mentoring under the microscope: An investigation of mentoring relationships and Latino adolescents' academic performance. *Journal of Community Psychology, 36*(4), 468–482.

25 How to match mentors and mentees effectively

George Quek

My experience in structured mentoring has involved helping to implement mentoring initiatives for more than 30 organizations throughout Asia Pacific in the past 10 years. In 2004, I launched the first and, to date, the only programme in Asia Pacific on 'How to Set Up a Structured Mentoring Programme' for HR professionals throughout Asia. Through all these, I discovered that a critical success factor in any mentoring programme is the effective matching of mentors and mentees. The need for this chapter is reinforced by the relatively vague treatment of this subject matter in existing books and literature on structured mentoring.

Situation

Yet this vital step of match-making is frequently a bottleneck with most mentoring programmes. The main reason is that putting two individuals together with the hope that they can get along and develop a meaningful relationship is so subjective. Numerous variables such as personality, generation gaps, gender/ethnic diversity, prior life and work experience, values, lifestyles, etc. come into play. This makes success in matching that much more difficult to predict.

I, therefore, set out with the goal of attempting to make the subjective as objective as possible. Through my work in helping to implement structured mentoring in organizations, I saw the need for a consistent and accountable methodology for matching mentors and mentees for the highest probability of success while considering the key variables mentioned above. The purpose of this chapter is to share this matching methodology with you in a practical way. To keep it real, I will be illustrating this process with a case from a client of mine.

The client is a leading global insurance organization that wanted to start a mentoring programme for its identified high potential mid-managers in Singapore. The intended mentors were members of the senior leadership team. As this was a pilot programme, it was decided to start small with just four mentees. There were about 10 senior leaders who were potential mentors. As mentoring is an off-line relationship, it was agreed that the CEO and the Human Resource Director take themselves out of contention as both could indirectly impact the performance evaluations of the mentees. That left the programme with eight possible mentors for four mentees.

The match-making process

In general, matching can take three approaches:

1   Mentees have no choice of mentors – pairs are assigned – forced pairing.
2   Mentees have a choice of mentors. This can take the following routes:

- Self-selection – the mentee is free to approach any identified mentor. The pairing depends on the mentor's consent to the relationship. The risk here is mentees might pick the more popular mentors without regard to compatibility with their own developmental needs.
- Preferred options – the mentee is matched with a few potential mentors deemed compatible. The mentee is then free to choose among them. The final choice depends on the coordinator who will consider availability and suitability. This option at least ensures that all recommended mentors can help the mentee with his/her needs. Mentors are shortlisted in this case.

3   Mentors get to pick mentees either through self-selection or preferred options. This option is rare as the emphasis of the mentoring programme is on the mentee who will have a bigger say in who can help him/her. This must be exercised with caution as it might lead to sponsorship in which the mentor is deemed to be directly enabling the career growth of the mentee. Again, the intent of the mentoring is developmental, not helping the mentee up the corporate ladder.

This client organization opted for preferred options as it believed that the mentees would be more committed to the relationship if they had a say in who their mentors were.

The matching methodology then follows a five-step process that is centred around a competency-based criterion. This process aims to give mentoring programme managers a transparent, documentable and justified means of matching mentors and mentees with a high probability of success. Success means the mentoring relationships can develop smoothly and effectively.

1   *Determination of key competencies to be focused on in the mentoring program*
    While we need to match based on stated preferences, let us not forget the whole point of mentoring is development. Thus, the foremost criterion should be who can best help the mentee with the desired development goals. And, as the mentoring initiative exists to develop the talent pool for the organization, the goals should revolve around the core competencies of the organization. The starting point, then, is identifying the competencies the organization wants to develop through the programme.
    In this case, the client chooses the following 14 leadership competencies:

Table 25.1 Client's leadership competency framework

DECISION QUALITY
- Makes good decisions (without considering how much time it takes) based upon a mixture of analysis, wisdom, experience and judgement
- Sought out by others for advice and solutions

PROBLEM SOLVING
- Uses rigorous logic and methods to solve difficult problems with effective solutions
- Probes all fruitful sources for answers
- Can see hidden problems/excellent at honest analysis
- Looks beyond the obvious and doesn't stop at the first answers

DEALING WITH AMBIGUITY
- Can effectively cope with change/shift gears comfortably
- Can decide and act without having the total picture
- Can comfortably handle risk and uncertainty

INNOVATION MANAGEMENT
- Is good at bringing the creative ideas of others to execution
- Has good judgement about which ideas and suggestions will work
- Has a sense about managing the creative process of others

PERSPECTIVE
- Looks toward the broadest possible view of an issue/challenge
- Can pose future scenarios
- Can discuss multiple aspects and impacts of issues and project them into the future

STRATEGIC AGILITY
- Can anticipate future consequences and trends accurately
- Is future oriented
- Can create competitive and breakthrough strategies and plans

MANAGING VISION AND PURPOSE
- Communicates a compelling vision or core purpose
- Can inspire and motivate entire units with possibilities and optimism
- Creates mileposts and symbols to rally support behind the vision

DELEGATION
- Broadly shares responsibility and accountability
- Tends to trust people to perform
- Lets direct reports and others finish their own work

DEVELOPING OTHERS
- Holds frequent coaching and development discussions
- Provides challenging and stretching tasks and assignments
- Is aware of each person's career goals
- Is a people builder

INFORMING
- Provides the information people need to know to do their jobs and to feel good about being a member of the team
- Provides individual information so that they can make accurate decisions
- Is timely with information

COMPOSURE
- Is cool/a settling influence under pressure
- Does not become defensive and irritated when times are tough
- Can be counted on to hold things together during tough times

LISTENING
- Practises attentive and active listening
- Has the patience to hear people out
- Can accurately restate the opinions of others even when he/she disagrees

MOTIVATING OTHERS
- Makes each individual feels his/her work is important
- Invites input from each person and shares ownership and visibility
- Can assess each person's hot button and use it to get the best out of him/her

BUILDING EFFECTIVE TEAMS
- Creates a feeling of belonging in the team
- Defines success in terms of the whole team's
- Blends people into teams when needed

Table 25.2 Leadership competency framework

	Select	*Select*
DECISION QUALITY	DELEGATION	
PROBLEM SOLVING	DEVELOPING OTHERS	
DEALING WITH AMBIGUITY	INFORMING	
INNOVATION MANAGEMENT	COMPOSURE	
PERSPECTIVE	LISTENING	
STRATEGIC AGILITY	MOTIVATING OTHERS	
MANAGING VISION AND PURPOSE	BUILDING EFFECTIVE TEAMS	

2   *Development and completion of Mentor and Mentee Profile Forms*
Next, each mentor and mentee is asked to complete and submit a profile form that will be later used to match. The questions asked in the form reflect the key matching criteria.

MENTOR/MENTEE PROFILE Form

Please take a couple of minutes to complete the following items to facilitate the mentoring initiative.

Name:

Position: Dept/Div: Mentor/Mentee

1   State a brief history of your career: job positions, work functions etc.
2   What do you hope to get out of the mentoring initiative?
3   What specific characteristics or qualities do you look for in a mentee/mentor?
4   State any of your interests, hobbies or experiences that might be of interest to a prospective mentee/mentor?
5   Review the following competencies below.

For Mentors: select 3 to 5 competencies that you can best help a mentee develop.
   For Mentees, select 3 to 5 competencies that you would like your mentor to help you develop. Add any other competency not identified here.

3   *Competency pooling*
Using the information collected from the profile forms, mentors and mentees who pick the same competency would be grouped together.

Competency: Dealing with Ambiguity

Mentors: Lau Sok Hoon

Yee Siew Eng

Competency: Composure

Mentees: Poh Huat

Magdalene Loh

Mentors: Lau Sok Hoon

Felicia

Goh Geok Cheng

Patrick Teow

Competency: Strategic Agility

Mentees: Poh Huat

Mentors: Tomas Urbanec

Duyen

Felicia

Mentees: Magdalene Loh

Lena Cheng

Poh Huat

Figure 25.1 Groupings of mentors and mentees by competency.

We can follow the mentee named Poh Huat. He picks three competencies that he would like to focus on in the mentoring relationship. The mentors listed were those who chose the same competencies they would like to provide support for. While one can argue that the competencies picked by the mentors might not be the ones they are truly competent in, we can safely work on the assumption that mentors, in general, are aware of their own strengths and they would not pick competencies they are not confident of. Allowing the mentors and mentees a free rein to pick competencies leads to a higher willingness and motivation as they enter the relationship.

At this stage, we have grouped the mentors and mentees by competency which serves as the first matching screen.

4   *Create a matching table for each mentee*

Now, we can shortlist the few mentors whose names keep appearing in all or most of the chosen competencies (they are the ones who pick the same competencies as the mentees). Mentors Patrick, Felicia and Lau Sok Hoon's names appear more than once. Hence, they are shortlisted.

Each of the three potential mentors has the capacity to meet the mentee's indicated needs. A matching table for each mentee is now used to do a second round of matching. Each potential mentor is rated against other secondary criteria. These criteria correspond to the questions asked on the Profile Forms.

- Cross-functional: mentor is not a direct superior to mentee (off-line).
- Background and interests: mentor and mentee share commonalities (questions 1 and 4 on the Profile Form).
- Preferences: as much as possible, match with stated preferred mentor/mentee; a common example is gender (question 3 on the Profile Form).
- Hierarchical: the mentor must be a certain number of grades higher than the mentee. A good rule of thumb is a mentor is at least two job grades above the mentees to ensure a wide enough experience gap that can result in a diversity of perspectives.

Each criterion is one star for a Slight fit, two stars for an Average fit and three stars for a Good fit.

Making the choice

The mentoring programme manager should form an ad hoc mentoring committee that will meet to determine the matching. This committee should be diverse, comprising representatives from different functions so that, when in doubt, there is a member who will know the mentor/mentee in question and offer perspective. The diverse committee will also ensure that the matching is objective and encompassing and not a Human Relations/Organizational Development/Learning and Development decision. The committee can number from three members including the programme manager.

Background/interest. Poh Huat indicates on his profile form that his entire career has been in Actuarial Science and in his free time he enjoys sports and travelling. Felicia has a background in Corporate Communication and loves

Table 25.3 Matching table for each mentee

Mentee: Poh Huat			
Criteria	Mentors		
	Felicia	Patrick	Lau Sook Hoon
Background/interest	**	**	*
Cross-function	***	***	*
Hierarchy/preferences	*	**	**
Total	6	7	4

Notes
 * = Slight fit;
 ** = Average fit;
 *** = Good fit.

working out and reading. Patrick is the Director of Agency Distribution and is into golf and travel while Lau is the COO and prefers gardening and cooking. All three potential mentors have spent a large part of their careers in the Insurance industry so the differentiating factor would be personal interests/hobbies. Felicia and Patrick both share Poh Huat's affinity for physical activities and travel so they both get two stars whereas Lau's preferences for sedentary home activities mean she does not have much in common with Poh Huat.

Cross-function. Here, the further the mentor is from the mentee functionally, the better. Lau's role as the COO means she works closely with the Actuarial department so she gets only one star while both Felicia and Patrick are in functions which have little direct dealings with Poh Huat, hence they both warrant three stars.

Hierarchy/preferences. Poh Huat indicates that, if possible, he likes a mentor with more business development and management experience. Felicia is a communications specialist who does not have direct business experience. She is one job grade above Poh Huat while Patrick and Lau are two job grades above Poh Huat. Thus, Felicia is given one star. Both Patrick and Lau are in the direct line of developing and operating the business so they get three stars each. What stops them from having three stars is they do not have profit-and-loss responsibility.

A weightage scheme can be used to give different weights for each criterion. For example, we can decide that background/interest is more important than cross-function and give it more weight. In this case, all criteria are equally weighted. The shortlisted mentors are those who score the most number of points. If the pairing is forced, Patrick will be the mentor picked. If options are allowed, we can offer Poh Huat either Felicia or Patrick as preferred options. However, we need to state, upfront, that while we will hope to give each mentee his/her first choice, we cannot guarantee it if some other mentee is a better fit for the same mentor.

A note on Personality and Communication Styles. Putting people with similar personality and communication styles together will increase the chance of better rapport and harmony. However, when two persons are too similar, they tend to have common blind spots. An introverted mentor might not be concerned about an introverted mentee's need to speak out more. Pairing two persons with different personalities would help with pointing out each other's blind spots but relationship building might take a longer time. Hence, we decide not to focus on Personality and Communication Styles as matching criteria. In any case, we believe that with proper mentor and mentee training that includes interpersonal interactive skills, well-trained mentors and mentees will be able to flex and adjust their communication styles to suit one another. Therefore, Personality, if used as a matching criterion, is not so much to ensure that people with similar or different personalities are paired, but rather to prevent people with extreme personalities being matched which may lead to conflict/disagreement or matching people with past cases of conflict from being put together.

Table 25.4 Summary of the matched pairs

Mentors	Mentees			
	Poh Huat	Magdalene	Duyen	Lena
Patrick Teow	X			
Felicia		X	X	
Tomas				
Lau				X
Goh				

Overall Mentor/Mentee charting. All mentors and mentees are cross-referenced to ensure that each mentor would have no more than two or three mentees in order not to overburden them.

Felicia is on the shortlist of three mentees: Magdalene (seven stars), Duyen (eight stars) and Lena (seven stars). Because we want to keep to a ratio of one mentor to two mentees, Felicia will be paired with the two mentees with the highest scores. However, there is a two-way tie between Duyen and Lena, both with seven stars. The mentoring committee then determines Lena can work with Lau though Lau is given just six stars. As a result, Lau is matched with Lena even if Lena prefers Felicia. This is indicative of the need to be flexible at the end of the day and reflective of the reality that we cannot please everyone.

The value of the match-making process

This matching process/methodology is an attempt to 'make the subjective matching endeavour more objective' and, therefore, is centred around a set of organizational competencies. The process is mentee-centric since it considers individual background/interests/preferences. Objectivity is ensured since the process involves multiple stakeholders in determining the criteria scoring. Importantly, the methodology allows for proper documentation of the process for future reference.

Part IV

Conclusions

26 Lessons learnt

David Clutterbuck, Anna Blackman
and Derrick Kon

Our case studies demonstrate that coaching and mentoring are thriving in the Asia Pacific region, with a wide diversity of application and approach. We see in the case studies an immense and sometimes naïve enthusiasm. It is clear that good practice is still in the process of being defined in the region overall – as it is to a lesser extent in America and particularly in Europe, where boundaries have begun to emerge and the focus on practitioner competence is well established. In Asia Pacific currently, we see a wide variation in the maturity of coaching, with Australia, New Zealand and Singapore being the most advanced.

To reach the same level of maturity, coaching and mentoring in other countries needs to tackle a number of significant issues.

Issues

Leaving aside the US/European split over mentoring (which is increasingly being resolved by the concept of mentoring being coaching plus experience) these continents have largely moved beyond the stage where anyone can attach the words coach or mentor randomly to any kind of activity. The authors rejected some potential case studies because they clearly were not about coaching or mentoring at all. We also see in the case studies within this book evidence of confusion in customers' minds. Coaches and mentors will need to continue to invest in educating the market.

Maturity. An indication of the maturity of a market or profession is when people are both able and willing to talk about failure as well as success. This is a limiting factor both in our book and in the profession as a whole in Asia Pacific. We were not able to access such cases for this edition, but look forward to doing so for future editions.

Fixed model coaching – in which the coach works to a highly prescribed model – is echoed in some of our cases. While this can be effective and appropriate at the basic levels of coaching, where the goal is clearly defined and relatively simple to achieve, at the more transformational levels of coaching, it is both limiting and sometimes counter-productive. Outside of Australia, New Zealand and Singapore, there is little evidence of coaching at the higher levels of coach maturity.

The four levels of coach maturity are:

1   Models-based (doing coaching to someone)
2   Process-based (coaching with someone)
3   Philosophy-based (integrating the coaching mindset with who we are – so, being a coach)
4   Systemic eclectic (supporting the client while they have the conversation they need to have with themselves).

Client experience. Similarly, we see in more advanced coaching environments an understanding and valuing of the role of the client and how the client can contribute to the effectiveness of the learning conversation. Neither the perspective of the skilled coachee nor the client experience are reflected in most of our cases and we were unable to find any relevant studies emanating from the region from our literature search. The case studies are from the coaches' perspectives with self-selected examples and nearly all chapters are descriptive rather than evaluative or self-reflective. These are still valid and useful examples; however, there needs to be further research to get an objective view of the process. This is an area in urgent need of research.

Quality standards and measurement. While some of our case studies indicate that coaches and organisations are applying quality standards, this is by no means universal. By and large, the effectiveness of coaching and mentoring and the competence of coaches and mentors seems to be taken on trust. If clients and organisations are to receive value for money – and if coaching and mentoring are not to do harm – then radical change is needed here. The ICF 2016 Global Coaching study (ICF, 2016) highlighted that professional coach practitioners place emphasis on training and credentialing. In addition, the research also reveals that managers/leaders using coaching skills place a similarly high premium on these markers of professionalism. It is worth noting that professional associations such as the International Coaching Federation (ICF), the Association for Coaching (AC) and the European Mentoring and Coaching Council (EMCC) are collaborating in the Global Coaching and Mentoring Alliance (GCMA) to develop credibility and professionalism of coaching and mentoring.

Supervision. We noted that very few of the coaches we contacted in our search for cases undertake supervision, yet this is demanded of all professional coaches and mentors by EMCC, AC, ANZI and recommended by ICF. The EMCC Guidelines for Supervision (EMCC, 2016) believe that coaches/mentors should undertake no less than one hour of supervision per 35 hours of practice, ensuring a minimum of four hours per year, evenly distributed if possible. The Australian New Zealand Institute of Coaching (ANZI) requires ongoing supervision for coaches to maintain their accreditation status, specifically 10 hours per year for associate coaches and six hours per year for professional coaches.

The cultural dimension of coaching. One of our aims in producing this book was to illuminate how culture impacts coaching and mentoring and the potential for different cultures to impact the wider world of coaching and mentoring. We feel that the chapters and cases have begun to achieve both of these aims – and that there is vast potential for more research and for more transfer of concepts and approaches between cultures, both within the region and with other regions. As an example, the concept of multiple kinds of smile, from Thai culture, has significant implications for mindfulness in coaching – an area of personal development and interest for many coaches and mentors in the Western developed countries.

Return on investment. Assessing effectiveness and business impact of coaching and mentoring is another area to work on as Asia Pacific organisations gain maturity in implementing coaching and mentoring practices. Coupled with the fact that coaching and mentoring may not be the only initiative that contributes to an organisation's improvement, there seems no universal adopted way to accurately measure this at this moment. Thus, defining the benefits expected and successfully measuring them will be an important topic that organisations will have to work on in implementing coaching and mentoring.

We believe coaching and mentoring in Asia Pacific will continue to grow and is not a passing management fad. The growing importance of competencies, standards and certification will strengthen the reputation of coaching and mentoring as a profession in this region. From this book, we hope researchers and practitioners have obtained a better understanding of coaching and mentoring in Asia Pacific, its key regional challenges and have gained new insights from the cases and learnings.

Coaching trends

A number of common themes have emerged from the cases provided; developing cross-cultural practice, introducing coaching into cultures/countries where it is not common, the value of coaching, the need to build respectful, positive relationships with coachees, coaches coming in to 'save' companies or managers. These themes fit nicely amongst some of the key trends identified within coaching and mentoring.

Professionalisation. To date, professionalisation in coaching has been, first, about developing training standards (where the ICF came in) and, then, about creating competences (where the EMCC began as it evolved from the research network of the EMC). Professionalisation has since moved on to supervision and is fast embracing team coaching. Internal coaches, typically seen as the Cinderellas of coaching, are now being drawn increasingly into professionalisation. A significant question therefore is: *how far can and should professionalisation go?* Closely allied to the theme of professionalisation is coach maturity and the four distinct stages as outlined above.

Integration of coaching and mentoring. In the past three or four years, we have also begun to see the stirrings of professionalisation in mentoring. It seems that retiring business executives want to be able to use their experience in a developmental role, rather than as a consultant. They don't want to become coaches, but they want all the non-directive, client-centred skills of a professional coach. John Leary-Joyce refers to this kind of mentoring as coaching plus – the plus being the use of wisdom and experience to provide context and craft questions, which are insightful because of their contextual insight.

Within organisations, internal developmental mentoring programmes have increasingly become the key to developing a coaching culture. Line managers, who lack confidence in applying coaching methods within their own teams, can learn non-directive developmental behaviours by becoming mentors to someone in a different part of the organisation.

Technology. Artificial intelligence, virtual worlds and even relatively simple algorithms have the potential to replace much basic-level coaching and, especially, coaching based on simplistic models, such as GROW. If it is a mechanistic process, it can be mechanised! This is at one level a threat – most of what coaches learn in initial training can now be done by machine – but at the same time it is an opportunity for increasing the professional competence and impact of coaches, as they acquire skills that can't be automated.

Goal orientation. In our research into how coaches use goals, it becomes increasingly clear that a lot of the literature is very simplistic. Goals more often emerge and evolve rather than appear as fixed objectives – at least, when coaching is done well. We are now seeing much more nuanced approaches to how coaches help clients set, manage and work with goals.

The team dimension. Most coaching today is carried out one-to-one, but increasing numbers of coaches are adding team coaching to their portfolio. This requires a much higher level of skill and knowledge that fits with their desire for continuous professional development. We are also seeing a shift away from the concept of the line manager as coach towards creating a coaching culture within work teams – one where everyone takes responsibility for the development and coaching of everyone else. This, of course, embeds coaching into the team's daily practice.

Mentoring trends

E-mentoring and multimedia mentoring. One of the most significant evolutions for mentoring in recent years has been e-mentoring. While e-mentoring lacks the communication richness of face-to-face dialogue, it provides built-in reflection time that can enhance the quality of both mentor questions and mentee responses (Clutterbuck & Hussain, 2010). For the future, we will see a much greater use of *multimedia mentoring* – relationships, which use a variety of media, including face-to-face, email, Skype, telephone and texting, as appropriate. Among the benefits of this approach are that differing needs of the mentee may be accommodated by selecting the most appropriate medium. In particular, some media are more time responsive than others – if an urgent dialogue is needed, text or email may be more effective than face-to-face.

Multimedia and e-mentoring are especially useful in distance mentoring, because the dialogue can be time independent. While there are potential issues with cross-cultural communication (and hence additional learning opportunities, too), there is some evidence that differences in hierarchical power exert less of an influence on the relationship – people can be more culturally and personally authentic; and they are able to give and receive a higher level of constructive challenge.

Coaching vs mentoring. Like mentoring, coaching in organisations has evolved over the past three decades, with the result that it's often not clear what the difference is between them. In general, coaching tends to be a shorter-term intervention, aimed at improving performance. Mentoring tends to be longer term, broader in its objectives and aimed at career development. In the next few years, we should see an acceleration of the trend to integrate coaching and mentoring as complementary approaches to developing talent in organisations. Some organisations already see both skills as essential for effective line management, with coaching primarily a relationship within the reporting line and mentoring always outside of it. To retain high potential employees, it will become increasingly important to provide both coaching and mentoring.

Mentoring variants. Almost all mentoring to date has been about individual, one-off relationships. However, we are seeing significant growth in three different alternative approaches. In *multiple mentoring*, an individual has several simultaneous mentors, each focusing on a different aspect of his or her life. In *sequential mentoring*, people move from one mentor to another, on a planned ladder of development. In *cascade mentoring*, people are simultaneously mentor and mentee, in different relationships. So, for example, graduate recruits may be mentored by a middle manager and may in turn mentor a youth at risk in the community.

Reverse mentoring. In reverse mentoring, the mentor is (often significantly) more junior than the mentee. Initially designed as a way to educate executives in new technology (particularly IT), reverse mentoring is increasingly becoming a practical means of promoting diversity/equal opportunity agendas. It is also starting to be used to create learning relationships, in which Gen Y can challenge the thinking of Gen X and baby boomers.

Integration of Human Resources and Community Social Responsibility mentoring initiatives. Until recently, mentoring programmes aimed at employees and mentoring for community social responsibility purposes were seen as separate activities, with separate budgets. Internally focused mentoring was about development; externally focused about corporate reputation and volunteering. The duplication of effort in having two sets of training and support systems had inevitably come under scrutiny. It's also become clear that the two kinds of mentoring programme have a lot to learn from each other. Cascade mentoring will increasingly be part of this integration – mentees, who take on a community mentoring role during their internal mentoring relationship, typically report that they become more appreciative of their mentor and better able to help the mentor help them.

Professionalisation. The pressure to professionalise coaching has been much greater than for mentoring, because of the large numbers of paid external (executive and life) coaches. All the main professional bodies – in particular, the International Coach Federation (ICF) and the European Mentoring and Coaching Council (EMCC) – have invested heavily in codes of conduct, accreditation and standards for coaching. The EMCC's standards and European Individual Award are the only ones to cover both coaches and mentors internationally. However, we can expect increasing professionalisation of mentoring. We can expect to see more organisations offering their mentors developmental ladders, ranging from simple foundation courses, to academically and professionally recognised certificate and diploma level qualifications.

Supervision. The requirement for coaches to be professionally supervised is a relatively recent development. It is a much stronger expectation in Europe than elsewhere – European companies often will not consider hiring an executive coach, who cannot demonstrate that they are adequately supervised. We will see increasing numbers of organisational mentoring programmes employing supervision.

Professionalisation for programme managers. The role of mentoring programme manager requires substantial skills of administration, participant support and stakeholder management. Programme managers also need to be role models for mentoring good practice. A handful of specialised training programmes have been around in recent years and some of these are now offering formal qualifications for programme managers. As programmes in multinational companies become larger, being able to demonstrate competence in the role will become a marketable commodity.

Accreditation of mentoring programmes. The International Standards for Mentoring Programmes in Employment (ISMPE) were established several years ago as an international benchmark of mentoring programme quality. The standards are being used in several countries and three continents. It is expected that they will become more widely applied in the future and that they will continue to adapt to innovation in mentoring.

Research. Research in coaching and mentoring has taken two very different paths. Most mentoring research is quantitative and positivist. Coaching research is mostly qualitative and experiential. So we have a lot more evidence for the efficacy of mentoring, but more understanding of the relationship dynamic in coaching. This is already changing and we can expect to see a more balanced research agenda in both areas.

One of the problems with much of the quantitative literature on mentoring is that it fails adequately to define the relationships that are being measured. There may be an assumption of a sponsorship model, but even then, there is often conflation of very different relationship dynamics – for example, mixing off-line relationships with 'supervisory mentoring', in which mentor and mentee are in a direct reporting line. The qualitative literature, on the other hand, can be difficult to extrapolate beyond the particular type and context of the mentoring relationship.

The quality of research is also benefiting from increasing interaction and networking between researchers around the world. The start of which is looking at different regions around the world and having researchers and practitioners collaborate to provide insight into what is happening within coaching and mentoring in that region. We expect to see these networks become stronger and better supported by both universities and professional associations.

References

Clutterbuck, D., & Hussain, Z. (2010). *Virtual coach, virtual mentor*. Charlotte, NC: Information Age Press.

European Mentoring and Coaching Council (EMCC). (2016). *Guidelines for supervision*. Retrieved 17 August 2017, from www.emccouncil.org/src/ultimo/models/Download/7.pdf.

International Coach Federation (ICF). (2016). *Global coaching study*. Retrieved 17 August 2017, from http://coachfederation.org/about/landing.cfm?ItemNumber=3936.

Index

Page numbers in *italics* denote tables, those in **bold** denote figures.

explore and appreciate 48; feminine in orientation 28; gap 58; impacts coaching 226; Indian work 109; individualistic 4, *80*; influenced by European 21; leadership 140, 142–3; Maori 121; national dimensions of 27; new 118; nuances of 19; optimisation programme 97; organisation 142, 152; organisational 88; paternalistic 69; patterns from 85; raise awareness of other 26; risk of stereotyping 30; role of 50, 55; role in work 25; safety 34; school 191; sensitivity to 47, 49, 65–6; seven dimensions of 29; shared learning 209; shift 20; storytelling 117; team 127; Thai 65, 68–70, 72, 74–7, *80*; unified 117; US 107; values 28; Western 4, 26, 49, 76; winning 161; work 120; work with diverse 78; working within 184; *see also* Asian cultures, coaching culture, different cultures
Curseu, P.L. *100*, 102

Dalton, F. 98, *100*
de Haan, E. 6, 57
Deloitte 31
development officers (DOs) 182–5
Developmental Model of Intercultural Sensitivity (DMIS) 30
different cultures 86, 116, 158, 227; diverse expectations of mentoring 43; diversity of 89, 111; executives from 79
disagreements 68–9, 220
disempowered 149; state of mind 108
Dowling, M. 194
Drake, D.B. *100*

Eby, L.T. 5, 205
embedded: coaching, in business environments 58; concepts in Thai culture 69, 72; core qualities 156; cultural charter 120; learning 146; practices of good coaching and mentoring 41; research 188; stage of developing coaching culture 34
embedding 124; coaching and mentoring culture 142; of learning through group coaching 125; mentoring 190, 193
Emotional Intelligence techniques 108
empowered 131, 135; both at work and at home 134; leadership team *100*; to make choices 176; to move forward 192; team members 163

empowering: individuals to achieve their goals 146; team mates to make decisions 99
empowerment 135; ensuring 117; generating *101*; post-coaching achievement 136; removing barriers to 134
European Mentoring and Coaching Council (EMCC) 6, 9, 13–14, 42, 60–1, 226–7, 230; General Council for Mentoring and Coaching 44; Guidelines for Supervision 226
expectations 124, 130, 134, 137, **189**; addressed 43; aligned 46; of coaching 78; in coaching relationships 72; conflicting 74; cultural 66, 79, 209; cultural discussion around 27; from customers 142; differing 90, 117; family circle 75; higher 67; incorrect 50; localised 4; meet 135; of mentoring from diverse cultures 43, 77; on nature and purpose of coaching 40; not living up to 74; perception of societal 151; pre-coaching 134; sharing 61; Thai behavioural 70

familial mentoring 209, 212–13
familial mentors 209–10
Franklin, J. 128

Garvey, B. 3, 5–6
Gen Ys 57, 229
Global Coaching and Mentoring Alliance (GCMA) 9–10, 226
goldminer's mentality 88
Goldsmith, M. 58, 124
good practice 6, 13, 39, 41, 57, 84, 106; coaching 60; integrating two approaches 18; mentoring 230; in process of being defined 225; recommended 18; research and development of 13; requires new mindset from managers and staff 42
Grant, A.M. 13
Grant Thornton 203
greng jai 72, 78, *80*
GROW model (Whitmore, J.) 7, 34, 122, 143

hai kiad 72
Hawaii 211; father-son mentoring relationship 209; mentoring relationships between families 213

Taylor & Francis eBooks

Helping you to choose the right eBooks for your Library

Add Routledge titles to your library's digital collection today. Taylor and Francis ebooks contains over 50,000 titles in the Humanities, Social Sciences, Behavioural Sciences, Built Environment and Law.

Choose from a range of subject packages or create your own!

Benefits for you

» Free MARC records
» COUNTER-compliant usage statistics
» Flexible purchase and pricing options
» All titles DRM-free.

Benefits for your user

» Off-site, anytime access via Athens or referring URL
» Print or copy pages or chapters
» Full content search
» Bookmark, highlight and annotate text
» Access to thousands of pages of quality research at the click of a button.

REQUEST YOUR **FREE** INSTITUTIONAL TRIAL TODAY

Free Trials Available
We offer free trials to qualifying academic, corporate and government customers.

eCollections – Choose from over 30 subject eCollections, including:

Archaeology	Language Learning
Architecture	Law
Asian Studies	Literature
Business & Management	Media & Communication
Classical Studies	Middle East Studies
Construction	Music
Creative & Media Arts	Philosophy
Criminology & Criminal Justice	Planning
Economics	Politics
Education	Psychology & Mental Health
Energy	Religion
Engineering	Security
English Language & Linguistics	Social Work
Environment & Sustainability	Sociology
Geography	Sport
Health Studies	Theatre & Performance
History	Tourism, Hospitality & Events

For more information, pricing enquiries or to order a free trial, please contact your local sales team: www.tandfebooks.com/page/sales

Routledge
Taylor & Francis Group

The home of Routledge books

www.tandfebooks.com